THE LOWEST FREEDOM

COLUMBIA STUDIES IN THE HISTORY OF U.S. CAPITALISM

COLUMBIA STUDIES IN THE HISTORY OF U.S. CAPITALISM

SERIES EDITORS: JUSTENE HILL EDWARDS, DEVIN FERGUS, BETHANY MORETON, AND JULIA OTT

Capitalism has served as an engine of growth, a source of inequality, and a catalyst for conflict in American history. While remaking our material world, capitalism's myriad forms have altered—and been shaped by—our most fundamental experiences of race, gender, sexuality, nation, and citizenship. This series takes the full measure of the complexity and significance of capitalism, placing it squarely back at the center of the American experience. By drawing insight and inspiration from a range of disciplines and alloying novel methods of social and cultural analysis with the traditions of labor and business history, our authors take history "from the bottom up" all the way to the top.

The Columbia Studies in the History of U.S. Capitalism series was founded in 2013 by Louis Hyman, Bethany Moreton, and Julia Ott to publish the best new work in the history of capitalism. In 2017, Devin Fergus joined the series board. In 2025, Justene Hill Edwards joined the series board.

Faith in Markets: Christian Capitalism in the Early American Republic, by Joseph P. Slaughter

The Rise of Corporate Feminism: Women in the American Office, 1960–1990, by Allison Elias

The Dead Pledge: The Origins of the Mortgage Market and Federal Bailouts, 1913–1939, by Judge Glock

Unfree Markets: The Slaves' Economy and the Rise of Capitalism in South Carolina, by Justene Hill Edwards

Histories of Racial Capitalism, edited by Destin Jenkins and Justin Leroy

Brain Magnet: Research Triangle Park and the Idea of the Idea Economy, by Alex Sayf Cummings

How the Suburbs Were Segregated: Developers and the Business of Exclusionary Housing, 1890–1960, by Paige Glotzer

Threatening Property: Race, Class, and Campaigns to Legislate Jim Crow Neighborhoods, by Elizabeth A. Herbin-Triant

Banking on Freedom: Black Women in U.S. Finance Before the New Deal, by Shennette Garrett-Scott

City of Workers, City of Struggle: How Labor Movements Changed New York, edited by Joshua B. Freeman

For a complete list of books in the series, please see the Columbia University Press website.

THE LOWEST FREEDOM

RACIAL CAPITALISM AND BLACK THOUGHT IN THE NINETEENTH CENTURY

JUSTIN LEROY

Columbia University Press   *New York*

Columbia University Press
Publishers Since 1893
New York   Chichester, West Sussex
cup.columbia.edu

Copyright © 2026 Columbia University Press
All rights reserved

Cataloging-in-Publication Data is available from the Library of Congress.

ISBN 9780231181983 (hardback)
ISBN 9780231223560 (trade paperback)
ISBN 9780231543941 (epub)
ISBN 9780231565714 (PDF)

LCCN 2026010486

Cover design: Elliott S. Cairns
Cover image: Mathew Brady, *Contraband School*, c. 1860–1865.
Mathew Brady Photographs of Civil War–Era Personalities and Scenes, 1921–1940, National Archives.

GPSR Authorized Representative: Easy Access System Europe,
Mustamäe tee 50, 10621 Tallinn, Estonia, gpsr.requests@easproject.com

*In memory of Cameron Philippe Leroy
and the millions more
for whom freedom was not enough*

Look into our freedom and happiness, and see of what kind they are composed!! They are of the very lowest kind—they are the very dregs!—they are the most servile and abject kind, that ever a people was in possession of!

—David Walker, *Appeal to the Coloured Citizens of the World* (1829)

CONTENTS

Acknowledgments xi
Introduction xv

1 Freedom's Dregs: Blackness, Indigeneity, and Racial Capitalism in Antebellum New England   1

2 The Radical Abolishment of Slavery: Abolitionist Encounters with Land and Labor Reformers   39

3 A Worse Condition Than in the Time of Slavery: Capital, Labor, and the Limits of Emancipation   81

4 Abolitionism Is Another Term for Communism: Abolition Democracy Against Racial Capitalism   121

Epilogue: Unending Histories   169

Notes 175
Bibliography 209
Index 233

ACKNOWLEDGMENTS

Writing this book is the hardest thing I've ever done. There were many times I thought I'd never truly finish, and the only reason that I have, even so belatedly, is due to the love and support of many friends, family members, mentors, and colleagues. As an undergraduate at Wesleyan University, I never dreamed that one day my earliest mentors Allan Isaac, Anita Mannur, and Kēhaulani Kauanui would become colleagues. José Esteban Muñoz was the first person to believe in me when I arrived at New York University as an eager MA student, and there's no one I'd have rather learned Marx from. In NYU's American Studies program I found an intellectual home I've missed ever since leaving. I am forever indebted to my dissertation advisers Jennifer Morgan and Nikhil Pal Singh, whose work influenced my thinking in ways that I could have never imagined. Martha Hodes taught me to think about academic writing as a craft, and I pass her lessons on to my own students. Ronak Kapadia got me into, through, and out of grad school. Laura Helton, Max Mishler, Samantha Seeley, and Shauna Sweeney made me feel intellectually brave, and they continue to push my thinking to new heights. I'm so proud of what you've all done. Manijeh Moradian, Thulani Davis, Stuart Schrader, Claudia Sofia Garriga-López, Liz Mesok, Eva Hageman, Marisol

LeBrón, Emily Hue, Elliott Powell, and Zenia Kish made taking this journey worth it.

During my time as a postdoctoral fellow at Harvard's Charles Warren Center, Walter Johnson gave more generously of his time than I deserved and encouraged me to explore the concept of racial capitalism more fully. Since then, I have been uncommonly fortunate when it comes to departmental colleagues. At the University of California–Davis, Mark Jerng and Greg Downs helped me make the transition from anxious postdoc to fully fledged faculty member. I am thankful to Mark especially for trusting me to build the Mellon Initiative on Racial Capitalism with him, which became my anchor at Davis. I will always be grateful to Thavolia Glymph for recruiting me to Duke, and I am still shocked that she remembered me after having met only once while on a panel together ten years prior. Tamika Nunley and Pete Sigal have offered sage guidance. Sarah Balakrishnan and I came to Duke at the same time, and she has been a tireless intellectual partner.

Over the years I've shared parts of this book at the University of Pennsylvania's Global Nineteenth Century Workshop, Stanford University's Approaches to Capitalism Workshop, Brown University's Nineteenth-Century U.S. History Workshop, and Princeton University's Department of African American Studies Faculty-Graduate Seminar. Critical feedback from these events has reshaped the book's core arguments in productive ways. Steve Hahn, Seth Rockman, Angela Zimmerman, Destin Jenkins, K-Sue Park, Manu Karuka, and Cameron Rowland have also been invaluable interlocutors as I struggled with how to frame this project.

Bridget Flannery-McCoy made me feel like this book was in safe hands at Columbia University Press, and Stephen Wesley has been both gracious about my yearslong silences and generous with his time once I committed to finishing. Bridget, Stephen, and the History of U.S. Capitalism series editors, Devin Fergus, Louis

Hyman, Julia Ott, and Bethany Moreton, have been incredible editorial partners whose support for this project has never wavered. I am also grateful to Tamara Nopper for developmental and line editing, and to my graduate assistant Shifa Nouman and copyeditor Zubin Meer for turning hundreds of incomplete citations into proper notes.

Ray Hsia, Stephen Kang, Jia Son, John Won, and Dave Zhou have lifted me up for two decades. They're the best best friends anyone could ask for. My father Jacques Leroy was my first writing teacher and has anticipated the completion of this book more eagerly than anyone, and my mother Carol Massoud-Leroy has had far more faith in my success than I ever have. Ryan Funk has spent more than ten years with a version of me shaped by the stress and anxiety of this project and loved me unconditionally anyway. I hope now I can be a better partner.

This book is dedicated to the memory of my brother Cameron Philippe Leroy. Like the thinkers I write about, he was guided by a sense of justice unbounded by legal authority or social propriety. I hope what I've written is up to his standards.

INTRODUCTION

In his masterful account of Reconstruction and its aftermath, W. E. B. Du Bois described how two visions for the South's future "clashed and blended" in the wake of the Civil War. "The one was abolition-democracy based on freedom, intelligence and power for all men; the other was industry for private profit directed by an autocracy determined at any price to amass wealth and power."[1] He wrote of Reconstruction as the tragic narrative of how an alliance forged between Northern capitalism and Southern white supremacy subverted a vision of *abolition democracy*—a future in which emancipation was the first step toward giving all poor and downtrodden people the economic, political, and educational tools necessary to become full participants in a racially egalitarian society.

For Du Bois, the history of emancipation was a history of labor struggle. He titled the first chapter of *Black Reconstruction*, which rehearsed the history of slavery, "The Black Worker," and later described enslaved people who fled plantations for Union lines during the war as engaged in a "general strike" against slavery. Du Bois also argued that abolition—"the emancipation of man"—was the first step toward Marx's notion of "the emancipation of labor," for the end of slavery meant "the freeing of that basic majority of workers who are yellow, brown, and Black." And, with no small degree of hyperbole, he noted approvingly that Reconstruction "showed certain tendencies toward a dictatorship of the proletariat," suggesting it was a thwarted preamble to the revolutionary socialism expressed most fully in the Russian Revolution.[2]

It was for these reasons that Du Bois characterized Reconstruction as "the finest effort to achieve democracy for the working millions which this world has ever seen."[3] The effort was short lived. Northern capital initially saw a fully enfranchised Black citizenry in the South as both a source of profit and a bulwark against the resuscitation of a Southern oligarchy opposed to Northern financial interests. But weary of the cost of defending freedpeople's interests and facing labor upheavals closer to home, in 1877 Northern industry allied themselves with Southern planters, solidifying their control of the federal government and establishing "a new dictatorship of property in the South through the color line" in the process.[4] Thus the pact between capitalism and white supremacy "murdered democracy in the United States so completely that the world does not recognize its corpse."[5]

Du Bois wrote of Reconstruction's experiment in abolition democracy as "a brief moment in the sun" set between two and a half centuries of chattel slavery and a post-emancipation labor regime that ushered freedpeople "back again toward slavery."[6] Yet *Black Reconstruction* articulated something of the abolitionist struggle that observers have little dwelled upon—that is, the relationship of land, labor, and capital to freedom in nineteenth-century Black thought. Like Du Bois, many Black abolitionists insisted that the promise of emancipation would not be fulfilled without economic self-determination, and, in turn, that economic dispossession could erase emancipation's significance. Before the end of slavery seemed possible and long after Reconstruction's demise, Black thinkers articulated a vision of abolition democracy in which the material conditions of Black life were a crucial component for making freedom meaningful.

FREEDOM OF THE LOWEST KIND

The Lowest Freedom is an intellectual history of how economic dispossession shaped the meaning of freedom in Black thought between the emergence of the antislavery movement and the dawn of Jim Crow. Throughout the nineteenth century, the evolving relationship between race and capitalism made economic deprivation a defining feature of free Black life, rendering formal emancipation in both the post-Revolution North and post–Civil War South less significant than it otherwise might have been. David Walker—the radical abolitionist whose words provide the inspiration for this book's title—described this type of proscribed freedom as "the very dregs" and "of the very lowest kind." Walker is one of the thinkers featured in this book, alongside Maria Stewart, William Apess, James McCune Smith, Frederick Douglass, T. Thomas Fortune, and Ida B. Wells. Many of these figures were quite well known and influential in their time. Du Bois himself admired and learned from most of them. He owned a rare first edition of David Walker's *Appeal to the Colored Citizens of the World*, listened to Frederick Douglass give a speech at the Chicago World's Fair in 1893, got his start in journalism by writing for T. Thomas Fortune's newspaper, the *New York Age*, and worked with Ida B. Wells in the Niagara Movement, one of the earliest national civil rights organizations.[7] Despite the prominence of these figures in the field of African American history, they are rarely taken up as economic thinkers or theorists of racial capitalism.

The Lowest Freedom argues that these thinkers prominently and persistently used themes of racial poverty, labor exploitation, and the denial of economic rights to characterize the conscripted nature of Black freedom. They revealed how racial violence operated through economic systems, and how those systems in turn constituted the limits of freedom within racial capitalism. They considered how the state—in the form of political parties, legislation, and the law—constricted Black labor and social mobility and helped organize the economy to maintain racial domination. These thinkers conceived of freedom not only as the end of the institution of slavery and equitable incorporation into the political forms of American democracy, but also, crucially, as a project to rework the relationship among land, labor, and capital. They circulated their ideas in books, newspapers, and speeches for others, including other Black reformers, to engage with. The Black press served as a key site of economic debate and for articulating theories about labor, capitalism, and class struggle. In responding to the endemic ways in which racial exclusion, dispossession, and extraction structured capitalism, they ultimately troubled any clear break between slavery and freedom.[8]

Of course, the refusal of legal rights, political disenfranchisement, and exclusion from the protections of citizenship diminished the horizons of freedom, and Black thinkers recognized this fact. However, any analysis of nineteenth-century Black thought that excludes economic questions or renders them subordinate to political and social questions cannot fully capture how Black reformers thought about the conscripted nature of their freedom or analyzed and campaigned against racial violence. The racialization of labor, property, and land was central to how early American capitalism functioned, no less so after emancipation than in the time of slavery.

Black intellectual history is well suited to excavating the relationships at the core of this book. Ideas about racial differentiation and notions of human nature as innately self-interested and acquisitive, both crucial to the naturalization of racial capitalism, owe no small debt to European intellectual history emerging from the Enlightenment. Black intellectual history offers a different way of knowing; as Brandon Byrd argues, the field coheres around the thought of those "who were defined as chattel, not thinkers, and denied full inclusion in Eurocentric conceptualizations of humanity." Centering Black thought confronts this genealogy of exclusion and "troubles post-Enlightenment ideas of progress and linearity by asking how ideas of the ostensible past might pertain to possible, liberated futures."[9] Guided by these principles, *The Lowest Freedom* makes three related interventions.

SLAVE EMANCIPATION

The Lowest Freedom emphasizes how capitalist development limited the scope of antislavery efforts and helped to reproduce the social and economic conditions of slavery even after emancipation. By orienting the whole of nineteenth-century Black history around the continuity of subjugation under capitalism, the book's first intervention is to challenge the moral claims embedded within narratives about progress from slavery to freedom and show how racial capitalism ensured the transferability of systems of domination across the slavery/freedom divide. *The Lowest Freedom* thus joins a growing body of work that explores the place of Black freedom within broader histories of nineteenth-century capitalism.[10]

Historians have long dispensed with the idea that slavery/freedom was a binary mediated by the singular moment of emancipation, instead situating Black life after slavery along a spectrum of unfreedom. There is a robust body of scholarship that identifies the abrogation of rights, racial violence, and criminal punishment as among the various methods that tied the project of emancipation to coercive regimes that shaped Black people's experiences of freedom in the United States and the wider Atlantic world.[11] Walker gleaned something of these dynamics when he described Black freedom in the North as "dregs" and the "lowest kind." His articulation of low freedom captured the indefinite suspension of emancipated peoples in the tenuous space between slavery and freedom.

The Lowest Freedom insists that one of the things that connected these diverse forms of coercion across the nineteenth century was their reliance upon the imbrication of race and capitalism. For Walker and the Black thinkers who came after, being truly free from slavery required an economic system that did not produce a racialized hierarchy of labor value enforced by racial subjugation and violence. Thus *The Lowest Freedom* is indebted to scholars who have suggested that emancipation projects forged in an ideology of liberal capitalism that both naturalized and valorized labor productivity were necessarily hostile to Black freedom as formerly enslaved people themselves imagined it.[12] Thomas Holt describes this dynamic as "the problem of freedom," which should be "understood as the task of socializing ex-slaves to respond to the work incentives of freemen."[13] In her now-classic account of the continuity between slavery and freedom, Saidiya Hartman describes emancipation as a "nonevent" whose aim was "transforming the formerly enslaved into rational, acquisitive, and responsible individuals." Hartman argues persuasively that "the question persists as to whether it is possible to unleash freedom from the history of property that secured it, for the security of property that undergirded the abstract equality of rights bearers was achieved, in large measure, through black bondage."[14] Similarly, Rinaldo Walcott uses the term "the long emancipation" to name the condition Black people have inhabited since the end of slavery, in contradistinction to freedom, which remains elusive. In Walcott's account, "such conditions mean that asserting a notion of freedom for Black people, one routed in the critique of capital, remains barely possible. The barely possible exists because the measures of life remain deeply rooted in capital and its subsidiaries, so to refuse capital is to refuse a sort of life."[15]

The reluctance of these scholars to embrace the terminology of freedom to describe formerly enslaved people's experiences of emancipation has much in common with nineteenth-century Black thinkers' own disappointment with the conscripted nature of freedom, which was at times so profound that they used the language of slavery to describe it.[16] Frederick Douglass, for example, often observed that without a robust set of political, social, and economic rights, Black people would become "slaves of society" rather than the slave of any one individual.[17] At the turn of the century, Du Bois described tenant farming, sharecropping, and convict leasing as methods of binding Black Southerners "to an economic slavery, from which the only escape is death or the penitentiary."[18] Neither mere metaphor nor factual description of reality, Black thinkers' persistent invocation of terms like "slaves of society" and "economic slavery" identified actually-existing Black freedom as an ideology of rule rather than a status of relief.[19] Like Walker when he described Black freedom as "of the very lowest kind," Douglass, Du Bois, and others indicted the persistent poverty, material deprivation, and exploitation that dared to call itself freedom. Crucially, *The Lowest Freedom* argues that these conditions were not the dying gasps of chattel slavery as it struggled to hang on to life, but evidence that even something so momentous as the emancipation of millions could not eliminate the suffocating force racial capitalism exerted over Black life.[20]

RACIAL CAPITALISM

Walter Johnson argues that "the history of racial capitalism . . . is a history of wages as well as whips, of factories as well as plantations, of whiteness as well as blackness, of 'freedom' as well as slavery."[21] By sketching how racial capitalism shaped freedom no less profoundly than it did enslavement and colonialism, *The Lowest Freedom* expands current frameworks for understanding the dynamics of racial capitalism before the twentieth century and makes its second intervention.

Racial capitalism encompasses a diverse set of practices and ideologies that structure the interwoven relationship between race and capitalism. The term describes how the violent dispossession required for capital accumulation creates, exacerbates, and relies upon racial difference. Race, in turn, naturalizes the inequalities capitalism produces, rationalizing the necessarily unequal distribution of power and resources under capitalism as consequences of race.[22] Using racial capitalism to encompass such a breadth of practices and ideologies purposefully gestures toward the enduring and persistent nature of the relationship between race and capitalism. Indeed, racial capitalism does not operate solely through the dispossession of land and the expropriation and exploitation of labor; it also operates through exclusion from economic life and, crucially, through forms of inclusion that obfuscate the requisite inequalities that capitalism produces.[23] As this book shows, emancipation was an example of this latter guise of racial capitalism.

Contemporary scholars owe much to Cedric Robinson for his popularization of the term *racial capitalism* in his landmark book *Black Marxism: The Making of the Black Radical Tradition*.[24] Robinson argued that "the development, organization, and expansion of capitalist society pursued essentially racial directions," and that, in turn, race permeated "the social structures emergent from capitalism."[25] He termed this development *racial capitalism*, and in doing so, offered a significant revision to Marxist theories of class formation. For Marx, part of the revolutionary potential of capitalism was its ability to scour away the forms of false consciousness—race, nation, gender, religion—that concealed the class conflict at the heart of all social relations. This would be capitalism's ultimate undoing, for once the proletariat became conscious of itself as a universal working class, it could then organize to overthrow capital. Robinson saw Marx as having it backward. Rather than erasing premodern forms of difference, capitalism exacerbated them, transforming variations in ethnicity, language, and culture internal to Europe into forms of racial differentiation that would eventually place the peoples of the world into strict hierarchies. Robinson concluded, "The historical development of world capitalism was influenced in a most fundamental way by the particularistic forces of racism and nationalism." But racism was not an ideology restricted to the ruling classes; Robinson argued that "in the intensely racial social order of England's industrializing era, the phenomenology of the relations of production bred no objective basis for the extrication of the universality of class from the particularisms of race." Having shaped the proletariat, racism would come to affect "the formative structures of socialist societies as they appeared" in the twentieth century as well.[26] Racial capitalism, then, would not be overcome by illusory ideologies of class universalism or even the advent of socialism. Far from erasing differences among labor, racial capitalism led to what Herbert Hill, longtime labor director for the National Association for the Advancement of Colored People (NAACP), described as "the historical development of working-class identity as racial identity."[27]

Originally published in 1983 to little fanfare, the republication of *Black Marxism* in 2000 has inspired a surge of new work that expands upon Robinson's theory of racial capitalism, bringing it to bear on the history of the twentieth century.[28] Even more recently, scholars have begun to apply the framework of racial capitalism beyond the Atlantic crucible that linked the histories of Africa, the Americas, and Europe.[29] And, while not directly connected to the renewed interest in *Black Marxism*, over the same period of time historians of slavery have come to embrace one of Robinson's central claims: That however else capitalism in the Atlantic world *might* or *could have* come about, in actuality its development was intertwined inextricably with chattel slavery.[30] The collective impact of this work on illuminating the relationship between race and capitalism can hardly be overstated. Yet its narrow focus on slavery in the nineteenth century juxtaposed against its expansive, global focus in the twentieth century has left a historiography that gives the incorrect impression that chattel slavery—alongside the attendant forms of Indigenous dispossession its expansion required—is the singular origin point of racial capitalism.[31] Careful attention to Black thought enmeshed in debates about colonialism, land reform, labor, unions, immigration, and international upheavals reveals that racial capitalism adapted to, and even thrived in, the context of nineteenth-century Black freedom.[32] *The Lowest Freedom* contends that post-emancipation forms of racial capitalism are not merely legacies of slavery but bequeathments of freedom.

ABOLITION DEMOCRACY

The Lowest Freedom's third and final intervention is to reimagine Black economic thought of the nineteenth century as both a history of and elaboration upon Du Bois's notion of abolition democracy, itself an instantiation of what Robinson called the "Black Radical Tradition." By abolition democracy, Du Bois meant "physical freedom, civil rights, economic opportunity and education and the right to vote" for freedpeople.[33] This economic opportunity would not be grounded in "New England capitalism and individualism," but the "demand for land."[34] And, just as it took a concerted wartime effort to abolish slavery, so, too, would a "dictatorship of labor" be necessary to enforce abolition democracy.[35]

In Du Bois's account, abolition democracy was a political formation rooted in the specific historical context of the Civil War and Reconstruction. He saw its possibility for success as contingent upon new alliances unleashed by the emancipation of four million enslaved people, the disenfranchisement of Southern planters, and the temporary support of Northern capital. For abolition democracy to successfully take advantage of this moment of opportunity would require a "union between the champions of universal suffrage and the rights of the freedmen, together with the leaders of labor, the small landholders of the West, and logically, the poor whites of the South" to command the power of the federal government against the combined strength of Northern and Southern capitalists, whose alliance "promised to become the greatest plutocratic government the world had ever known."[36] At the heart of Du Bois's conception of abolition democracy was the joining of egalitarian political and social relations with redistributive forms of economic production upheld through the active involvement of the state. This involvement could range from policies designed to curb the oppressive power of capital to the use of force in response to white supremacist violence.

While achieving abolition democracy on a national scale might have seemed possible to Du Bois for but a brief moment, its core tenet of bringing about political, social, and economic equality through the mobilization of federal power in the service of an expansive democracy would have been familiar to the Black thinkers who are the subject of this book. Across the nineteenth century, their thought paired demands for democratic rights with a critique of how racialized poverty and economic dispossession limited the meaning of Black freedom. By pointing out white Americans' refusal to abide by the language of the nation's founding documents and amplifying the antislavery, and later, pro-Reconstruction trends in party politics, they articulated the necessary role of federal power in realizing their demands. Abolition democracy, in other words, aptly describes the aims of nineteenth-century Black economic thought both before and after the short period Du Bois described in *Black Reconstruction*.

Jesse Olsavsky argues that while contemporary scholars and organizers have invoked abolition democracy to name their aspirations for radically egalitarian, noncoercive forms of freedom, "this tendency often separates the idea of 'abolition-democracy' from the concrete history of abolitionism, which produced it, and from later socialist and anti-colonial revolutions, which were its heirs." Even as these theorists assert a relationship between uprisings of the enslaved and anticolonial, anticapitalist rebellion, they "often uncouple organized, interracial abolitionism from that revolutionary history." As a result, "the profound role of abolitionism in the making of twentieth century black revolutionary traditions" has remained obscured.[37]

The Lowest Freedom uses these historical linkages to place Black thinkers' theorization of abolition democracy into conversation with a broader set of ideas Robinson dubbed the "Black Radical Tradition." "An accretion, over generations, of collective intelligence gathered from struggle," Robinson argued that "the Black Radical Tradition was distilled from the racial antagonisms which were arrayed along a continuum from the casual insult to the most ruthless and lethal rules of law" and that "inevitably, the tradition was transformed into a radical force" whose aim was to overthrow racial capitalism.[38] Usually reserved to describe intellectual and political efforts of the twentieth century, the notion of a "Black radical tradition" situates Black Americans alongside West Indians and Africans as part of global anticolonial and socialist movements. Like *Black Reconstruction* and *Black Marxism*, scholarship in this tradition challenges both liberal and Marxist histories of political economy that ignore the importance of race. Although slavery is crucial to the emergence of capitalist modernity in the Black radical tradition, it rarely acknowledges the long history of Black abolitionism as its precursor.[39]

By framing Black economic thought of the nineteenth century as a theory of abolition democracy, *The Lowest Freedom* suggests a new way of tracing the emergence of the Black radical tradition. To call this nineteenth-century tradition "radical" is not to say that all forms of the Black radical tradition are reducible to one another nor to posit an unbroken continuity; differing historical contexts created abolition democracy and anticolonial socialism, which in turn were animated by differing ideologies. The Black radical tradition, like all traditions, looked different over time depending on the particular circumstances that produced it. Rather, the act of juxtaposition recovers the radical potential of Black thought to illuminate how racial capitalism subverted Black freedom in the nineteenth century in ways that would anticipate how racial capitalism's enduring presence would undermine future Black emancipatory achievements, such as the overthrow of colonial rule in Africa and the West Indies and the end of white supremacist apartheid regimes in the Southern United States and South Africa.

ORGANIZATION OF THE BOOK

The Lowest Freedom unfolds across four chapters. Chapter 1 focuses on the writings of David Walker, Maria Stewart, and William Apess, all reformers in antebellum Massachusetts. Their work documents a system of racial capitalism at work in New England. This system was distinct from that of the South and was built upon Black freedom and Indigenous presence rather than Black enslavement and Indigenous removal. Chapter 2 reconsiders tensions between Black abolitionists and white labor reformers in the decades before the Civil War. Although the two groups disagreed about whether property in man or property in land was the worse sin, the challenges labor reformers made to abolitionist arguments forced Black abolitionists to integrate critiques of wealth and landed property into their attacks on slavery. Chapter 3 focuses on Frederick Douglass's changing views on the relationship between capital and labor after the Civil War. Over the course of the 1870s and 1880s, the worsening condition of Black Southern labor led Douglass to frequently frame wealth and capital paired with white supremacy as a threat to Black freedom. Finally, chapter 4 traces journalists T. Thomas Fortune's and Ida B. Wells's diagnoses of the racial and economic conditions of the Black South in the final decades of the nineteenth century.

THE LOWEST FREEDOM

1

FREEDOM'S DREGS

Blackness, Indigeneity, and Racial Capitalism in Antebellum New England

Slavery was the engine of capitalist development in the antebellum United States, and dispossessed Indigenous land its fuel. Between 1776 and 1860, the United States seized nearly 800 million acres of Native territory, most of which would become the plantation states of the Deep South. The land's new masters, in turn, stole the labor of four million enslaved people. This labor produced the cotton that the United States sent into global markets, and was the nation's largest export. On the eve of the Civil War, the value of enslaved people was greater than that of all other financial assets combined, including banks, railroads, and manufacturing. The only thing more valuable was the very land they cultivated.[1] The sheer scope of chattel slavery and the Indigenous dispossession required for its expansion has made the history of these parallel processes invaluable in excavating the beginnings of racial capitalism in the United States. Yet racial capitalism is not merely a project of raw violence; it relies, too, on the idioms of freedom and progress. Nowhere were these dynamics more visible than New England in the first decades of the nineteenth century.

Black and Native people were disproportionately poor and powerless in antebellum New England. They were free, but just so. In the decades following the American Revolution, whites increasingly saw the degraded status of these groups as the result of natural and immutable racial inferiority. Black and Native people themselves understood their impoverished condition as the result of long and ongoing histories of racial plunder. At stake were competing explanations for poverty and its amelioration, the durability of past forms of dispossession, and the value of freedom in the face of labor exploitation and economic predation. In some ways, it is surprising that white New Englanders gave any thought at all to Black and Native people. Unlike in the South, exploited racial labor did not form the basis for New England's economy. In 1830, Black people made up just over 1 percent of New England's population. In Boston, the region's largest city, Black residents numbered fewer than two thousand, or 3 percent. Even taking into account that these figures likely exclude fugitive slaves, seamen, and others whose precariousness might make it wise to avoid census takers, Black New Englanders made up a tiny fraction of the population.[2] New England's Indigenous population was even smaller, at only a few thousand. The largest communities, who lived on reservations, were made up of only a few hundred individuals, and it was a common sentiment among whites that Native people were "disappearing," destined to die out.[3]

These tensions surrounding the role of Black and Native people in New England despite their small numbers reveal a way of understanding the intertwined relationship between race and capital accumulation distinct from that which prevailed in the South. Rather than clearing Native land for enslaved labor, this form of racial capitalism centered on racializing poverty and social disorder. It criminalized forms of interracial contact that might threaten white racial solidarity in the face of divergent class interests, and justified the racialized economic hierarchy of New England as the natural result of Black and Indigenous inferiority rather than a consequence of centuries of dispossession, both organized and idiosyncratic. Most importantly, this form of racial capitalism adapted to the conditions of freedom and did not rely upon slavery or Indigenous removal to thrive.

The intellectual production of the reformers David Walker, Maria Stewart, and William Apess documented this connection between racialized poverty and histories of dispossession between the late 1820s and mid-1830s. While each of these figures had the opportunity to advocate for New England's Black and Native communities in ways that few others did, the social and economic forces that they criticized shaped their lives in ways typical for people of color in antebellum New England. Walker was born in 1796 to an enslaved father and free mother in Wilmington, North Carolina. As a young man he moved to Charleston, likely drawn by its much larger free Black community and the economic opportunities the city offered. By 1825, Walker had settled in Boston. He opened a used clothing shop and quickly embedded himself in Boston's free Black community. Stewart was likewise born free in Greenwich, Connecticut, in 1803. Orphaned as a young girl, she spent her childhood and adolescence bound as an indentured servant to a white clergyman and his family. After her indenture ended around 1818, she worked as a domestic servant while pursuing any scraps of education and religious instruction available to her, eventually making her way to Boston. Stewart, too, was involved with Boston's vibrant Black community. Apess was born in Massachusetts along the Vermont border in 1798 to one of the few Pequot families remaining in the region. He grew up with his maternal grandparents in Connecticut. They were abusive, and to remove him from their care the town's overseers bound Apess as an indentured servant to a local family. He ran away from his master and fought in the War of 1812 before traveling throughout New England as an itinerant preacher.[4]

Most Black and Indigenous people in this period were illiterate. Neither group possessed the right to testify in court, and there were vanishingly few newspapers or other public forums in which they could respond to the racism that they confronted. Thus, the published writings and political speeches of Walker, Stewart, and Apess are invaluable for documenting the relationship between race and poverty from Black and Indigenous perspectives before the expansion of Black print culture in the late 1830s.[5] But they were neither solitary nor isolated figures. For the most significant years of their public lives, Walker and Stewart lived in Boston, New England's most dynamic Black community. Although Apess never lived in Boston, he, too, was influenced by the ideas that circulated there. Boston in the 1820s buzzed with Black political activism as it never had before, and it was in this context that Walker, Stewart, and Apess produced among the most impactful writing and speeches of the early antebellum period.[6] The African Meeting House was founded in 1806 as the city's first Black church and tended to the community's spiritual needs. Several other Black churches soon followed. These spaces were important physical sites for gathering and organizing. The African Society, a mutual aid society founded in 1796, acted as a community shield against the economic precariousness endemic to Black life, while the African Masonic Lodge, the first Black fraternal organization, founded in 1776, offered an important sense of community for the city's Black men.[7] In 1832, Boston's Black women formed the Afric-American Female Intelligence Society "for the diffusion of knowledge" and to protect members from destitution if they became too sick to work.[8] And, from its founding in 1826, members of the Massachusetts General Colored Association forcefully articulated a burgeoning ethos of antislavery and social equality.[9]

Walker's 1828 speech before the Massachusetts General Colored Association prefigured many of the arguments in his only written work, *Walker's Appeal, in Four Articles; Together With A Preamble, to the Coloured Citizens of the World, But in Particular, and Very Expressly, to Those of the United States of America*.[10] Often referred to today as

David Walker's Appeal, the publication of its first edition in 1829 was a watershed moment in the history of American abolition. Walker demanded "the complete overthrow of the system of slavery in every part of the country" and "all over the world."[11] The arguments of the *Appeal*—a call to end slavery, an appeal to Black racial unity, the claim that enslaved people had built the nation with their stolen labor, and the rejection of Black biological and moral inferiority—had appeared in fits and starts in Black oratory going back to the turn of the century. But Walker's *Appeal* was "the first sustained written assault upon slavery and racism to come from a Black man in the United States."[12] It is no exaggeration to say that his text set the stage for an abolitionist movement grounded in demands for the immediate, rather than gradual, abolition of slavery that emerged soon after its publication.[13] Using a network of Black seamen—perhaps including Stewart's husband James—Walker was able to distribute the *Appeal* across the Atlantic coast of the United States. The text left slaveowners apoplectic, forced white abolitionists to consider Black people as agents of their own freedom, and motivated others, including Stewart and Apess, to expand on the arguments and themes Walker laid out.[14]

Reading the *Appeal* spurred William Lloyd Garrison, one of the nation's most prominent antislavery reformers, to reject a gradual approach to abolition and embrace uncompromising immediatism. In 1831, he founded *The Liberator*, an abolitionist newspaper supported predominantly by Black subscribers.[15] It was in the pages of *The Liberator* that Stewart published her first political tract, *Religion and the Pure Principles of Morality*. Building on the themes of Walker's *Appeal*, Stewart made a series of public speeches in Boston over the course of the early 1830s—the first American woman to do so before mixed-gender audiences—in which she argued not only for the end of slavery and degrading labor, but also for Black women's rights. *The Liberator* printed these speeches as well, and in 1835

Garrison published a collection of Stewart's speeches and writings under the title *Productions of Mrs. Maria W. Stewart*.[16]

After fleeing his indenture as an adolescent, Apess traveled throughout New England and New York. In 1825 he settled in Providence, and an interest in religious instruction led him to become an ordained Methodist minister. Apess was involved with Providence's Black community, which was fighting discriminatory and exclusionary laws that, while primarily directed at Black people, also targeted Indians. In 1829 Apess left Providence for New York City, and published the first autobiography by a Native American, *A Son of the Forest*. Apess's subsequent works were more explicitly political, and bore marks of his engagement with Black and Native communities: "An Indian's Looking-Glass for the White Man" (1833), *Indian Nullification of the Unconstitutional Laws of Massachusetts, Relative to the Marshpee Tribe: Or, The Pretended Riot Explained* (1835), and *Eulogy on King Philip, As Pronounced at the Odeon, in Federal Street, Boston, by the Rev. William Apes, an Indian* (1836).[17]

It might seem odd to place Walker and Stewart, Black abolitionists, alongside Apess, a Pequot reformer. To be sure, Black and Native communities had distinct histories in early nineteenth-century New England. But they also overlapped in significant ways. And perhaps at no other moment in U.S. history were Black and Indigenous people so closely linked in white racial ideologies. Although he did not identify as Black in any of his extant writings, Apess, like many people of color in the antebellum period, was of mixed descent and possessed African heritage through his mother. Beginning in the eighteenth century, intermarriage was common between Black and Indigenous people. In the wake of devastating seventeenth-century Indian wars, Native communities experienced gender imbalances skewed toward women. And before the abolition of slavery in New England, the majority of enslaved people were men. Native women and Black men encountered one another working in white households and in segregated urban neighborhoods. Although white people became increasingly concerned with precise and discrete racial classification by the early nineteenth century, census takers and other officials were often unable to visually distinguish Black and Native people. Indeed, the very same person could be classified as "Negro," "Indian," or "mulatto" depending on who was doing the classifying. Mixed race individuals sometimes, like Apess, emphasized political and community ties to a single part of their identity; other times they shifted their way of identifying over time. But regardless of how any given individual chose to classify themselves or was classified by white census takers, white people often elided the differences between the two groups with the ambiguous category "persons of color."[18]

Walker, Stewart, and Apess each drew upon these overlapping histories and ideological ambiguities in their work. These writers narrated their own racial subjugation by linking the origins of the United States to the intertwined dynamics of enslavement and genocide. Most importantly, the history of Indigeneity disquiets any simple dichotomy between an enslaved South and free North in the post-Revolution period. The forms of dispossession Indigenous people were subject to did not hinge on the distinction between slavery and freedom; in fact, during this period the U.S. government crafted new forms of legal dependency to take advantage of Native people's ambiguous status.[19] Placing Blackness and Indigeneity side by side is to insist that racial capitalism could operate with equal facility in New England as it did in the South.[20]

Focusing on the political thought of Walker, Stewart, and Apess, this chapter proceeds in two parts. First, it describes the impoverished conditions under which Black and Indigenous people lived in antebellum New England. It also explains the strategies Walker, Stewart, and Apess advocated for ameliorating these conditions, including how they challenged the idea that Black and Native poverty was the result of natural racial inferiority by historicizing the legacies of enslavement and genocide in New England. Second, this chapter charts Walker, Stewart, and Apess's opposition to colonization (the resettlement of free Black people outside of the United States) and guardianship (white political authority over Native communities). To many white New Englanders, these propositions seemed more efficient and just solutions to the problem of Black and Indigenous poverty than extending those groups full political, social, and economic rights. Ultimately, the works of Walker, Stewart, and Apess reveal how racial capitalism thrived in a society that was not economically reliant upon racialized labor and had only a small population of people of color.

RACIAL CAPITALISM AND ITS DISCONTENTS IN ANTEBELLUM NEW ENGLAND

Walker's first biographer concluded that despite owning his own business, "Mr. Walker, like most reformers, was a poor man—he lived poor, and died poor."[21] This description captured the conditions that Black and Indigenous New Englanders lived under almost without exception. Black Bostonians, for example, were vastly overrepresented in the city's almshouses in the first decades of the nineteenth century. By midcentury Black people had nearly disappeared from almshouse rolls, less a testament to their social mobility and more a suggestion that their access to limited forms of social welfare narrowed over time.[22] Black New Englanders "constituted the most deprived and destitute element in the urban population."[23] Their circumstances were so dire, in fact, that in one public lecture, Stewart declared, "tell us no more of Southern slavery; for with few exceptions . . . I consider our condition but little better than that."[24] Racial prejudice excluded Black people both from avenues of economic advancement as well as public assistance, yet white people increasingly saw Black poverty not as the avoidable consequence of such exclusion but the expected result of innate racial inferiority.[25]

Racial capitalism in New England operated at the intersection of legal ambiguity and customary forms of social and economic exclusion. Only in rare cases were rights explicitly denied by statute. Formal segregation was intermittent and limited, and both Black and Native people possessed a range of legal rights. In Massachusetts, for example, Black men possessed the right to vote, and Black people generally had the rights of contract, property, and lawsuit (although they did not serve on juries until 1860).[26] Native people were not citizens and could not vote; the rights they did possess were upheld by a logic of paternalism.[27] Racial capitalism worked precisely because it was so diffuse—widespread white beliefs in racial inferiority articulated with institutionalized, but not legally codified, forms of exclusion (from higher education and apprenticeships, for example), market subversion (white workers' refusal to work alongside workers of color and to admit them into unions), and the calculated risk that fraud or theft against Black and Native people would go unpunished (stealing resources from Indian reservations). All were undergirded by the notion that such was the natural state of things. Walker, Stewart, and Apess challenged this order first by documenting it and then by arguing that it was not natural at all, but rather the cumulative effect of regimes of racial capitalism that began with enslavement and colonialism and continued into the antebellum period.

Black men and women in New England's cities were barred from all but the most marginal forms of labor. This reality was a distinct shift wrought by emancipation. Because enslavement offered opportunities for slaveowners to profit from the skilled, specialized, and professional labor of their Black property, there was no prohibition on enslaved people learning trades. As emancipation cut off the ability to exploit Black skill, Black people's access to skilled work disappeared. This state of affairs was not the inevitable outcome of emancipation or of white people's racist beliefs. It was largely the result of organized exclusion on the part of white laborers, who feared that the newly free Black population would be satisfied with a lower standard of living than whites, and could thus undercut white workers by accepting lower wages. As a result, many Black men were relegated to employment as day laborers on the docks of port cities like Boston or Providence—seasonal work that was interrupted by icy winters—and both Black men and women were vastly overrepresented as domestic workers. In fact, the majority of Black women who worked for wages did so in white households. Service was a racialized occupation in the antebellum United States; one visiting Englishman noted that it was "considered as degrading by all untainted with the curse of African descent."[28] Stewart came to the similar conclusion that "few white persons of either sex, who are calculated for anything else, are willing to spend their lives and bury their talents in performing mean, servile labor."[29]

Indigenous people in New England faced economic marginalization similar to that of free Black people as the region's capitalist economy developed, and "Indians formed part of a larger transient class that contributed to, but barely benefited from, the rise of industrialization, agrarian improvement, and consumer culture in southern New England."[30] Although the largest tribes held reservations of several thousand acres—and more than ten thousand in the case of the Mashpee, New England's largest Indigenous community—the U.S. government did not recognize them as sovereign nations. Communities governed these reserves through an evolving combination of traditional practices and English laws regarding the commons, and while every member of a community held reservation lands in common, they did so under the auspices of state governments, who appointed guardians to make decisions about a community's resources and whose ultimate authority superseded that of tribal leaders.[31] As a result, New England's Indigenous people possessed only limited political autonomy to combat the pressures that the changing economy placed upon their communities. As newly developing industries, such as mills, laid claim to lands that poor white farmers used to draw subsistence and supplement other forms of work and survival, whites began to poach fish and steal wood from reservations. Environmental transformations wrought by capitalism affected the health and course of rivers, further affecting traditional modes of subsistence. And Native people themselves were not exempt from the turn toward a consumer-based, rather than subsistence production–based, economy. While they could meet many of their needs through the land, Indigenous people also experimented with wage work, sold goods to white settlers, and even leased timber-cutting rights to whites. Amid these shifts, the guardian system meant that Indians ultimately had few tools with which to combat white predation.

In addition to these forms of structural exclusion, New England's people of color were also persistently vulnerable to theft, fraud, and plunder. Despite possessing some formal rights, Black and Indigenous people had little legal power and few prospects for securing their interests in court. Walker noted early in the *Appeal* that even if Black people could find enough success to acquire a bit of land or property, whites readily cheated them out of it. "Can a man of colour buy a piece of land and keep it peaceably? Will not some white man try to get it from him, even if it is in a *mud hole?*" Walker asked. "I must, really, observe that in this very city, when a man of colour dies, if he owned any real estate it most generally falls into the hands of some white person. The wife and children of the deceased may weep and lament if they please, but the estate will be kept snug enough by its white possessor."[32] Even if working Black men and women of Boston accepted the degraded conditions in which they labored in an effort to find some measure of economic security, they were still subject to such individual acts of exploitation. In fact, Stewart found herself in the very situation Walker described. Stewart's husband, James, was a veteran of the War of 1812 and a businessman of no small success. Stewart described him as "a light, bright mulatto," and James's complexion may have in fact allowed him to pass as white before his marriage to Stewart as he was building his shipping business.[33] James died three years after he and Stewart wed; he drew up a will just before his death, and, as one of Stewart's friends recounted, "left her amply provided for; but the executors literally robbed and cheated her out of every cent."[34] The executor, Daniel Badger, absconded with the original will and submitted in its place a version in which Stewart was left with only a single bed, the remainder of the estate bequeathed to Badger himself. While a judge eventually rejected the false will, Badger then successfully claimed that James owed him and other creditors a large sum.[35] Stewart was left with nothing but what she called "poverty's dark shade."[36]

Apess experienced similar forms of fraud, and attributed these experiences to his economic vulnerability as an Indigenous person. Like James Stewart, Apess fought in the War of 1812, convinced that enlistment was preferable to indenture.[37] Apess felt little in the way of patriotic fervor, writing in his autobiography, "I could not think why I should risk my life and limbs fighting for the white man, who had cheated my forefathers out of their land."[38] Recruits were promised a monthly wage, an enlistment bonus, and 160 acres of land, but Apess, like other Indigenous people who fought in the war, received no back pay, no bonus, and no land.[39] His experiences in the war led Apess to conclude, "I could never think that the government acted right towards the '*Natives*,' not merely in refusing to pay us, but in claiming our services in cases of perilous emergency, and still deny us the right of citizenship."[40] After the war, Apess made his way to Montreal, where he became "addicted to drinking rum" and held a series of odd jobs.⁴¹ Dissatisfied with the work, he traveled to Kingston, Ontario, and found employment as a shipboard cook. Apess recounted, "I was onboard the vessel some time, and when we settled, the captain cheated me out of twelve dollars," a full month's pay.⁴² Apess eventually returned to Connecticut, where he resolved "to go to work and be steady."⁴³ He hired himself out to a white farmer, and after "a month or two" asked for his wages. The farmer refused, and Apess recounted, "when I wanted my pay, he undertook to cheat me out of it, and thinking to treat me as he would a degraded African slave," the farmer chased Apess off with a wooden stake.⁴⁴ Apess concluded that white people were "ready at all times to speculate on the Indians and cheat them out of their rightful possessions."⁴⁵ He made sense of the theft of his wages as part of a larger pattern of racialized dispossession rather than episodes of personal misfortune.

In a speech before the Massachusetts Colored General Association, Walker reluctantly admitted "that the major part of us are ignorant and poor, I am at this time unprepared to deny."⁴⁶ Stewart came to a similar conclusion when she observed that "most of our color have dragged out a miserable existence in servitude from the cradle to the grave. And what literary acquirement can be made, or useful knowledge derived, from either maps, books, or charts, by those who continually drudge from Monday morning until Sunday noon?"⁴⁷ Although organized exclusion from skilled trades and pervasive theft on the part of whites were the causes of this poverty, it was New England's people of color whose criminality went unquestioned. In 1821, the Massachusetts legislature reported of Boston that "the good order, and tranquility of this town, has of late years, been *often* and *much disturbed* by violent riots at that part of the town, where persons of colour are collected in great numbers."⁴⁸ Black people were overrepresented in Boston's prisons four times over, especially for theft and crimes of vice such as intoxication and transgressive sexual activity.[49] Compared with whites, Black people were more likely to be convicted, more likely to be sentenced to prison (rather than paying a fine), and more likely to serve a longer sentence.[50] To the Massachusetts legislature, these statistics—and the fact that neither Black nor Indigenous people had the right to sit on a jury or serve as judges—were not evidence of racism but of Black disorderliness. For white people, such logic further naturalized the very poverty for which they were responsible. Similarly, to white observers, New England Indians, who survived through a combination of wage labor, hunting, fishing, and subsistence farming, were a backward people. In their view Natives existed at the margins of society because of their unfortunate attachment to racialized cultural practices and enduring savagery, when in fact, all poor people, including white people, relied upon a similarly eclectic range of work to get by.[51] Walker, Stewart, and Apess set themselves to the task of countering these beliefs. They did so by encouraging their communities to reject racialized and gendered forms of servility, invoking the long histories of racial dispossession that had shaped the economic fortunes of the nation, and supporting a range of mutual aid efforts meant to provide a bulwark against economic immiseration.

The vast majority of Black Bostonians were day laborers, servants, or worked in similarly marginal professions, and many did not have the time, inclination, or ability to protest their conditions. This reality meant that Walker and Stewart had to criticize poverty without denigrating the labor of the poor. They did so by exalting the will to thrive and sustain family life expressed in the willingness to perform marginal labor, while rejecting the racial hierarchy implied by Black people's overrepresentation in this type of work. A central pillar of their argument was that white greed was a primary cause of Black poverty. Walker used the term "avarice" in connection with white people dozens of times in the *Appeal*, and reminded his readers "that it is the greatest desire and object of the greater part of the whites, to keep us ignorant, and make us work to support them and their families."[52] Such a wretched state of affairs could only come about through the indoctrination of Black subservience. Walker recounted a conversation with a Black bootblack whose only aspiration was to have a steady supply of shoes to clean. Walker left the conversation disgusted. He wrote, "I do not mean to speak against the occupations by which we acquire enough and sometimes scarcely that, to render ourselves and families comfortable through life. I am subjected to the same inconvenience, as you all." Walker clarified that his objections were reserved for "our *glorying* and being *happy* in such low employments."[53] This incident, and others like it, led Walker to conclude that the reason white people were "able to keep their feet on our throats" had nothing to do with whites' natural superiority but the "mean, servile spirit" of Black people, which, Walker believed, prevented them from questioning their subservience.[54]

Stewart touched upon similar themes in her work, and came to the same conclusion as Walker regarding humble labor. In one public address, Stewart said, "I do not consider it derogatory, my friends, for persons to live out in service. There are many whose inclination leads them to aspire no higher; and I would highly commend the performance of almost anything for an honest livelihood."[55] Yet doing such work without a word of protest could also lead whites to believe that they were correct in their assertions that servitude was the natural place for Black people. "They boldly assert that did we possess a natural independence of soul, and feel a love for liberty within our breasts, some one of our sable race, long before this, would have testified it, notwithstanding the disadvantages under which we labor." Stewart described a nearly impossible situation, for even as whites understood Black people's quiet acceptance of such labor as evidence of their satisfaction, "if we complain, it is considered the height of impertinence."[56] Stewart also expressed concern that continual manual labor "irritates our tempers and sours our dispositions" until "we care but little whether we live or die."⁵⁷ Although she acknowledged that free Black people were not subject to the commodification and violence of slavery, she saw little opportunity for their betterment while they were trapped in service and domestic labor.

Stewart rejected not only racial servitude but gendered servitude as well. In her speeches and writing she often drew parallels between white expectations for Black obeisance and Black women's deference to the men of the race. "How long shall the fair daughters of Africa be compelled to bury their minds and talents beneath a load of iron pots and kettles?" she asked. Stewart was adamant that if Black women accepted servitude as their natural place they could never improve their own condition or that of Black people more generally. She refused the notion that Black women should be confined to performing domestic labor in white households or their own, leaving advocacy of the race to men. Stewart often chided the men in her audiences, justifying her unconventional public role by alluding to the idea that if men were unable or unwilling to do what was necessary to improve the fortunes of the race, then the task would fall to a woman. "I am sensible of former prejudices; but it is high time for prejudices and animosities to cease from among us," she wrote, calling publicly for Boston's Black community to support women's aspirations.⁵⁸ Stewart knew that articulating her position so forcefully ran the risk of alienating much of her audience, but it remained a constant theme in her work until her last address, in which she left her audience with the advice "let us no longer talk of prejudice till prejudice becomes extinct at home. Let us no longer talk of opposition until opposition till we cease to oppose our own."⁵⁹ Stewart was among the first reformers to analogize race and gender, suggesting that ameliorating the condition of free Black people must also include advocating for women.

Walker, Stewart, and Apess also justified their rejection of ideas about natural racial inferiority by looking to history. There they found alternative explanations for the differing conditions between whites and people of color. Such histories were rendered invisible when white people recast their effects as, in words of one historian, "simply the working out of natural laws, the inevitable consequence of . . . racial inferiority."[60] For each of these three reformers, the low status of Black and Indigenous people in New England was an extension of the racial dispossession that was foundational to building the United States. Although all poor and working people were vulnerable in the emerging capitalist economy, Walker, Stewart, and Apess each argued that people of color experienced such vulnerability as an extension of earlier forms of racialized expropriation.

Stewart aptly captured this view when she described how whites had long derived status and power from the theft of Black labor. "Cast your eyes about, look as far as you can see; all, all is owned by the lordly white, except here and there a lowly dwelling which the man of color, midst deprivations, fraud, and opposition has been scarce able to procure. Like King Solomon, who put neither nail nor hammer to the temple, yet received the praise; so also have the white Americans gained themselves a name, like the names of the great men that are in the earth, while in reality we have been their principal foundation and support."[61] Walker was even more stark in his assessment of the role of slavery in building the nation, writing "America is more our country, than it is the whites—we have enriched it with our *blood and tears*. The greatest riches in all America have arisen from our blood and tears."[62] And they were correct. Both the survival and economic success of colonial New England relied upon trade with the emerging center of the Atlantic capitalist economy, the West Indian plantation complex.[63] Early settlers enslaved Indigenous peoples during seventeenth-century Indian wars—including Apess's people, the Pequots—and sold them to planters who primarily enslaved Africans. These planters constituted the primary market for all New England goods, not just human chattel, and trade with them undergirded the region's economic development.

Just as trade in slaves was crucially important to New England's early economic success, so, too, was labor of enslaved people.[64] In eighteenth-century Boston, New England's economic center, enslaved people made up as much as 15 percent of the population at midcentury, a much higher percentage than the antebellum free Black population. They were a vital part of the city's laboring population, particularly when it came to specialized artisanal labor. One historian argues that enslaved people were "so vital, in fact, that if they suddenly disappeared from the historical landscape, Boston's economy would have collapsed."[65] Outside of Boston, New England's enslaved people were concentrated in professional and wealthy households, where their labor freed male heads of household to secure their family's economic interests away from the home. Part of the value of enslaved labor, then, was in "easing the transition from a household-based to a market-based economy" for those who could afford it.[66] Given this history it was no wonder Walker lamented, "Now, what can be more aggravating, than for the Americans, after having treated us so bad, to hold us up to the world as such great throat-cutters? It appears to me as though they are resolved to assail us with every species of affliction that their ingenuity can invent."[67] Doing so contributed to the erasure of the very histories that entangled racial plunder and wealth accumulation in New England.

In his most influential book, *Indian Nullification of the Unconstitutional Laws of Massachusetts*, Apess, writing in the third person, recounted that "the author has often been told seriously, by sober persons, that his fellows were a link between the whites and the brute creation, an inferior race of men to whom the Almighty had less regard than to their neighbours, and whom he had driven from their possessions to make room for a race more favoured."⁶⁸ Apess countered such ideas about racial atavism by historicizing the ongoing dispossession of New England's Native people. Apess drew his readers' attention to stolen land, suggesting that the theft and fraud he and other Indigenous people experienced in the nineteenth century was but a microcosm of the larger theft of land that New England Indians suffered in the seventeenth and eighteenth centuries. According to Apess, on their arrival, the first English settlers to Plymouth, "without asking liberty from any one . . . possessed themselves of a portion of the country, and built themselves houses," finally writing a treaty and commanding the Indians to "accede to it."⁶⁹ Thus Apess concluded "it has been considered as a trifling thing for the whites to make war on the Indians for the purpose of driving them from their country, and taking possession thereof. This was, in their estimation, all right, as it helped to extend the territory, and enriched some individuals."⁷⁰ The seizure of Indigenous lands was not the long-finished consequence of Indian wars centuries past, but an ongoing process that continued to inflect Native life.

What was once achieved through war was accomplished in Apess's time through law: "It is a sorrowful truth that, heretofore, all legislation regarding the affairs of Indians, has had a direct tendency to degrade them, to drive them from their homes, and the graves of their fathers, and to give their lands as a spoil to the general government, or to the several States."⁷¹ Bringing together Black and Indigenous histories of racial capitalism, Apess argued that the beliefs of the first settlers, "pretended pious, has been the foundation of all the slavery and degradation in the American Colonies, towards colored people." These histories, combined with the racial indignities Apess suffered throughout his life, led him to conclude that "the doctrines of the pilgrims has grown up with the people," meaning the attitudes toward Native people in the antebellum period were more mature versions of an earlier century's.⁷² Although in the nineteenth century white people viewed their relationship with Native New Englanders as one of benevolent paternalism, Apess saw a direct continuity from seventeenth-century enslavement and genocide to the present. He possessed a special disdain for missionaries, whose purpose in proselytizing to Indians was "to degrade them worse, to bring them into society where they must welter out their days in disgrace merely because their skin is of a different complexion."[73] Going even further, he wrote, "nothing has more effectually contributed to the decay of several tribes than the course pursued by their missionaries."[74] As white New Englanders turned to new theories of race that emphasized natural and inalienable difference even as they disavowed their investments in slavery and colonialism, Walker, Stewart, and Apess narrated racial dispossession as the result of centuries of racial capitalism that survived the slavery/freedom divide to the era of burgeoning industrial capitalism.

Walker, Stewart, and Apess paired their rejection of racial servility and revisionist histories with support for a range of community-building and mutual aid projects, both formal and informal. Black Bostonians participated in Freemasonry beginning in 1775 during the British occupation of Boston. In 1787, Boston's Black Freemasons received their own charter as African Lodge No. 457.[75] The African Lodge was an important tool for political education and organizing in the postrevolutionary decades, and it was one of the earliest antislavery organizations in the city. Black Freemasons paid membership dues to the lodge, which provided the organization with a reservoir of cash that it could use to aid members who became sick or unemployed. If a member passed away, the African Lodge could pay for funeral costs and support surviving family members. Soon after his arrival in Boston, Walker joined the lodge. Alongside the Massachusetts General Colored Association, the African Lodge served as a testing ground for Walker's ideas, which he later expanded upon in the *Appeal*.[76] Walker also used his clothing shop as a gathering space for the community, and he took in boarders as well. His biographer recalled that "his house was the shelter and the home of the poor and needy."[77] Such an arrangement doubtless helped Walker make ends meet, but it also ensured that others would not become indigent.

Stewart carved out a role for women in such mutual aid projects. Boston's African Society, the city's oldest mutual aid organization, was an all-men's organization. In exchange for dues, it offered a limited form of health insurance, burial funds, and generally socialized economic risk to the extent possible among an impoverished community. While Philadelphia, the city with the largest free Black population in the early nineteenth century, had a robust network of women's mutual aid societies, Boston did not.[78] Stewart did not let that limit her opportunities to rally the Black community. She enjoined her readers and audiences to pool funds for the construction of Black schools. "Let our money, instead of being thrown away as heretofore, be appropriated for schools and seminaries of learning for our children and youth," she told one audience.[79] Education played a unique role in antebellum Boston's history of Black poverty. The city's public school system dates to the early seventeenth century, and, until after the Revolution, Black children could attend these institutions, which were not formally segregated. But the harassment, racism, and hostility Black students experienced made Boston's public schools terrorizing environments. Truancy was frequent, and Black Bostonians felt that their children were being functionally denied an education. Beginning in 1787, the community asked the Massachusetts legislature to fund all-Black schools; the request was denied, and again in 1798. Finally, in 1812, the Boston School Committee agreed to fund Black schools, but did not give the Black community authority over appointments or administration. The system consisted only of primary and grammar schools, and the Black schools were more poorly funded than white schools.

Black Bostonians thus paid the same taxes as whites, but received less in compensation. Although prevalent racism meant that education was far from a guarantee of steady employment, the denial of equal education contributed to the relegation of Black people to the lowest forms of work.[80] Thus Stewart imagined a collective economic project that might extend Black educational attainment and keep authority in the hands of Black parents, driven by the efforts of women. She entreated, "Let every female heart become united, and let us raise a fund ourselves; and at the end of one year and half, we might be able to lay the corner-stone for the building of a High School, that the higher branches of knowledge might be enjoyed by us."[81] Stewart's efforts represented an effort to recognize Black women's economic contributions to the Black community and her belief that women should take a leading role in such political organizing.

While New England Indians did not form the same kinds of urban communities as Black people, and thus did not establish formal aid societies, reservations served a similar function. By the antebellum period, many Native people worked as servants in white households or took on various forms of precarious wage and day labor that took them away from their communities and reservations. While total self-sufficiency was no longer possible, these communities could offer temporary respite from labor in the outside world. Apess himself benefited from such generosity and spent time among both the Haudenosaunee and Mashpee peoples during periods when he wished to escape the predations of wage labor. The Black and white refugees of capitalism also sometimes found succor on reservations; in the case of Black people, this was most frequently due to familial ties created through intermarriage. The idea that Indian reservations could be refuges from the imperatives of capitalism rather than simply quaint time capsules that preserved the disappearing traditions of Indigenous people perturbed white observers, who associated racial mixing among the poor with dangerous social disorder and the subversion of natural laws, and evidence that Indians could neither assimilate into capitalist social relations nor preserve traditional lifeways without white oversight.[82]

White New Englanders naturalized, and even profited from, the economic precarity that was a legacy of racial dispossession. Yet the presence of Black and Native people always carried with it the threat or social disorder, and in the antebellum period whites attempted to stem this threat by reimagining the place of the region's people of color. While whites would think of these projects as informed by benevolence and the antithesis of the racial violence that white Southerners depended upon for their wealth, Walker, Stewart, and Apess saw yet further continuities.

COLONIZATION, GUARDIANSHIP, AND THE PROBLEM OF RACE

Racial capitalism took on a regionally specific appearance in New England. Forms of racial inequality first wrought by enslavement and dispossession remained intact even as those systems receded due to the ways people of color were especially vulnerable to poverty in the emerging capitalist economy. To white people, such inequality seemed timeless and inevitable, yet also threatening to social order. By the early decades of the nineteenth century, these enduring conditions of racialized economic inequality led white New Englanders to explore methods for resolving this tension in ways that further eroded Black and Native people's limited existing rights. These methods—colonization for free Black people, and guardianship for Indigenous communities—seemed benevolent to many white people, generous solutions to a problem of racial poverty in whose origins whites acknowledged no culpability. Compared with Black chattel slavery and forced Indigenous removal in the South, both of which rapidly expanded in this period, white New Englanders' schemes for colonization and guardianship seem insignificant. Yet forms of racial capitalism that can articulate alongside notions of freedom, benevolence, and improvement have proven far more durable than those that rely upon the raw violence of slavery and removal. In contesting colonization and guardianship, Walker, Stewart, and Apess argued that these projects would neither benefit people of color nor stabilize New England society. To the contrary, they revealed that colonization and guardianship bore traces of earlier forms of dispossession that Black and Native New Englanders had struggled against for centuries.

The social arrangements of Black and Indigenous communities seemed threatening to white people. Although these arrangements were often either the result of racial poverty or acts of resistance to it, whites tended to understand them as further evidence of people of color's inherent backwardness. Indeed, economic success, or the lack thereof, or the refusal to engage in wage labor at all could each be a sign of racialized disorder.

Throughout New England, an interracial working class gathered in port cities and centers of trade such as Boston, drawn together by taverns, brothels, and boarding houses. This group consisted of seamen, day laborers, the precariously housed, and the transient poor of all stripes. As early as the 1790s, white New Englanders were concerned about how the presence of free Black people would depreciate property values, since New England cities were not segregated by law or policy but by the economic pressures of real estate. Black people were pushed out of all but the poorest neighborhoods, and those neighborhoods became associated with Blackness despite the fact that the Black population was too small for Black people to ever make up the majority of residents. And the forms of working-class social life that flourished in such environments, such as illicit sex, interracial intimacy, extralegal economic activity, and revelry that fell outside middle-class moral norms—in short, the refusal to comply with social expectations—became associated with racial disorder. Unable to abide a household that might, for example, consist of a widowed Black woman who took in male boarders, white mobs assaulted Black neighborhoods indiscriminately, making no distinction between the specific targets of their ire, such as brothels, and Black residences more generally.[83]

Yet white New Englanders were no more satisfied by Black economic success. Against all odds, and despite the great poverty of the majority, New England's cities were home to a Black professional class. While small in number, the very existence of Black professionals who could scrape together something resembling economic security gave lie to the idea that racial nature, rather than law or policy, kept Black people at the bottom of the economic hierarchy. White workers both skilled and unskilled feared that the presence of free Black people in the labor market would incite a race to the bottom for wages. Indeed, "whites found any degree of success among blacks—any evidence of free people of color *living like white people*—to be as disruptive of the social order as the presence of indigent, dependent, transient, or publicly rowdy ones" and thus endeavored to maintain a clear racial hierarchy by controlling access to labor and employment.[84]

In the early nineteenth century, Indian reservations and villages began to seem similarly threatening to whites. Although Native New Englanders worked on ships, in white households, and as day laborers, leaving their communities of origin for long periods of time, when they had the opportunity to return, these communities "acted as reservoirs of antimarket forces," providing Indigenous people with access to care, shelter, and sustenance—in short, a reprieve from the demands of capitalism.[85] Oftentimes non-Indian people had access to these "antimarket" refuges as well. Because of the frequent intermarriages between Indigenous women and Black men who either served in white households with Indian women or on ships with Indian men in the late eighteenth and early nineteenth centuries, Black husbands could become part of Native kin communities. The white and Black poor who were unrelated by kinship could also sometimes find sanctuary in Native communities. One Boston newspaper complained that local Indian villages were places where "the vagrant, the dissipated, and the felonious do congregate," while the guardian of Apess's people, Connecticut's Mashantucket Pequots, found that they were "extremely hospitable to all vagabonds; receiving, without hesitation, all that come to them, whether white, mulatto, Indian, or negro."[86] These white observers associated poverty with immoral behavior, and, since Indians possessed many immoral cultural traits, such as unsanctioned marriages, improper gender roles, and collective property rights, it made sense to them that the white and Black poor found common ground with Indians. What escaped their notice was the possibility that these people were refugees of capitalism, a possibility that was obscured by the racialized language of a shared immorality.

The solution to these problems of racial disorderliness took two distinct forms. For free Black people, it was colonization, or their removal beyond the borders of the nation. Although the notion of colonization had eighteenth-century roots, Northern emancipation after the Revolution led to the founding of the American Colonization Society (ACS) in 1816, which founded the African colony of Liberia for the purpose of expelling the newly freed Black population. For whites, slavery controlled and suppressed Black people's naturally disorderly disposition, and the absence of slavery meant that free Black people would be a perpetual threat to the stability of the nation. Something like the opposite was true in their minds about Natives. Both the preservation of Indigenous people's traditional cultures and the possibility of their assimilation were interrupted by the corrupting influences of the poor and criminal, both white and Black. Only by instituting even further restrictions upon the autonomy and self-governance of Native communities could white overseers curb these tendencies. Beginning in the eighteenth century, governments of the New England colonies appointed guardians to make legal decisions for these communities. Many Indigenous groups subject to guardianship were able to successfully petition the British government for the restoration of autonomy over the course of the century, but after the Revolution, New England state legislatures reestablished the system.

Mobilization against colonization was one of the landmark issues for Black Northerners in the 1820s and 1830s, and Walker, almost single-handedly, turned the emerging antislavery community in New England against colonization by framing it as a scheme to further entrench slavery in the South rather than provide economic opportunities for Black emigrants to Liberia. Colonization was one of Walker's major targets of opprobrium in the *Appeal*. At the inaugural meeting of the ACS, Henry Clay, then Speaker of the House, imbued the promise of Black people's removal to Liberia with providential significance. Clay hoped settlement in Africa "might be rendered instrumental to the introduction into that extensive quarter of the globe, of the arts, civilization, and Christianity." And, by sending Black Americans as its emissaries, Clay asked, "may we not hope that America will extinguish a great portion of that moral debt which she has contracted to that unfortunate continent?"[87] Walker remained unconvinced that exiling Black people to Africa would pay any debt white Americans owed to either party. He dismissed "Mr. Clay and his slaveholding party" as "men who are resolved to keep us in eternal wretchedness," and asked his readers if they would trust a scheme thought up by those "who have always been our oppressors and murderers, and who are for colonizing us, more through apprehension than humanity."[88] Walker was right to be suspicious, and right to claim colonization was borne from white apprehension about Black freedom. White supporters of colonization ranged from Northern reformers who genuinely hated slavery but could not fathom a place for free Black people, to Southern slaveowners who worried free Black people might threaten the institution of slavery by inciting rebellion or serving as an example to the enslaved. Regardless of motivation, by refusing to imagine a place for Black freedom within the borders of the United States, colonization did not just represent the separation Black and white people spatially; it contributed to the production and sharpening of racial categories themselves.[89]

Although Clay and other supporters presented colonization as a philanthropic scheme, the racially exclusive vision of freedom championed by the ACS also had several overlapping economic motivations. With memories of the failed rebellion of Denmark Vesey still fresh, many white Southerners feared that free Black people would inspire further revolts among the enslaved, their very presence proof that there was no inherent connection between Blackness and enslavement. Exiling these potential subversives would protect the institution of slavery and maintain the economic system built on it. Colonization also allowed white Americans to oppose slavery without having to accept multiracial democracy as the result. This line of reasoning was especially persuasive in the North, where white laborers feared competition with free Black people for unskilled labor would drive down their wages. And, while Clay spoke of Black colonists' relationship to Africans as one of benevolence, the ACS had commercial motives and expected an American presence on the African continent to facilitate trade and access to natural resources. Colonization served the racial and class interests of white Northerners and Southerners alike.[90]

Despite the participation of Northerners, white and some Black, Walker remained convinced that colonization was a proslavery scheme, a "colonizing trick." To him it was nothing more than a slaveholders' plan "to get those of the coloured people, who are said to be free, away from among those of our brethren whom they unjustly hold in bondage, so that they may be enabled to keep them the more secure in ignorance and wretchedness, to support them and their children, and consequently they would have the more obedient slaves."[91] Should the ACS be victorious, the presence of free Black people would no longer muddy the border between Blackness and enslavement, whiteness and freedom. Black labor creating white wealth would continue to be the natural order of things.

Stewart, too, directed her ire at white compatriots in the North who claimed they were performing a charity for Black people. Stewart challenged the motives behind colonization when she said, "if the colonizationists are the real friends to Africa, let them expend the money which they collect in erecting a college to educate her injured sons in this land of gospel, light, and liberty; for it would be most thankfully received on our part, and convince us of the truth of their professions, and save time, expense, and anxiety." Their refusal to do so would seem to confirm that the ACS was moved principally by the desire to scour any traces of Blackness in the North; any benefit Black people might derive from their exile was incidental. Stewart was convinced that "their hearts are so frozen toward us they had rather their money be sunk into the ocean than to administer it to our relief: and I fear, if they dared, like Pharaoh, king of Egypt, they would order every male child among us to be drowned."[92] Although she drew from biblical history rather than the recent past of her own country, Stewart, like Walker, associated colonizationists with regimes of slavery. She reminded her audience that white Americans had already driven Native people from their homes and refused to meet the same fate, sooner choosing death. "They would drive us to a strange land. But before I go, the bayonet shall pierce me through."[93]

Colonization indeed allowed American reformers with a wide range of opinions on the institution of slavery to find common ground in their desire for a white republic. Central to that common ground was the idea that while Black freedom could not find purchase within the borders of the United States, colonization could mirror the emigration in search of freedom so central to American mythology; each ship full of free Black people bound for Liberia was a potential *Mayflower*.[94] Historian Nicholas Guyatt has described the drive to exile free Black people so that they might fulfill the promise of liberty elsewhere as a precursor to separate-but-equal ideology.[95] Indeed, colonization allowed whites to reconcile the tension between dedication to white supremacy and to ideals of freedom. Supporters of colonization imagined a spatial separation from free Black people but not an absolute political break; the pioneers in Liberia would be expected to serve American religious and economic interests in Africa, bolstering the nation's own imperial ambitions across the Atlantic even as Indian removal facilitated expansion to the west.[96] Walker and Stewart were representative of free Black people's widespread rejection of this vision of Black freedom. Indeed, the intellectual and political battles against colonization were central to Black understandings of freedom and democracy throughout the antebellum period.[97]

During his travels as an itinerant preacher, Apess spent time with the Mashpee, a Wampanoag people and one of the largest Indigenous communities in New England. The Mashpee reservation was located in Barnstable County, Massachusetts, better known as Cape Cod. The region had long been the epicenter of the New England whaling industry, but by the antebellum period, Indian whalers had largely been pushed out of the industry as technological advances led to increased crewman pay, making the work more appealing to white seamen.[98] Like all New England Indians, the Mashpee lacked communal autonomy, and when Apess arrived in Mashpee, they were engaged in an ongoing struggle against their overseers. With Apess's help, the Mashpee successfully won the right to govern themselves with the same degree of independence as white communities, one of the most significant political victories in Native New England history.

After the catastrophic violence of King Philip's War at the end of the seventeenth century, colonial officials appointed ministers to act as guardians to protect and preserve the Mashpee, with all the paternalism and condescension the term implies. In 1760, the Mashpee petitioned King George III in an effort to gain greater political autonomy, and at the Crown's insistence, in 1763 the Massachusetts legislature granted the Mashpee the right to elect their own town officials, offering a counterweight to the single appointed guardian. However, after the Revolution, Massachusetts replaced elected town officials with a board of overseers appointed by the governor, with broad and sweeping authority, including "full power to regulate the police of the plantation; to establish rules for managing the affairs, interests, and concerns of the Indians and inhabitants. They may improve and lease the lands of the Indians, and their *tenements*; regulate the streams, ponds, and fisheries; mete out lots for their particular improvements; control and regulate absolutely, their bargains, contracts, wages, and other dealings, take care of their poor, and bind out their children to suitable persons."[99] Guardianship had its origin in the idea that Indians were a dependent category of persons, such as children, who could not make their own legal, political, or economic decisions without oversight; in 1816, the Massachusetts Supreme Court described Native people as "unfortunate children of the public, entitled to protection and support."[100] In some cases, the high social standing and legal fluency of guardians and overseers could achieve their stated goal of protecting Indian communities from white encroachment by enforcing prohibitions against selling land to non-Natives and by facilitating legal responses to theft of resources or game, but just as often guardians abetted these forms of dispossession. By the turn of the nineteenth century, New England

Indians increasingly saw guardianship as a form of domination rather than aid, and demanded the same right to self-governance as predominantly white New England communities. "Guardians chosen from the region's elites were generally concerned with maintaining social order in a time of rapid and threatening changes, while Indians increasingly shared the conditions and concerns of the laboring poor," and thus the revival of guardianship was central to the ways that New England's Indigenous people experienced the rise of capitalism.[101]

By the time Apess arrived in Mashpee in 1833, the tribe had been petitioning the state legislature to have greater independence for decades. Five years earlier in 1827, the legislature granted the Mashpee and other Native communities in Massachusetts the right to elect their own overseers. Their guardian, however, still exerted tremendous influence over the Mashpee's affairs. The issues at play were bound up with the tensions brought about by New England's transition to capitalism. Guardians, usually white elites invested in traditional forms of social deference and hierarchy, were often critical of both too much democracy as well as the social dislocations of capitalism. They thought of their duty to Indians as protecting them against both white theft as well as rash decisions about how to interact with the new capitalist economy, which prevented the communities from benefiting from the voluntary sale of collective resources. Guardians were at once invested in both the preservation of an unchanging vision of Indigenous communal values and Native assimilation. Although in theory the two positions were contradictory, holding them simultaneously allowed guardians to justify nearly any decision as legitimate in their role as paternal stewards. They could, for example, demand that Native land be divided into privately owned parcels rather than held in common, on the one hand, while preventing the owner of such a parcel from selling timber cut on their land as a profit-making venture. The Mashpee did not all agree on the proper use of their community's resources or the best way to hold land, but they did demand the right to make such decisions without white oversight.¹⁰²

Apess built his case against the Mashpee's guardianship by arguing that it was a form of economic exploitation rather than benevolence. When he first came to the reservation, Apess was surprised to find that religious services at the tribe's meetinghouse were attended exclusively by white congregants from surrounding towns. Although the state levied taxes and fees against the Mashpee for their religious education, they did not have the right to choose their own preacher. The Congregationalist assigned to their community did not fit with their more evangelical sensibilities, so most Mashpee declined to attend sermons. To Apess, this state of affairs functionally redistributed Native resources to the white parishioners, since the Mashpee were the ones paying for the services. Pushed on by this example, Apess attempted to calculate the sum stolen from the Mashpee by the fact that they paid far more in taxes than they derived in benefits over nearly a century and a half of guardianship. He also included the wage theft of those who were bound into indenture and were not paid for their labor in white households. The latter was no insignificant amount, and Apess quipped, "I could tell of one of our masters who has not only supported himself and family out of the proceeds of our lands and labors, but has educated a son at Harvard, at our expense."¹⁰³ After his investigation Apess concluded, "though it is manifest that we have cost the government absolutely much less than nothing, we have been called State paupers, and as such treated. Those are strange paupers who maintain themselves, and pay large sums to others in the bargain. Heigho! It is a fine thing to be an Indian. One might almost as well be a slave."¹⁰⁴ The guardianship policy of Massachusetts created, or at least exacerbated, the very conditions among the Mashpee that it purported to ameliorate, and in doing so it looked something like slavery to Apess's eye.

Reflecting upon his time with the Mashpee, Apess wrote that guardianship "laws were calculated to drive the tribe from their possessions, and annihilate them, as a people."[105] The charge of pauperism articulated well alongside other justifications for eliminating Indigenous sovereignty, proof that Indians could not rationally or reasonably manage their own land and resources without white oversight. Whites stole Indian resources in the legally sanctioned form of taxes and wage theft, and the unsanctioned form of poaching, and then used that very same lack of resources as evidence of inferiority to justify policies that would further impoverish the Mashpee. Apess pointed out to Bostonians the hypocrisy of decrying the injustice of the two Supreme Court Cases that facilitated Cherokee removal, *Cherokee Nation v. Georgia* (1831) and *Worcester v. Georgia* (1832), while ignoring the ways that the guardianship system dispossessed New England Indians: "Perhaps you have heard of the oppression of the Cherokees and lamented over them much, and thought the Georgians were hard and cruel creatures; but did you ever hear of the poor, oppressed and degraded Marshpee Indians in Massachusetts, and lament over them?"[106] In New England, Indians' poverty became a mark of their inferior racial status and the impossibility of uplift, while the role of both state policies and capitalism in producing that poverty disappeared. Apess refused to think of this process as any less destructive than the forced removal of the Cherokee.

Apess's arrival and response to the white parishioners in the spring of 1833 empowered the Mashpee to escalate their campaign to escape guardianship. They adopted Apess as one of their own, giving him the right to speak for and advocate on behalf of the tribe. The Mashpee decided they would no longer tolerate whites taking resources from their land, either illegally, as through poaching, or legally, as when overseers sold resource rights without the tribe's consent. They informed the governor of Massachusetts of their decision and immediately began to make good on their promise.

Although he offered few details, Apess reported that he and other Mashpee physically prevented white men from taking timber sold to them by the overseer and retook control of the meetinghouse from their white preacher. Having foiled one group of white men caught in the act, "the Indians now made it part of their business to watch their property; being determined to disappoint the rapacity of the whites."[107] An investigator sent by the governor described the Mashpee as "in a state of open rebellion against the laws of the Commonwealth," but was able to broker a truce until the Mashpee could make their case to the state legislature the following January.[108]

While in Boston pleading their case, the Mashpee's plight and ensuing revolt garnered sympathetic coverage in the press, including *The Liberator*, and Apess and his companions gave public speeches in support of Mashpee autonomy.[109] The Mashpee's petition argued that "if things were conducted differently . . . and if we had what has been squandered, as we believe from circumstantial evidence, we all should be in a better condition than we are now."[110] The petition was successful. The legislature dissolved the guardianship system and granted Mashpee the same local autonomy as non-Native townships. While this victory did not fully resolve the issue of Indian poverty, it was one of the most significant Native political projects in nineteenth-century New England. Although New England's white reformers presented Black colonization and Indigenous guardianship as forms of racial benevolence, Walker, Stewart, and Apess gave voice to the idea that these schemes fostered racial dispossession rather than its opposite.

CONCLUSION

David Walker died a wanted man. The *Appeal* struck terror into the hearts of Southern legislatures, where memories of the Haitian

Revolution, Gabriel's Rebellion, and Vesey's Rebellion were still fresh. The governor of Georgia put a $10,000 bounty out for his capture, a tremendous sum. When Walker was found lying dead at the entrance to his home in August of 1830, rumors quickly circulated throughout Boston's Black community that he had been poisoned in retaliation for the *Appeal*. In reality, Walker likely succumbed to tuberculosis. As it turned out, neither a price on his head nor assassination by poison would be necessary to bring ruin to Walker and his family. After his death, Walker's widow, Eliza, could not make payments on their house, and it ended up in the hands of a white man—precisely the scenario that Walker described as commonplace in the *Appeal*.[111] Stewart fared little better. Like Eliza Walker, she was cheated out of her inheritance when her husband died. And her demand that Black men confront their own prejudices against women seemed a bridge too far even for Boston's liberal reform community. She left the city in 1833 and there are few records of her ever speaking in public again, despite the fact that her devotion to a life of service never wavered. Apess, too, met an ignominious end. After he led the Mashpee to victory in their struggle against guardianship, he became deeply indebted to multiple creditors, and in a tragic twist, one of the suits against him was brought by a young Mashpee woman who accused him of improperly harvesting tribal resources.[112] By 1836, Apess fled his New England debts, leaving his wife and children behind; they later ended up in a poorhouse, while he began anew in Manhattan. After a brief illness, Apess died in a New York City boardinghouse in 1839. Perhaps indulging in racial stereotypes about Indians and alcoholism, the city's medical examiner attributed his death to complications from drinking.[113] It is no surprise that Walker, Stewart, and Apess themselves fell victim to the dynamics of racial violence and dispossession that they revealed in their work. The life tragedies of these reformers punctuate how difficult it was for even New England's most exceptional people of color to escape impoverishment, fraud, and debt.

To see the origins of racial capitalism in only the raw violence of enslavement and Indian removal is to miss the adaptability that is one of its defining features. Racial capitalism thrived even as racial rights and freedoms expanded over the course of the nineteenth century. On this dynamic, to paraphrase Walter Johnson, the history of Massachusetts is more illuminating than the history of Mississippi.[114]

2

THE RADICAL ABOLISHMENT OF SLAVERY

Abolitionist Encounters with Land and Labor Reformers

James McCune Smith was unique among Black abolitionists for the depth of his skepticism that the Civil War would end slavery. By 1864 he knew as well as anyone that a Union victory was overwhelmingly likely, and with that victory would come emancipation. But, emancipation, McCune Smith predicted, would not mean the genuine eradication of slavery. "There is neither in the political, nor religious, nor philanthropic worlds of the American people, any agency at work that can encompass the entire abolishment of slavery," he wrote in a letter to the *Weekly Anglo-African* newspaper. His pessimism came from the fact that unlike most of his abolitionist allies, McCune Smith did not see enslaved and wage labor as moral, ideological, and economic antitheses. Rather, he understood the difference between Northern and Southern labor regimes as one of degree, not kind. "In slave society, there is *no conflict* between capital and labor; labor lies prostrate, and capital dictates its own terms, which are perpetual subjugation; in other words, perpetual slavery," he wrote. By translating slavery into economic language that transcended its regional specificity, McCune Smith was able to assert that the end of slavery in law did not mean its end in fact. He feared that emancipation could, in a bitter twist, result in the extension of one of slavery's defining features—capital's command over labor. "So far from this war diminishing the wish or power of capital to own labor, it will increase both. Colossal monopolies are parceling out even the free States for their ownership. The slave in the South will have namesakes in fact, if not in title, North of Mason and Dixon's line." Emancipation, in other words, would not interrupt the relations of power underlying slavery despite enslaved laborers winning the title of freedmen and women. Worse still, the expansion of capital would ensure that Northern laborers worked under conditions that increasingly resembled slavery. The condition of the enslaved could not be elevated to that of free laborers, because the notion of free labor itself was an illusion when the ownership of land and capital was concentrated among a small elite. McCune Smith argued that "the word *slavery* will, of course, be wiped from the statute book . . . but the 'ancient relation' can just as well be maintained by cunningly devised laws."[1] In McCune Smith's vision of the postwar future, the abolition of slavery was not the first step toward fulfilling the promise of equality for all, but a way of cheating its own death and surviving even without statutory sanction.

McCune Smith's despairing view of emancipation was a stark contrast to that of Frederick Douglass, his close friend and ally. Douglass arrived in New Bedford, Massachusetts, in the autumn of 1838 as a fugitive from slavery. He soon found work loading whale oil onto a ship, and seven years later, in his first autobiography, he famously described the experience of earning a wage as transformative. "I was now my own master," he wrote. "It was a happy moment, the rapture of which can be understood only by those who have been slaves. It was the first work, the reward of which was to be entirely my own . . . I worked that day with a pleasure I had never before experienced."[2] When he penned these words, Douglass was a rising luminary of the abolitionist movement, and he would go on to become arguably the most prolific and influential Black intellectual of the nineteenth century. A decade later, in his second autobiography, Douglass again reflected upon his first job in New Bedford with similar reverie: "That day's work I considered the real starting point of something like a new existence."[3] The fact that Douglass tethered the transformative possibilities of freedom to the experience of earning a wage seemed to punctuate—sharply—the absolute distinction between enslaved and free labor that animated abolitionist discourse in the middle third of the nineteenth century.

At the root of McCune Smith's view, far more contrarian than Douglass's, was his conviction that emancipation would not shift the deep imbalance between labor and capital, nor would it give freedpeople the tools for genuine economic autonomy. Whereas Douglass exalted the symbolic power of receiving a wage as an expression of freedom early in his career, McCune Smith thought of wages without ownership of land or capital as merely a more sophisticated form of slavery. For McCune Smith, freedom would not be found in transforming millions of slaves into wage laborers; he thus approved of plans to divide plantations among the formerly enslaved, calling them "eminently fair and just." Such plans would be a "radical abolishment of slavery" because they "made the freedman owner of his own labor, and also an owner of a fair share of the land." He did not blame the failure of such plans on persistent Southern racism, but on the more diffuse forces of capital, which "took the alarm" and "bought up the rest of the land, or at least placed it beyond the reach of the freedmen."[4] McCune Smith recognized the ways the federal government was "the minion of capital" and abetted the continued abjection of Black labor despite a formal commitment to emancipation and legal equality, and concluded his letter with the grim prediction: "For these reasons, we do not see that American slavery will go out of existence as an issue or result of the present war."[5]

In the decade leading up to the Civil War, the ideology of free labor united a Republican coalition against the power of Southern slave owners.[6] In his now-classic account of Republican ideology, Eric Foner has argued that "to think of free labor as coexisting in ideological tension with slave labor . . . suggests that the free labor ideology could not develop without a sharpening of the actual dichotomy between slavery and freedom."[7] In other words, in the middle decades of the nineteenth century, the notion of a diametric opposition between enslaved and free labor was an argument, not a settled fact. For much of the antebellum period, working for a wage carried an association of dependency that made it seem closer to indenture and enslavement than independent yeomanry in the minds of many white people. Amy Dru Stanley lays responsibility for the shifting understanding of wage labor squarely at the feet of abolitionists, arguing that "through their attacks on slavery," abolitionists "transformed the cultural meaning of wage labor, dissociating it from domestic dependency." Instead of "defining a condition of dependency less profound than chattel slavery, the wage contract had become the very token of freedom."[8] Indeed, William Lloyd Garrison made such arguments in his very first issue of *The Liberator* in 1831. In an article titled "Working Men," Garrison argued against attempts "to inflame the minds of our working classes against the more opulent, and to persuade men that they are contemned and oppressed by a wealthy aristocracy."[9] For Garrison, the only aristocracy the working classes need concern themselves with was that of the slave-owning variety. From its outset, then, the abolitionist movement seemed to be in irreconcilable tension with labor reform.

Although recent scholarship has challenged the idea that abolitionists offered an alibi for the exploitative social relations of wage labor, the question of the relationship between abolition and capitalism is still, after decades of debate, profoundly unresolved.[10] Black abolitionists have rarely figured into these debates, with the noteworthy exception of Douglass's aforementioned valorization of the wage.[11] Yet the idea that abolitionist thought was a bourgeois tool for legitimizing capitalist domination over wage workers oversimplifies a much more complex story hinted at in McCune Smith's letter to the *Weekly Anglo-African*. Despite his joy at receiving payment for his labor, the negative impacts of capitalism upon working people did not escape Douglass's critical gaze. Both men mobilized abolitionist ideas to critique wealth disparities, economic inequality, unfair labor conditions, and class immobility for workers of all races.

A series of debates with land reformers in the press throughout the 1840s and early 1850s prompted Douglass, McCune Smith, and other abolitionists in their circles to deepen their understanding of what emancipation should mean. They looked to the recent past to imagine a future yet to come, using the successes and challenges of British West Indian emancipation in 1834 to make claims about what would be necessary for the post-emancipation South to be truly free. Land reformers sought the redistribution of land owned by the federal government to urban wage laborers, allowing them to become economically self-sufficient. They also wished to limit the concentration of landed property, so that land ownership could not be a means of hoarding wealth and exploiting the labor of others, and were certain that slave emancipation without land reform would simply substitute one form of enslavement for another. Unlike land reformers, abolitionists never disavowed the revolutionary possibilities of personal liberty even in the most precarious of economic conditions. However, they did begin to think carefully about how material dispossession and capital's domination of labor shaped the meaning of Black freedom. This branch of antislavery thought never resolved the tensions that created it. It did not produce a choate economic philosophy, and existed alongside a more conventional moral critique of slavery. Yet it provided the basis for what would become a decades-long challenge to the terms of emancipation in the South, and allowed McCune Smith, Douglass, and others to identify economic continuities between slavery and freedom even as the Civil War and

Reconstruction transformed formerly enslaved people's legal, political, and social identities. In short, this strand of antislavery and post-slavery thought framed slavery as a problem of capital's domination of labor, suspending—even if only momentarily—faith in the world-shaping power of emancipation to reveal the equally world-shaping resistance of capitalism to enduring transformation. In turn, these intellectual struggles reveal the inability of formal racial equality to erase the racialized economic inequalities structured in capitalism.

This chapter unfolds in two sections. The first, on land and labor, argues that in criticizing the language of "wages slavery" used by land reformers, abolitionists clarified which aspects of slavery they thought of as uncomparable while also expressing support for labor and land reform movements.[12] While land reformers argued that the abolition of chattel slavery would simply subject formerly enslaved people to the even more precarious condition of wage slavery, abolitionists came to argue that slavery was the total domination of labor by capital, and this domination could not be undone without abolition. The second section focuses on how these encounters with land reformers shaped abolitionists' perspectives on the meaning of freedom. Although abolitionists never saw eye to eye with land reformers, they did internalize some of their arguments, and the debates of the 1840s and 1850s transformed how abolitionists thought of Black poverty in the North, how they evaluated West Indian emancipation, and what they expected of emancipation in the South.

Black abolitionists and their white allies had to contend with Southern proslavery ideologues and Northern labor radicals who agreed on one thing, if nothing else: white wage laborers suffered more at the hands of their employers than enslaved people did at the hands of planters. They navigated this unlikely convergence by arguing that as theft of the self, chattel slavery represented the purest form of unjust property relations. It was, however, part of the same spectrum of racial and economic domination that immiserated the free poor, Black and white alike. In cultivating these arguments, Douglass, McCune Smith, and others developed sophisticated ways of describing the deleterious economic effects of slavery and interrogated how questions of wealth, labor, and land would shape the meaning of Black liberty. This framework allowed them to expand and extend their critique of racial capitalism after emancipation to explain the continued dispossession of Black life in the decades after the Civil War.

DEBATING LAND AND LABOR IN THE 1830S–1840S

In the 1830s and 40s, abolitionists, slave owners, and land reformers crafted competing narratives about the nation's proper social order by theorizing the relationship between capital, labor, and property. The role of chattel slavery connected these narratives, and Northern reform newspapers were an important staging ground for debates between abolitionists and land reformers on these issues.

Black abolitionists considered questions of labor and capital in the Black press from its earliest days. Samuel Cornish, a minister, founding member of the American Anti-Slavery Society, and editor of the *Colored American*, one of the first Black newspapers, suggested that abolition was deeply connected to wider forms of inequality. In April of 1837, Cornish republished an article titled "The North and South Contrasted" from *The Philanthropist*, an Ohio antislavery newspaper. In the article James Birney, white editor of *The Philanthropist*, described South Carolina senator John C. Calhoun's defense of racial slavery in the South as an existential threat to white workingmen in the North. Abolitionist attacks on slavery excited Southern politicians to wild-eyed defenses of the institution, depicting it as a positive good that exemplified the proper relationship between labor and capital. Abolitionists, in turn, used such statements as evidence that slave owners wished to dominate all laboring people, not merely those who could be enslaved because of their race. Summarizing Calhoun's logic, Birney wrote, "the capitalist, the planter, the manufacturer, should be raised entirely above the productive class, the laborers, the working men; he should be totally independent of them—he should own them." While white Southerners were happy to use race as the justification for enslavement, Birney insisted that should Black people disappear, planters "would sanction the enslavement of the laboring part of the white population." He encouraged Northern workers to oppose the extension of slavery to more territories, because the same principles upholding Black slavery could be used to justify white enslavement "should capital ever be able to wield enough power." Cornish included a brief introduction to his republication in which he reiterated the link Birney had made between the power of capital and the entrenchment of slavery, writing that Calhoun "would gladly see the laboring classes of the community reduced to the most humiliating vassalage" and that "of all aristocracy, that of wealth and slavery is to be most dreaded."[13]

As one of the very few Black newspapers during the 1830s, the *Colored American* offered a unique platform for Black readers to challenge Southern politicians' defense of slavery as the natural and preferable organization of society—not merely in terms of white over Black, but capital over labor. Its pages hosted abolitionist responses encouraging white workingmen to see slave owners as their common enemy. For example, Cornish republished an article that warned readers, "the laboring men of the North are sadly mistaken, if they suppose that the slaveholders do not look with a jealous eye upon their liberty." This article, like Birney's before it, linked the fates of enslaved and wage laborers through the implication that planter capitalists wished to own both. The author posited that slave owners "claim a peculiar affinity with the capitalists and would-be aristocracy of the North, to whom its laboring population, they affirm, hold substantially the relation of slaves to masters."[14] While Northern capitalists rejected such a comparison, and Northern workers embraced it as evidence of their degraded condition, Southern capitalists saw it as confirmation that the ownership of labor was both natural and proper.

Cornish returned to these topics over the course of his paper's brief life. In 1838, Cornish published an article penned by Gerrit Smith, a white New Yorker of extraordinary wealth who was committed to broad social reform and immediate abolition. Smith argued that all laborers of every race must be united against slavery, offering a corollary to the idea that slaveholders wished to dominate all labor regardless of race. He wrote, "The same spirit which enslaves and tramples upon the liberty and rights of the Black man, would as readily, were he out of its power, brutalize and enslave the poor white man and his posterity. That Slavery is at war with all the interests of the laboring classes of community, admits not of a doubt. The whole system is one of despotism, and destructive of the rights and interest of the poor." Smith quoted a recent speech delivered by Francis Wilkinson Pickens, South Carolina congressman and cousin to Calhoun, to prove his point. Pickens had declared, "all society settles down into a classification of capitalists and laborers" and that "the former will own the latter." Putting things even more simply, Pickens said, "slavery is the universal condition of laborers!!!"[15] There could be no clearer declaration of what the Southern plantocracy thought of the white working classes of the North.

Although these early exercises in establishing the power of capital as the common basis for the oppression of both enslaved and wage laborers did not mature into a comprehensively egalitarian pro-labor abolitionism, they did establish the foundation for future intellectual projects. When Cornish left his position as editor of the *Colored*

American in 1839, the owners, Black abolitionists Phillip Alexander Bell and Charles Bennett Ray, appointed McCune Smith as his replacement.[16] Although the paper stopped publication in 1841, McCune Smith, Ray, and Gerrit Smith worked together several years later when Smith decided to grant a portion of his vast land holdings in New York to free Black people to use for farms in 1846. Smith was the wealthiest man and largest landowner in New York thanks to an early inheritance from his father, a land speculator and business partner of John Jacob Astor. Smith was involved in reform movements from a young age and was an active abolitionist. Encouraged by others in his reform circles, Smith, in the 1840s, set about giving away the majority of his land in the form of several thousand grants in upstate New York. Smith wrestled with the decision of who would be eligible for these grants, but because of limits to even his own holding in lands, because he knew Black people were "the poorest of the poor," and because Black people had few other opportunities to improve their condition, he limited his grants to Black New Yorkers. He also believed that each example of improvement in the condition of free Black people would strike an ideological blow to slavery.[17]

To find eligible applicants for his land grants, Smith enlisted the aid of McCune Smith, Ray, and Theodore S. Wright, a Black abolitionist, reverend, and, like Cornish, a founding member of the American Anti-Slavery Society. In a public address celebrating Smith's grants, the trio of Black abolitionists proclaimed, "Too long have American usages and American caste consigned us to dependent employments at reduced wages,—to fortuitous labour, embracing but a portion of the year—thus creating that feeling of dependence and uncertainty, which ever crushes the energies and deadens the faculties of men."[18] They hoped that land would offer an escape from such conditions, giving Black families economic independence, which would in turn combat racial prejudice. McCune Smith, Ray, and Wright encouraged recipients of grants not to mortgage their farms and fall into debt, and extolled the importance of both self-reliance and "mutual reliance"—that is, looking to other Black people for care, support, and aid. They concluded with the hope that an agricultural life would serve as a form of "self-emancipation from the drudgery of the cities," linguistically linking the privations free Black people suffered in urban housing and labor markets to a kind of enslavement.[19]

Unfortunately, this self-emancipation did not come to pass. Very few of the three thousand grantees ever claimed their land. Both Smith and his Black allies underestimated the difficulty a mostly urban population would have establishing farms from nothing, and may have overestimated how centrally located and fertile these lands were. McCune Smith, Ray, and Wright proposed practicing economy as a means of saving to buy the necessary equipment to start their farms, which they estimated to be $100. Although they argued that both irregular employment and habits of frivolous consumption had led to a lack of economy among New York's free Black population, no amount of thrift could surmount such a high cost of entry—$100 represented four month's average daily wages for laborers in New York, and Black laborers were the least likely to have steady employment and most likely to be underpaid.[20] Despite these challenges, McCune Smith remained hopeful. Relating a conversation he had with two land grantees, McCune Smith wrote to Smith in 1848 that ownership of land allowed these Black settlers to enjoy a degree of autonomy that would be unthinkable had they been accountable to a landlord or employer.[21]

The very same day McCune Smith reported to Smith, Douglass published a letter that described a different, yet likely much more common, set of experiences among aspiring Black landowners.[22] By 1848 Douglass had established himself in Rochester, New York, where he founded the *North Star* newspaper. His coeditor, Martin

Delany, reported that free Black homesteaders who migrated to the Midwest from the South encountered shopkeepers who offered them only "old horses and plows and other farming utensils, worn out and good for nothing," which were "sold to them at high prices." This dynamic led some "to say that they would rather be back in Virginia again."[23] Even without having to clear the hurdle of purchasing land, Smith's grantees would have faced similar challenges as those Delany described.

Although Smith's hopes for Black people to thrive as farmers on the land he gave them went unrealized, the project represented an important intellectual confluence between the abolitionist and land reform movements. Smith recognized that racial and economic dispossession worked together to make free Black people the neediest of the poor. Therefore, he opposed slavery on both moral grounds, and because he saw it as a threat to all working people. Smith's position was unusual. More frequently, white land reformers considered the abolition of slavery to be a lesser struggle than that for the abolition of private land ownership. While they did not support slavery, they believed the dominion of slave owners was an outgrowth of the right to own land, and that slavery would necessarily disappear once private land ownership was dispensed with. This position frustrated most abolitionists. Even more alienating was land reformers' insistence that the exploitative conditions of urban labor, which they referred to as "wages slavery," was worse than chattel slavery.

A chief architect of this movement and its language in the 1840s was George Henry Evans, a British American reformer, editor of the first American labor newspaper, the *Working Man's Advocate*, and cofounder of one of the nation's earliest labor organizations, the Workingmen's Party. Evans was a fixture of the New York labor reform movement of the 1830s, and after the Panic of 1837—an economic crash caused in large part by land speculation—he began to incorporate ideas about land reform into his labor organizing.[24] In

1844, Evans founded the National Reform Association, an organization dedicated to land reform policies as a solution to the conditions of urban wage labor. The following year he began publishing *Young America*, the official newspaper of the National Reform Association.

Evans was an opponent of slavery and supporter of Black rights, but he often antagonized abolitionists for what he perceived to be their aristocratic leanings. In one *Young America* editorial, he accused Garrison and *The Liberator* of ignoring the plight of the white poor in Britain even as the paper celebrated British West Indian emancipation. The editorial prompted an ally of Garrison's, Wendell Phillips, to reply. Phillips was a white abolitionist who came from a wealthy Boston family, and despite his strong support for labor, perhaps typified in Evans's mind the association between abolition and urban capital. Phillips insisted that Evans's charges were unfair and untrue, arguing "that a man robbed of land is worse off than one robbed of himself" was an idea that appealed to a "corrupt public sentiment" and proposed to achieve white advancement by sacrificing Black rights. Evans responded that "the paragraph in question has had its intended effect," implying that the purpose of his editorial was to provoke abolitionists into engaging with the intellectual platform of the National Reform Association. Evans claimed that if, as he believed, "that the men robbed of their land *are* robbed of themselves most effectually," abolitionists would find that enslaved people were emancipated into a new slavery of wages. "The National Reform measures would not merely substitute one form of slavery for another, but would replace every form of slavery by entire freedom," Evans concluded. National Reform, in other words, aimed to abolish both wage and chattel slavery, whereas abolition would simply eliminate one form of slavery.[25]

This rhetoric baffled abolitionists, who found comparisons between enslaved people and wage laborers overwrought at best and morally dishonest at worst. In 1842, Jeremiah Sanderson, member of a small network of Black abolitionists in Lowell, Massachusetts, wrote to fellow reformer and Black abolitionist William Cooper Nell after having observed young white women at work in textile mills. "I have before now, heard their condition compared, degradingly, to the slaves of our country," he wrote. Yet, according to Sanderson, these women looked "more like the Daughters of capitalists than slaves."[26] To Sanderson, wage labor was incommensurable with slavery.

Frederick Douglass came to a similar conclusion when he confronted widespread white poverty on his first trip to Ireland. Douglass published an autobiography in 1845, and its success drew more attention than was prudent for a fugitive of slavery. He fled to Britain that summer and lectured there for more than a year. In a letter to Garrison, Douglass confessed that he assumed stories he had heard about Irish oppression were exaggerations meant to diminish the severity of American slavery by comparison. Seeing the reality firsthand, Douglass wrote that "the half has not been told." He wrote that he could not relate to Garrison within the confines of a single letter "any thing like a faithful description of those painful exhibitions of human misery, which meet the eye of a stranger at almost every step . . . the streets were almost literally alive with beggars, displaying the greatest of wretchedness." He went on to describe mutilated bodies—"mere stumps of men," "horribly deformed" with "crooked limbs"—covered in tattered rags, "emaciated forms" living in miserable huts. Though he had many times before, and would many times after, insist upon the exceptionalism of chattel slavery, Douglass admitted in this letter that in Ireland, "men and women, married and single, old and young, lie down together, in much the same degradation as the American slaves. I see much here to remind me of my former condition." Yet Douglass remained deeply ambivalent about the reasons for the poverty he witnessed. Even as he recounted these horrific conditions to Garrison, Douglass insisted "the *immediate*, and it may be the main cause of extreme poverty and beggary in Ireland, is intemperance."[27]

If Douglass was ambivalent about his encounter with Irish poverty, his introduction to land reform was decidedly negative. During his British tour, Douglass lectured with the white abolitionist John Collins. According to Douglass, Collins drew attention away from the plight of the enslaved by espousing radical land reform ideas. Collins told audiences that "the anti-slavery cause is a mere dabbling with effects," whereas restricting property in land would "do more for the Slave than the anti-slavery movement."[28] While Douglass was not opposed to the ideas of the land reform movement, he objected to the way that Collins used those ideas to diminish the work of abolition. Even as Douglass's thinking on land reform became more sophisticated in the coming years, he would always bristle at the notion that slavery was unexceptional, merely one form of economic exploitation among many.

When Douglass returned from his British sojourn in 1846, the abolitionist press was still engaged with *Young America*, offering swift and energetic responses to Evans's provocations. In a series of articles published in the spring of 1847, Gamaliel Bailey, editor of the newly founded abolitionist newspaper the *National Era*, vigorously tested the arguments of *Young America*, probing Evans's claims with a greater degree of sophistication than previous land reform skeptics. Bailey insisted that like land reformers, abolitionists sought to elevate all people. "Right measures, wisely directed, for the protection of labor against the oppressive impositions of capital, will always command our support," he noted. "That there are serious evils arising from the absorption, by a few property holders, of large landed estates; from the influence of overgrown wealth, and the too great dependence of the laborer; and that labor-saving machinery has generally added more to the power of the employer than employed, few will deny." Yet Bailey ultimately could not accept the conclusions of land reform ideology, even if he shared some of its goals. Just as Evans questioned the intellectual basis of abolition, Bailey questioned the most radical premise of Evans's brand of land reform—the idea that land ownership should be severely circumscribed. Bailey pointed out that the United States had already done away with primogeniture in order to encourage the breaking up of large estates, and wondered if there could be further reform to land ownership laws "without seriously discouraging and obstructing the enterprise necessary to the growth of society." He also argued that concentrated land ownership was not the only source of inequality—a person whose wealth came from "bank stocks or factories" would be "as apt to be oppressive, as much to be dreaded, as the vast landholder."[29]

These counterarguments perhaps missed the point; had Bailey been more familiar with Evans's thought, he would have known that the purpose of limiting land ownership was, in theory, to make land available for grant without cost, giving urban wage workers the option of becoming farmers, which, in turn, would make labor more scarce and drive up wages for those who remained in cities.[30] But just as Evans feared that slave emancipation would not lead to true freedom for Black workers, Bailey questioned the outcome of the land reformers' goals. To have inalienable possession of land—that is, to be prohibited from selling it—would not free the wage worker, he argued. It would consign him to be bound to the land without hope of changing profession or attempting anything else in life. Bailey went so far as to argue that land reformers' policies would make the working man "a slave to the soil." Society would be forced to "a dead, eternal level, from which it could no more rise than a society of beavers."[31]

Although Evans professed support for abolition, to Bailey his invocation of wage slavery seemed to "admit and confirm all that the proslavery propagandists of the South have declared concerning the degradation of Northern working men, and the superior blessedness of Southern slaves." The tension seemed irresolvable. Bailey utterly rejected the idea that being compelled to work by the threat of starvation was identical to the threat of physical violence, or that worrying about earning enough to support one's family was anything like the fear of being forcibly separated and sold away from spouse and child at the whim of one's owner.[32]

These debates shaped Douglass's thinking when he relocated to Rochester, New York, in 1847. Douglass wished to establish himself as a journalist and be able to advocate for his race without oversight from white abolitionists, and once settled in Rochester he founded his first newspaper, the *North Star*. The paper's relationship to land reform began inauspiciously; in one of his first issues, Douglass was forced to defend himself from a calumnious attack in the land reform paper the *Homestead Journal*. The paper charged that "250,000 White Factory Slaves were worked up and slaughtered; to pay some part of this Black Man's freedom!" After Douglass fled to England to escape possible capture, his British abolitionist allies purchased his freedom. The *Homestead Journal* implied that the funds they had used to do so were the ill-gotten gains of their brutal exploitation of British workers. The paper further accused Douglass of ignoring the plight of the white poor in favor of shedding light on the evils of slavery and other social ills. "Crushed Black Slaves are the only Slaves he will advocate—the wages Slave of the North has no wrongs."[33] This was land reform ideology taken to such an extreme that its logic began to fray, but Douglass was compelled to defend his reputation. He dignified the charges only with a brief reply: "For any man to talk about white slavery in this country in connection with Black slavery, is to use words deceitfully."[34]

Yet Douglass committed himself to learning more about the land reform movement and writing more on the topic once his thinking "shall have reached an intelligent maturity."[35] Douglass had able help in this endeavor. Gerritt Smith, who had distributed portions of his land to free Black people the year prior, introduced himself to Douglass in 1848, which marked the beginning of a close friendship. And Douglass's printer for the *North Star*, John Dick, was a white abolitionist with land reform sympathies. By late 1848, these influences began to shape Douglass's work. In a speech before a convention of Black men in Ohio that September, Douglass told his audience that although there was no shame in the most menial of labor, the fact "that such employments have been so long and universally filled by colored men . . . that it has established the conviction that colored men are only fit for such employments" severely conscripted the freedom Black people experienced in the North. Douglass argued, "in the Northern states, we are not slaves to individuals, not personal slaves, yet in many respects we are the slaves of the community."[36] Despite abhorring the notion of wage slavery, Douglass found the language of slavery useful to describe the way that low employment became enmeshed with racial prejudice to justify the economic dispossession of free Black people.

Even as Douglass held the movement at arm's length, he would often print and reprint articles on land and labor reform. The *North Star* curated a space for debates about land, labor, and capital even as Douglass maintained that slavery was an exceptional form of dispossession both in kind and degree. He reprinted articles that outlined the case for land reform in detail and made arguments for the necessity of land ownership to republicanism; that framed the power of capital over labor as the present-day equivalent of rank and privilege in feudal times; and that pleaded for public lands to be used for the benefit of individuals and families rather than land speculators.[37] Douglass also reprinted articles that reinvigorated the abolitionist critique of slave owners' belief that capital should own labor as property and urged such laborers not to support the expansion of slavery, because it was "the condition, not color, that is the mark of degradation in the eyes of slaveholders."[38] Finally, Douglass reprinted work that explored the argument that slavery degraded all labor, especially free white labor in the South, because proximity to slavery made such labor servile and dependent.[39]

As the *North Star* provided a space to wrestle with the relationship between chattel slavery, wage labor, and land ownership, the *National Era* began to publish less combative pieces on land reform. The paper also continued to condemn slave owners as the most oppressive version of the capitalist class. Bailey printed and reprinted articles meant to persuade his readers that slavery was a threat to free labor by using slave owners' own words, and, more importantly, by adopting the land reform movement's language of labor and capital. One of the paper's correspondents wrote an article paraphrasing South Carolina congressman Francis Pickens's oft-quoted 1836 speech before Congress, charging Pickens and other Southern politicians with formulating "a new definition of Democracy," which asserted "that the best form of society is that in which the capitalists own the laborers."[40] Touching on similar themes, the author of one letter submitted to the *National Era* lamented, "we see, in the system of slavery, a perfect demonstration of the same tyrannical disposition" that could be found "in the rules and regulations of every department of business, to a greater or lesser extent."[41] Another letter denounced land speculation and the concentration of land in the hands of the few, claiming that these practices render "the poor the servant of the capitalist."[42] Yet another letter reported approvingly on a strike at Rhode Island cotton mills, and warned that the logic mill owners used to rationalize reduced wages reproduced the very logic of slavery. The letter's author wrote that manufacturers justified wage cuts to workers by telling them that the cuts would not reduce them to starvation, an argument "which rests upon the unhallowed assumption that the laborer has no natural or legal or social right to anything more than a bare livelihood. This is the vital element of slavery, and it will probably continue to haunt the minds of the capitalists, and depress the hearts of laborers, till the relations of capital and labor are materially modified."[43] In each of these cases, the *National Era* at once validated many of the central tenets of land reform while turning those ideas to the cause of abolition. In this synthesis, chattel slavery was not a mere symptom of the disease of land ownership; it was the epitome of the very capitalist forces land reformers railed against.

By 1850, Bailey was conceding analytical ground to land reform ideas in ways that would have been unthinkable a decade earlier. Refuting an article he had read whose author asserted that abolition was a ploy by the wealthy to reduce the wages of workingmen, Bailey wrote in an editorial of his own that "there may be great wealth in a slaveholding State, but the tendency of it is to concentrate in a few hands. This, we admit, is the tendency of capital, even under the wages system—for the simple reason that, although the working man is paid his stipulated wages, he is excluded from any share of the profits of the enterprise in which his labor and the money of his employer are invested." But although the concentration of capital at the expense of those who labored to produce it characterized both Northern and Southern economies, Bailey argued that "the tendency referred to is far stronger under the chattel system, because the capitalist engrosses not only the entire net profits of the joint enterprise in which he and his slaves are employed, but also retains what the latter ought to receive as wages, allowing them only so much as will barely keep them in good working condition."[44] The editor of the *National Era* was no longer simply dismissing the language of wage slavery by enumerating the horrors of chattel slavery and asserting the value of workingmen's self-ownership; he was amplifying many land reformer arguments, and in the process theorizing chattel slavery as the most complete form of capital's domination of labor.

Thus, it was perhaps no surprise that when Bailey reported on land reform debates taking place in the Senate in early 1850, he noted, "the large slave-owners naturally regard Land Reform and Anti-Slavery cause as affiliated enterprises." Bailey went on, "slave labor requires extensive tracts of land for its profitable employment," and so "the occupation of the public lands by small cultivators, restricting its range, would tend to diminish its profits, and finally make it worthless. Hence it is to the interest of this large class of slaveholders . . . that the public domain be secured *against* extensive occupation by small farmers."[45] Using the language of capital and labor, Bailey was able to advocate for both the white poor and the enslaved by criticizing the aims and beliefs of slaveholders *as capitalists*.

A similar transformation was underway in the Black abolitionist press, thanks in part to Douglass's friendship with Gerritt Smith. Abolitionists newspapers were rarely financially stable, and the *North Star* was no exception. Smith, who ran for president as the Liberty Party candidate in the election of 1848, facilitated the merger of the party's organ, the *Liberty Party Paper*, with Douglass's *North Star* to form a new venture, *Frederick Douglass' Paper*. Formed in 1840 as the first explicitly antislavery political party, the Liberty Party integrated land reform into its 1848 platform as a result of Smith's advocacy. Although Douglass retained editorial control, John Thomas, former editor of the *Liberty Party Paper*, assisted Douglass, and handled day-to-day operations when Douglass went on lecture tours. The articles Thomas wrote and published in *Frederick Douglass' Paper* made it a site of advocacy for some of the most radical articulations of racial and economic equality in the early 1850s. Through Thomas's efforts, *Frederick Douglass' Paper* put land reform and abolition into friendly dialogue rather than contentious debate. For example, Congress began debating a Homestead Bill in 1852 that would grant a homestead of 160 acres of public lands to any white family who wanted one.⁴⁶ The bill represented the possibility that one of the major political aims of the land reform movement would become a reality. Thomas reported on the bill for *Frederick Douglass' Paper*, and noted that his "one objection" was that it would grant land only to male heads of household, "whereas, it should likewise give that amount to any person, male or female, Black or white, who has arrived at the age of twenty-one years."⁴⁷ By couching his support for the bill in the broad racial and gender inclusivity that was a hallmark of abolitionism, Thomas imagined how land reform efforts could give poor people of all races and genders a more meaningful experience of freedom.

The following month, Thomas published another article hopeful about the Homestead Bill's passage but noted that "aristocrats and monopolists" were arrayed against its success. Adopting the abolitionist stance that slavery made slave owners despise manual labor, Thomas wrote, "The difference between a monopolist and a poor man, is, that the latter is robbed of his rights that the former may have more than his rights.—The natural condition of the latter is changed, that the former may live in ease and luxury upon the others' dependance and destitution." Without taking recourse to the language of wage slavery, Thomas suggested a parallel between how slave owners captured the rights and labor of enslaved people to enrich themselves, and the way that the Northern capitalist did the same. In the same article, Thomas made another move to shift the arguments of abolition and land reform into closer alignment. He wrote, "A man may as lawfully sell himself, as sell his interest in the earth."⁴⁸ Rather than argue about whether being denied the right to self-ownership through enslavement was commensurate with being dispossessed from the land, Thomas suggested that the right to the earth was in fact a part of the right of self-ownership, making land reform a fundamental component of the abolitionist struggle.

Thomas drew out such connections between the two movements' ideologies throughout his writing for *Frederick Douglass' Paper*, and sometimes made his case for land reform in ways that may have made Douglass himself uncomfortable. In one article, Thomas wrote, "Next to slavery and the rum trade, if not equally with them, does land monopoly impoverish, oppress, and degrade mankind, and curse the country . . . Of a certainty, slavery is dependent on it for its existence, and must die with it."[49] Thomas linked the fate of chattel slavery and land monopoly, but he came dangerously close to the notion, long rejected by abolitionists, that abolition did not need to be advocated as a *particular* issue because slavery would disappear once the *general* problem of land monopoly was solved. In an article ruminating upon the origins of capital, Thomas framed "land, light, air, and personal rights" equally as divine birthright, and claimed that poverty and domination were the result of the clash of the right to acquire for some overtaking these sacred rights of others. "Hence, what is called *capital* becomes monopoly," Thomas wrote. "Hence, one man owns his thousands of acres, and sells to his equal brother his right to till on the earth; while another is a millionaire, and regulates stocks and prices, and settles the conditions in the form of rents, by which the poor are allowed a home on the earth. Hence, too, one is a master and another a slave. Hence the monstrous accumulations on the one hand; and the want and degradation, depravity and sorrow on the other."[50] For Thomas, a slave owner's infringement upon the enslaved's right to self-ownership and the land monopolist's infringement upon the universal right to the soil both represented a deep misalignment between labor and capital. But rather than setting up a tension between white poverty and Black enslavement by constructing an oppositional relationship between chattel slavery and wage labor, Thomas instead framed slavery as part of the grand question of capital's domination of labor. More importantly, Thomas transformed freedom into a question of how to escape and transform capital's domination rather than a simple legal status.

Thomas's efforts made *Frederick Douglass' Paper* such an enthusiastic supporter of land reform that Douglass had to defend the content of the paper to some of his abolitionist allies. Although Thomas made land reform more central to his writing than Douglass did, Douglass stood fully behind Thomas's work. Douglass said of his paper at the 1852 annual meeting of the American Anti-Slavery Society, "That it advocates 'Land Reform,' only proves that while it is as good an abolition paper as any other, it is sufficiently comprehensive in spirit and feeling, to embrace the landless poor in its beneficent concern; and he who would make the advocacy of *Land Reform* a reason for the discontinuance of the paper, only shows that the principle he applies to slavery, he is *un*willing to apply to other forms of oppression."[51] Douglass's defense of his paper punctuated a broader shift in his own thinking and that of his closest intellectual allies. In the span of just a few short years, the *North Star*, *Frederick Douglass' Paper*, and the *National Era* went from seeing land reform as a movement that advanced proslavery propaganda through the language of wage slavery, to considering it an allied movement, even adopting some of its foundational claims. In the decade leading to the Civil War, abolitionists would continue to integrate land reform ideas into their own conceptions of Black freedom.

DEBATING CAPITAL AND FREEDOM IN THE 1850S

As debates with land reformers reshaped abolitionist attitudes toward capital and labor, Black abolitionists and their allies began to integrate these themes into their notions of what rights and protections freedom should entail. They looked to the recent history of emancipation in the British West Indies and the conditions of free Black Northerners to assess what demands to make of emancipation in the South once it became clear that a Union victory in the Civil War would mean the end of slavery. Two questions loomed large over each of these discussions: what forms of economic security were necessary to ensure that freedom did not resemble slavery by another name, and what forms of labor were so exploitative that they could not reasonably be called free?

In 1842, the governor of Jamaica famously described the emancipated West Indies as "the theater of a great experiment" to determine whether free labor could be as productive as enslaved labor.[52] Both abolitionists and American slave owners eagerly followed news about the productivity of West Indian plantations and the efficiency of free labor following emancipation. The British Parliament passed the Slavery Abolition Act in 1833, which liberated enslaved people throughout the British West Indies when it went into effect on August 1, 1834. Emancipation did not lead directly to freedom; until 1838, formerly enslaved people were subject to an exploitative apprenticeship system meant to acclimate them to a form of freedom predicated upon wage labor rather than subsistence agriculture. Despite these limitations, it was clear to both American critics and defenders of slavery that the outcome of British emancipation had the power to shape public opinion toward slavery in the United States.[53] Abolitionists leaped upon any evidence that suggested the end of slavery was not just a moral victory but an economic one.

After speaking to "a member of the Legislative Council in one of the crown islands of the B. West Indies," Samuel Cornish, editor of the Black newspaper the *Colored American*, wrote glowingly of the accomplishments of emancipation. These accomplishments, according to Cornish, were in stark contrast to "the ruin of the islands and the vagrancy of the emancipated" predicted by defenders of slavery. He reported that emancipation had created a new Black middle class, "quite numerous and prosperous," overturning the former system under which there existed only wealthy planters and human property. Cornish predicted that this new class would break down the island's aristocracy, and that free labor, far from ruining the economy, made it more diversified and efficient.[54] The *Colored American* periodically published brief updates on the West Indies until it ceased publication in 1842, emphasizing the theme of continued economic productivity and the triumph of free labor. "The universal cry from all parts of the island is, that there is no want of laborers," Cornish reported in one article.[55] "Employers and laborers now regard each other's interests more as identical," he wrote in another.[56]

The white Bermuda-born abolitionist Charles Stuart made a similar assessment. In 1839 he wrote to Theodore Wright, the Black reverend who would work with McCune Smith to distribute Gerritt Smith's land grants to Black New Yorkers, with laudatory reports from Jamaica. Stuart was of the opinion that the state of Jamaica was "exceedingly happy" and that "lawful liberty reigns, in practice as well as by legislation." He noted that wages were high and "consuming poverty" did not exist on the island, but conceded that the franchise was restricted to the wealthy, a group he described as a "malcontent, selfish and dangerous oligarchy." While Stuart was impressed with freedpeople's embrace of free labor and reported that idleness was uncommon, he pointed out that they operated under the false assumption that they had legal rights to their customary provision grounds, small plots of land on plantations enslaved people used to grow food.[57] Such an assumption came dangerously close to the idea that land redistribution was a right of freedom. Stuart was also concerned that formerly enslaved people thought "nine hours' labor per day was too much." Yet overall Stuart was impressed by the achievements of freedpeople in such a short period of time, especially since former slave owners "still felt *like* slaveholders." As he put it, former slave owners dreamed of enacting a feudal system that would bind laborers to the land that they worked upon, "that liberty should be abolished and a species of villenage put in its place."[58] Although Stuart was clear that such a system would be an assault upon free labor, he did not connect the desire of planters to exert more control over freedpeople's labor to his criticism of their oligarchical political power.

Within a decade, Black abolitionists began to reevaluate the simple narrative that the productivity of emancipated laborers in the West Indies proved the superiority of free labor. They did so both by investigating reports of labor exploitation and by criticizing the very terms of West Indian emancipation, which included financial compensation for slave owners but not enslaved people themselves. In doing so, they advanced arguments about the necessity for legal freedom to be paired with economic rights. William Wells Brown, an American fugitive from slavery residing in Britain, experienced an abrupt change in opinion about conditions in Jamaica after meeting with labor recruiters tasked with finding workers to immigrate to the island. In July 1851, Wells wrote to the *London Times* suggesting that because of the hardships fugitive slaves experienced finding work in England, their most promising destination might be Jamaica. Fugitives' experience with plantation agriculture, Brown reasoned, meant that they could be easily employed on Jamaican sugar plantations.[59] Later that month, Brown wrote much the same in a letter to Douglass, encouraging enslaved fugitives to go to Canada or the West Indies rather than England due to the likelihood of economic hardship there.[60] By October, after having had "interviews with West India Agents and Proprietors, who are not only willing but desirous to secure the emigration of colored citizens to Trinidad and Jamaica," Brown reversed course. Although these men assured

Brown that fugitive laborers would be going to the West Indies under conditions of "the utmost freedom," Brown had heard rumors that such labor agents were "dissatisfied" with abolition and that "a species of slavery had been carried on under the name of emigration." He began to suspect that fugitives might be enticed to the West Indies with promises of good employment only to find themselves trafficked into bondage. He wrote to Douglass again, sharing his concerns. "I take the earliest opportunity of warning all colored men to be on their guard, how they enter into agreements, no matter with whom, white or colored, to go to the West India islands, lest they find themselves again wearing the chains of slavery."[61]

Henry Highland Garnet came to a similar conclusion. Born enslaved in Maryland, Garnet and his family escaped to New York City when he was a child. He was educated alongside McCune Smith at the African Free School and trained as a minister. Garnet was skeptical of the possibility for Black equality in the United States, and was a staunch advocate for Black emigration to South America, the West Indies, and Africa. In 1852 he and his family relocated to Jamaica. Garnet wrote to *Frederick Douglass' Paper*, reporting that planters were desirous of Black American workers, and explained this was due to the fact that "the Creole is naturally indolent" and held "some very ridiculous and silly notions about labor," in contradistinction to the "*go-ahead* enterprise" of Americans.[62] Garnet agreed with the planters, and brought with him to Jamaica an idea common among Black Americans—namely, that West Indians, both Black and white, were not sufficiently inculcated to the benefits of hard work.[63]

By the following year, Garnet's opinion had changed markedly, and he attempted to set the record straight among fellow abolitionists who still held his former views. In 1846, Parliament ended preferential tariffs for British West Indian sugar, exposing it to competition with cheaper, slave-produced Cuban sugar.[64] The British and Foreign Anti-Slavery Society, the chief British abolitionist organization and a major ally in the struggle to end slavery in the United States, however, took the stance that declining productivity on West Indian sugar plantations was instead due to cultural deficiencies and unwillingness to work among Black laborers. Seeing such views presented in one of the Society's publications, Garnet took the opportunity to write about his new understanding of Jamaica. While Garnet maintained that the laboring classes of Jamaica were not as industrious as those of Europe or the United States, he described them as "orderly, and law-abiding." After living on the island for more than a year, Garnet now understood that Jamaicans did not dislike work due to any cultural deficiency, but because "they do not consider their wages to be sufficient and just," which was the main principle "upon which the people refuse to do more work."[65] Wages were so low that laborers preferred subsistence farming, cultivating the same small plots they did under slavery and selling any excess produce for cash. And although many laborers wished to own more land than their small provision grounds, white plantation owners often refused to sell to freedpeople lest they lose control over their labor, and did not like to break up plantations, making purchase completely out of reach for most laborers. Garnet made it clear that he blamed planters for this state of affairs. "To speak plainly," he wrote, "the habits of too many of the whites, are wicked, disgusting, and beastial." He concluded that "it is becoming more, and more apparent, that the emancipated people, use their liberty with more moderation, and propriety, than their former masters, exercise government over them."[66] Although Garnet did not object to wage labor in principle, he came to see the only labor problem in Jamaica as one of former slave owners using economic means to hinder and impoverish emancipated people to whatever extent possible.

McCune Smith found even more fundamental faults with West Indian emancipation. Writing to *Frederick Douglass' Paper* on its twenty-second anniversary, he argued that "the British Emancipation act was a compromise act, inasmuch as it paid masters, so called, twenty millions of pounds for property which they never owned, thus admitting *that man held property in man*. Surely that is a principle which no abolitionist can admit, much less celebrate."[67] McCune Smith's claim was highly unusual; taken to its logical end, it would have precluded abolitionists from purchasing the freedom of runaway slaves because doing so would concede the idea that human beings could be purchased as property. Many abolitionists roundly rejected such arguments, and Douglass, whose own freedom was purchased, disagreed with McCune Smith's evaluation of West Indian emancipation. Yet McCune Smith raised important questions about who truly benefited economically from emancipation. Not only did West Indian emancipation recognize the property rights of slave owners, if only obliquely, by compensating them for property lost, the British made no equivalent offer of support to freedpeople.[68] "A paltry twenty thousand pounds was appropriated for the education of the freedmen . . . that is all given to the former slave in consideration of the robbery and embruting which had been perpetrated on him for centuries." The small sum Britain contributed to the elevation of freedpeople as compared to the compensation for those who enslaved them offended McCune Smith's sense of justice. Rejecting the celebratory tone surrounding emancipation's commemoration, McCune Smith wrote, "in looking at these shortcomings of the British people, in regard to their Black fellow subjects, we do not feel like sounding their praises for the little they have done, in view of how much they have left undone."[69] While freedom could not be reduced to any monetary sum, his criticism suggested that full emancipation should have meant a compensatory component for the enslaved, not their enslavers. In other words, McCune Smith raised the question of what forms of economic security might be necessary to call the work of emancipation complete.

Douglass's view of West Indian emancipation approached the hagiographic. In an 1857 Emancipation Day speech in upstate New York, Douglass invited his audience to think of West Indian emancipation as a "transaction of vast and sublime significance, surpassing all power of exaggeration." While McCune Smith sought to tether economic questions to emancipation, Douglass wrenched them apart. Yet in doing so, he did not excuse emancipation's shortcomings, but rather indicted the way that Americans' commitment to justice could be tempered by financial concerns. To Douglass, the very terms of debate surrounding emancipation—whether free labor was efficient and productive—were hopelessly insufficient, the equivalent of using "a microscope to view the stars, and a fish line to measure the ocean." Evaluating emancipation by asking whether it would affect the cost of commodities or affect the supply of sugar was a result of "the gross materialism of our age and nation," an example of "the great American question (viz.) *will it pay?*" In the first years after West Indian emancipation, abolitionists sought to vindicate it by celebrating the economic productivity of free labor; here, Douglass illustrated how misguided such efforts could be. "Money is the measure of morality, and the success or failure of slavery, as a money-making system, determines with many whether the thing is virtuous, or villainous, and whether it should be maintained or abolished."[70] Douglass's celebration of West Indian emancipation was a rebuke of the idea that profit could determine virtue and that freedom should be contingent on productivity.

Douglass's Emancipation Day speech the following year was similarly laudatory. He reiterated the idea that trying to judge whether emancipation was a success or failure was to miss its significance entirely. If emancipation could be considered a failure at all, Douglass argued, it was because "it has failed to keep Slavery under the name of Liberty," and "failed to change the name without changing the character of the thing." Emancipation had "failed to keep the lands of Jamaica in the hands of the few and out of the hands of the many," and "failed to make men work for a planter at small wages, when they can work for themselves for larger wages."[71] The failure of emancipation, then, was in slaveholders' inability to reforge it in the old image of slavery. Douglass's assessment of West Indian emancipation bordered on the Whiggish, and it certainly did not comport with Brown and Garnet's firsthand reports on the efforts of planters to control Black labor and limit land ownership. Emancipation did in fact keep land in the hands of the few and force freedpeople to sell their labor to their former owners. Yet even as Douglass misapprehended some of emancipation's realities, in his hopefulness he rendered a vision of what emancipation *could* and *should* entail. Douglass outlined a set of economic rights—high wages and land redistribution—that would make freedom wholly distinct from slavery.

McCune Smith's and Douglass's writings on the economic dimensions of West Indian emancipation reflected a broader shift within abolitionist literature of the 1850s. After a decade of debate on land and labor in their newspapers, abolitionist editors were less concerned that highlighting labor struggles in Jamaica and elsewhere would vindicate the proslavery forces in the United States who deemed Black people unwilling to work absent the threat of the lash. They expressed openness to the idea that reluctance or outright refusal to work on the part of freedpeople was an indictment of the low wages offered by former planters rather than a reflection of racial indolence. In the pages of the *National Era*, Bailey defended the economic benefits of free labor, but noted that these benefits were of lesser import than the improvements emancipation produced among freedpeople themselves. Consideration for the formerly enslaved "never enters into the cold calculations of selfish capitalists," Bailey charged, who "seem to underrate the social amelioration of the negroes, and to look exclusively to the tables of exports, as the criterion of success."[72] The *National Era* objected to the idea circulating among planters of introducing laborers from China or Africa who might undercut upward mobility among Jamaican freedpeople by driving down wages. Bailey saw such plans as "a monstrous piece of wickedness" that would bring unnecessary competition to the West Indies "for the purpose of reducing wages to the starving point."[73] The debate about West Indian emancipation became terrain upon which the *National Era* could theorize the ways that "selfish capitalists" could infringe upon the promises of freedom.

Mifflin Wistar Gibbs, a freeborn Black Philadelphian who lectured with Douglass before settling in British Columbia in 1858, used similar language to defend Jamaican freedpeople. Responding to an article from the *London Times* republished in a local newspaper that deemed West Indian emancipation a failure because Black laborers refused to work long hours on plantations, Gibbs wrote to the editor that emancipation could only be seen as a failure to "the avaricious, and devotees of unrequited toil."[74] He asserted that laborers who "refuse to work for mere nominal wages for others when they can admirably sustain themselves by the cultivation of their own soil" were not "refusing" to work but merely refusing untenable conditions.

The language that land reformers used to defend the rights of labor and rail against the excesses of the capitalists who employed them proved useful for abolitionists in their defense of West Indian emancipation. It would be similarly useful as abolitionists debated the meaning of freedom closer to home.

As they were reconsidering how to narrate the significance and outcome of West Indian emancipation, abolitionists in the 1850s also articulated disappointment with the constricted terms of Black freedom in the North. Although they did not directly reference *Young*

America and the land reform debates of the previous decade, abolitionist thinking on the limitations of Black freedom and what would be necessary to make it meaningful bore distinct traces of those exchanges. Douglass, McCune Smith, and others wrote about labor exploitation, the ethics of accumulating wealth, and access to land as they considered the economic rights they might pair with demands for political rights and social equality. A speech McCune Smith delivered to a group of Black clergymen in 1851 in New York City reflected these shifts. Speaking on the present condition of free Black people, McCune Smith told his audience that for most, the disadvantages of city life outweighed the advantages. These disadvantages included reduced lifespan, exclusion from industrial and artisanal work, and diminished self-reliance as the result of perpetual menial employment. He argued that "the enormous combination of capital" taking over the city "must tend to grind the face of the poor in the cities, and render them more and more the slaves of lower wages and higher rents." McCune Smith found the conditions of free Black life in New York so circumscribed that he thought it apt to describe them as a kind of enslavement to the power of capital. Persuaded by McCune Smith's speech, the assembly of clergymen adopted a resolution encouraging Black people to pursue country life and agrarian autonomy, thus avoiding the "employments of dependency" to which urban capitalism subjected them.[75]

Like McCune Smith, Douglass began to use the language of slavery to describe the experience of Black freedom in the North. In an editorial for *Frederick Douglass' Paper*, he observed that recent immigrants from Europe created competition for jobs as coachmen, servants, cooks, and porters—labor that had long been racialized and thus accessible to Black workers. Douglass encouraged his readers to learn trades or be "elbowed out of employment completely" and left "at the mercy of the oppressor to become his debased slaves."[76] Elsewhere, he argued that without access to education and stable employment, Black Northers were reduced to the condition of "*semi*-slave." Absent these things, Black freedom hardly deserved the name. Black people would be vulnerable to the whims and exploitations of white employers, which Douglass described as "emancipation from master *individual*, to master *society*."[77]

William J. Wilson, a frequent contributor to *Frederick Douglass' Paper* under the pen name Ethiop, expressed frustration that after a quarter-century of freedom, Black New Yorkers still faced such conditions. "Why do they not make greater improvement?" he asked. "Why not possess a part of the wealth? Why not do a part of the business? Why not possess a part of the valuable property of the city?"[78] Wilson was convinced that only "a *black aristocracy*, and nothing short of it" could shatter the racial prejudice and discriminatory laws Black New Yorkers suffered under.[79] A critic of the deleterious effects of capital accumulation, McCune Smith stood firmly against the idea that the pursuit of wealth was the route to Black uplift. Responding to Wilson using his own pen name Communipaw, McCune Smith challenged the idea that the accumulation of wealth would ultimately be a path to security. He wrote, "the wealthy are never a progressive class; they are by necessity conservatives," suggesting that even if a small number of Black New Yorkers became wealthy, they would not necessarily contribute to the prosperity of the less fortunate.[80] McCune Smith punctuated his argument with the lines, "hundred thousand dollar black men would be no better than hundred thousand dollar white men. So much for gold as an end."[81] McCune Smith's rebuke of Wilson's call for Black wealth brought to the surface a tension that had until this point remained unarticulated in abolitionist thought. If slavery did in fact represent the power of capital so unrestrained that it could claim ownership over life itself, how could the causes of antislavery and Black freedom be served by pursuit of that very same power?

Douglass also took interest in questions of wealth during the 1850s. He could not bring himself to reject the potential of Black wealth out of hand as McCune Smith did, a position Douglass described as "standing so straight . . . as to lean backward."[82] But, like McCune Smith, Douglass thought the concentration of wealth to be inimical to social reform, and his remarks and writings on the subject bore traces of his earlier debates with land reformers. In a speech at the annual convention of the Western Anti-Slavery Society in Salem, Ohio, Douglass asserted that abolition was "the poor man's work. The rich and noble will not do it." The moral clarity necessary to stand against the blighting slave system, masters of the plantation, and their Northern allies was only to be found among the humble. "It is not to the rich that we are to look but to the poor, to the hardhanded working men of the country, these are the men who are to come to the rescue of the slave." Several of Douglass's allies in the abolitionist movement—not least among them Gerrit Smith—were men of wealth. Douglass's language was not meant to convey a factual truth but rather his conviction that the interests of "the poor, and the bound everywhere" were aligned.[83] While over the course of his career Douglass did raise the possibility that Black capitalists might do some good for the race, he was firmly opposed to vast wealth being concentrated in the hands of the few. He approved of the desire to escape poverty and accumulate a modest degree of capital, but denounced the "unlimited hoarding of wealth, and monopolies of land, which has converted almost the entire civilized world into an abode of millionaires and beggars; which renders the enslavement of the peoples of the world possible, and shrouds the future of liberty with gloom."[84] Douglass had adopted the idea, borrowed from land reformers, that land monopoly enabled and abetted chattel slavery and posed a deep threat to liberty even for those who were not enslaved. Becoming capitalists in the same vein as masters of the plantation and factory could not be the horizon of Black freedom.

Once the Civil War began, abolitionists were eager to apply the theories they had developed through debate about capital, labor, and freedom to the context of the South. In the wake of South Carolina's secession in December 1860, Thomas Hamilton, editor of the *Weekly Anglo-African*, conjectured that one of the primary motivations behind South Carolina leaving the Union was the repudiation of its debt. "The cotton States owe the Northern merchants and capitalists more than the entire States are worth or can yield for years to come," he wrote. Hamilton left no doubt as to the significance of his theory, revisiting the idea of slave owners as capitalists with an unending desire to commodify in the name of profit. "Having lived for years on the unpaid labor of Black men, they are educated up to the point of appropriating the unpaid capital of white men—for a man is a man."[85] Hamilton positioned slave owners' economic function as appropriating unearned labor, and, if they could manage it, unearned capital. Douglass expressed similar views in the first weeks of the Civil War. He predicted that should the Confederacy emerge victorious, "they would place an iron yoke upon the necks of freemen, and make the system of Slavery the great and all commanding interest of the whole country." Their goal, in Douglass's view, was "for a government in which Slavery shall be National, and freedom no where, in which the capitalist shall own the laborer; and the white non-slaveholder a degraded man."[86] For Douglass the war was not a conflict between a free, capitalist North and an unfree, precapitalist South, but a contest to place limits on the power of slave-owning capitalists.

Similar arguments circulated throughout the abolitionist press, and other publications warned that without uniting to end slavery, a Southern victory would mean that distinctions between enslaved and free, Black and white would no longer matter—all labor would be owned and dominated by slave owners. The *Christian Recorder*, the official organ of the African Methodist Episcopal Church, reported on Virginia's secession debates in late 1861. The paper noted that the constitutional amendments under debate were intended to "establish an oligarchy" that would prevent the "masses" from challenging the absolute authority of the "moneyed few." Representatives of the Virginia convention argued that shoring up the power of capital was necessary because of the forces of labor arrayed against it. These forces included "homestead bills," "Fourierism and communism," and, worst of all, "abolitionism." Virginian representatives saw slavery as "an effectual barrier against that tendency to antagonism between labor and capital which exists at the North." By collapsing land reform, communism, and abolition together as threats to Southern capital, these secessionists prompted abolitionists to do the same, further entrenching the idea of economic rights and security as an essential component of emancipation. The *Christian Recorder* concluded, "having first got the poor Black under the yoke, the effort now is in Virginia to deprive the poor whites of their liberty. The question of color is but a convenient accident by which the enormity of oppression is concealed from superficial thinkers. These Virginians, it is plain, regard labor as degrading, whether performed by Blacks or whites, and hence, no matter what a laborer's blood, he is to be deprived of his dearest rights."[87] To contest the logic of slavery, the paper framed the abolitionist cause as a defense of the rights of labor.

The claim that slave owners wished to have dominion over all labor by subjecting it to utter commodification had circulated in the abolitionist press for decades, but it was only with the onset of the Civil War that Black abolitionists used this idea as the basis for articulating their desired terms for Southern emancipation. In 1862, Douglass laid out the stakes of the war: "The work before us is nothing less than a radical revolution in all the modes of thought which have flourished under the blighting slave system." The most important component of this revolution would be the idea "that the liberty of a part is never to be secured by the enslavement or oppression of any." Douglass was clear that "the work does not end with the abolition of slavery but only begins." Without vigilance, emancipation would not produce freedom for Black people, who Douglass feared would "exchange the relation of slavery to individuals, only to become the slaves of the community at large, having no rights which anybody is required to respect."[88] Douglass considered the repression of Black labor to uplift white, the degradation of *any* labor, and the belief that capital should dominate labor as baleful ideas that had all "come from Slavery." As evidence he offered the fact that he had never seen "such contempt for poor white people as in the South," reasoning that if the poor, white and Black alike, were the most hated class in the South, then the South's labor system—slavery—was behind similarly negative ideas about labor in the North.[89] In other words, Douglass blamed Southern ideas about the proper relation of labor to capital that upheld slavery for the more universal capitalist devaluation of labor in the United States.

As the war raged on, these ideas developed into an economically inflected notion of what emancipated people deserved. In a speech before the Massachusetts Anti-Slavery Society Douglass defined freedom for his audience: "It is the right to choose one's own employment. Certainly it means that, if it means anything; and when any individual or combination of individuals undertakes to decide for any man when he shall work, where he shall work, at what he shall work, and for what he shall work, he or they practically reduce him to slavery." And so, at last, Douglass could countenance the idea that economic dispossession and the conspiracies of capital to dominate labor could "practically" be slavery. He argued that without both political and economic rights, free Black people "might as well almost retain the old name of slavery," for they would be "not the slave of the individual master," but "the slave of society."[90] Douglass did not abandon his faith in free labor, duly protected; he expected that after emancipation, so long as freedpeople possessed true legal, political, and social equality, they would be able to participate in the labor market without being reduced to a state comparable to slavery. Yet, after two decades of debating land reformers and evaluating the outcome of emancipation in the West Indies and the North, Douglass came to the conclusion that free people could indeed experience a kind of slavery if capital dominated labor. Just as slave owners considered slavery the ideal system for ensuring this state of affairs, labor's freedom from such domination was now a crucial component of liberty for Douglass.

CONCLUSION

McCune Smith died of heart failure just weeks before the ratification of the Thirteenth Amendment could prove false his apocalyptic prediction—"that there is neither in the political, nor religious, nor philanthropic worlds of the American people, any agency at work which can compass the entire abolishment of slavery." Yet, had he lived, he may have remained unconvinced that emancipation constituted anything like the "entire abolishment of slavery." Whereas Douglass expressed hope that wage labor, with sufficient protections, could form the basis of a just economic system, McCune Smith was far more skeptical about the future. "The thousands of colossal fortunes which this war has already created will find no better investment than buying up the lands of the rebel States. And, owning the land, the ownership of labor also will speedily accrue to them. What defence can the landless, penniless, outlawed *emancipado* make against the land-monopolizing, monied, lawmaking capitalist—who says to him, work for this pittance or get you gone and starve!"[91] McCune Smith had to look no further than the failure of the Port Royal project on the Sea Islands of South Carolina. When the islands' slave owners abandoned their plantations after the Union navy arrived in 1861, the remaining enslaved people divided the plantations among themselves and shifted their agricultural labor toward personal subsistence. Even before the end of the war, Union occupiers put an end to the project by forcing the islands' Black residents back to work producing cotton, and auctioned confiscated land to the highest bidder. Unsurprisingly, Black people ended up largely without land and rather than being able to produce for subsistence they worked for wages on the same plantations on which they were enslaved. McCune Smith approved of Port Royal as a blueprint for the coming emancipation of the entire South, but powerful forces were arrayed against such an outcome. "Capital, however, took the alarm. Capital . . . bought up the rest of the land, or at least placed it beyond the reach of the freedmen." The Union—the very force that was meant to bring freedom to the enslaved—reversed this enactment of what McCune Smith described as a radical form of abolition. Disillusioned, he wrote that "the special manner in which capital will seize upon and own labor in the reconstructed States requires no foretelling." No matter who the law said was free, capital could thwart emancipation by restricting access to land. Despite the revolutionary outcome of the war, "the white man, owning the land, the capital and the lawmaking, already owns labor." McCune Smith predicted that while capital might initially pay lip service to emancipation and "deck its victim with the garlands of freedom," it would do so "only to make the sacrifice more complete in the end."[92]

It is unlikely that McCune Smith, Douglass, and the other abolitionists who wished to protect emancipated Black people from the violence of capital would have come to the positions they did if not for sustained debate with white land and labor reformers. They never accepted such reformers' notion that wage slavery was worse than chattel slavery, but these encounters forced abolitionists to sharpen their own ideas about the relationship between capital and labor, free and unfree. Far from acting as uncritical proponents of wage labor who turned a blind eye to the system's exploitative realities, by reflecting upon the conditions of the post-emancipation West Indies and free Black people in the North, McCune Smith, Douglass, and their cohort began to articulate an economically-inflected understanding of freedom, or, as McCune Smith put it, "the radical abolishment of slavery." McCune Smith's fiery voice lay silent after the Civil War, but Douglass would continue to wrestle with questions of capital and labor and the meaning of Black freedom in the South for the remainder of the century.

3

A WORSE CONDITION THAN IN THE TIME OF SLAVERY

Capital, Labor, and the Limits of Emancipation

F our million enslaved souls were freed from chattel bondage by the end of the Civil War. It was a momentous achievement, the culmination of decades of antislavery agitation. Yet, by the close of the century, Frederick Douglass, who intimately knew the horrors of slavery and had dedicated himself completely to the abolitionist cause, could not help but conclude that emancipation was a failure. Douglass delivered his last major public address, "The Lessons of the Hour," in 1894 at the Metropolitan African Methodist Episcopal Church in Washington, DC. Primarily a condemnation of lynching and racial violence, toward the end of the address, Douglass turned his attention to other ways that white Southerners attempted to prevent formerly enslaved people and their descendants from experiencing meaningful freedom. He noted that it "seems to give pleasure to our enemies" to assert "that the condition of the colored people of the South has been made worse; that freedom has made their condition worse."[1] Douglass did not denounce this sentiment, but rather embraced it. He told his audience, "I even concur with them in the statement that the Negro is in some respects, and in some localities, in a worse condition to-day than in the time of slavery."[2] While former slaveowners attributed the degraded condition of Black people to a racial incompatibility with freedom,

Douglass laid responsibility at the feet of those who refused to accept emancipation.[3] "To my mind, the blame for this condition does not rest upon emancipation, but upon slavery. It is not the result of emancipation, but the defeat of emancipation. It is not the work of the spirit of liberty, but the work of the spirit of bondage, and of the determination of slavery to perpetuate itself, if not under one form, then under another. It is due to the folly of endeavoring to retain the new wine of liberty in the old bottles of slavery. I concede the evil but deny the alleged cause."[4] Listeners might be forgiven for wondering whether Douglass truly believed that freedom could leave one in a "worse condition . . . than in the time of slavery." Of course, "only a willful misreading could interpret the disappointments of freedom constantly reiterated in slave testimony as a longing for slavery. To the contrary, what haunts such laments is the longing for an as yet unrealized freedom, the nonevent of emancipation, and the reversals of slavery and freedom."[5] Douglass's words, uttered in the final year of his life, sit uneasily among much of the rest of his work. They cry out for purposeful consideration.

Even during the height of Reconstruction, freedpeople faced widespread political violence meant to circumscribe their enfranchisement and limit their ability to choose where, when, or even if to work. White assaults on Black freedom grew more intense after the end of Reconstruction in 1877. Across the rural South, Black laborers continued to toil on plantations, compelled by debt, exploitative labor contracts, the withholding of wages, threat of violence, or some terrible combination of all these things and more.[6] Douglass argued that such a labor regime could provide the economic benefits of slavery without ideological investment in the institution itself. He noted, "with this power over the Negro, this possession of his labor, you may easily see why the South sometimes brags that it does not want slavery back. It had the Negro's labor heretofore for nothing, and now it has it for next to nothing and at the same time is freed from the obligation to take care of the young and the aged, the sick and the decrepit."[7] Douglass blurred the boundary between slavery and freedom using the language of economic dispossession.

"The Lessons of the Hour" illustrated both the critical potential of Douglass's economic thought as well as its limitations—namely, the strands of abolitionist thought he could not bring himself to abandon. For Douglass, the capture of labor constricted Black freedom and seemed to represent "the spirit of bondage" and "the determination of slavery to perpetuate itself," and this capture caused "the defeat of emancipation" that rendered freedpeople worse off than slaves. Douglass's formulation, then, suggested that labor exploitation could embody the negation of freedom and a failure of emancipation. By arguing that the attempt to buy Black labor "for next to nothing" disavowed slavery while being tantamount to it, Douglass was neither resigning to a future of endless misery nor ignoring the very real differences emancipation made. He was, however, insisting upon an economic and material component to freedom. Douglass enjoined, "let the South abandon the system of 'mortgage' labor and cease to make the Negro a pauper, by paying him scrip for his labor." And he reminded his audience that "in old times when it was asked, 'How can we abolish slavery?' the answer was 'Quit stealing.' The same is the solution of the Race problem to-day."[8] Douglass could see clearly that without economic security, the work of emancipation was incomplete at best, or a failure at worst. He used the language of slavery to describe freedom absent such security, when earlier in his career he viewed enslavement and poverty as incommensurate evils. But he could not fully reconcile this support for the rights of Black labor with the reality of a capitalist social order in which subjection to the will of employers was a defining feature of free labor. Douglass, in other words, could conceive of the oppression of Black labor only as a return to slavery, not as the very nature of free labor under regimes of racial capitalism.

For much of his career, Douglass was optimistic that once nationwide emancipation became a reality, Black people's enthusiastic participation in the free labor economy would be a vehicle for demonstrating their capabilities and hastening the erasure of any lingering racial prejudice among whites. Although Douglass considered vast concentrations of wealth to be a social ill, it was one he believed would be resolved with emancipation, as planters and their proslavery allies in the North were, to Douglass's mind, the most glaring examples of capitalist excess. And while Douglass understood that industrial capitalism had the capacity to produce an exploited underclass, once the United States embraced equality before the law and universal male suffrage through the passage of the Fourteenth and Fifteenth Amendments, he had faith that the nation's political institutions would prevent such a fate from befalling American workers. Douglass's bitter evaluation of emancipation at the end of the century came only after wrestling with challenges to these ideas over the course of decades. This chapter traces Douglass's changing attitudes on race, labor, and capital from the end of the Civil War to the end of his life. As Southern revanchism and Northern apathy allowed new racialized labor regimes to take hold throughout slavery's former territories, Douglass grew disillusioned with the possibility that Black people could secure the economic rights necessary to make their freedom meaningful. And as Douglass confronted these new realities, his speeches and writing reveal how racial capitalism maintained its grip on Black life even in the wake of something so momentous as the abolition of slavery.

DEFENDING BLACK LABOR

Douglass was a lifelong advocate for the rights of working people of all races. He was also deeply suspicious of organized labor unions, seeing their aims and methods as at odds with the cause of racial equality. This tension was a defining feature of Douglass's economic thought, but it was a generative one. Douglass often articulated how the power of capital constrained Black freedom with profound clarity; at times he also wholly misapprehended the realities facing Black labor in the wake of freedom. Before the Civil War, the institution of slavery shaped the working conditions of the vast Black majority, and by naming enslavers as the worst of the capitalists, the two groups became inextricably linked in Douglass's mind. After emancipation, Douglass had difficulty conceiving of continued capitalist domination of labor as anything but a backward slide toward slavery. And while he could not see such domination as a defining feature of capitalist social relations, he was as committed to fighting against its effects as he was to the cause of abolition. To do so, Douglass adopted an evolving and eclectic set of ideas anchored by the conviction that Black freedom could not truly be realized without dignity and economic security for labor.[9]

Douglass lived in Baltimore for much of his adolescence, and the city shaped his earliest attitudes about the relationship between white labor and Black freedom. While in Baltimore from 1826 to 1838, Douglass lived with Hugh Auld, brother to his enslaver Thomas Auld. Douglass worked in Auld's shipbuilding business, and, after the business failed, Auld arranged for Douglass to apprentice as a caulker with another shipbuilder. When Douglass began his apprenticeship in 1836, he worked alongside ship carpenters who were both white and Black. Soon after, however, the white carpenters went on strike, refusing to go back to work until their employer fired all free Black carpenters. Their reasoning, according to Douglass, was that "if free colored carpenters were encouraged, they would soon take the trade into their own hands, and poor white men would be thrown out of employment." Although Douglass was not fired, the white apprentices felt "it degrading to them" to work alongside a slave, and soon after returning to work beat Douglass severely while dozens of more senior white workers looked on without intervening.[10] Auld was furious and arranged for Douglass to apprentice elsewhere, but was unable to take any recourse, since none of the white observers would testify to the beating, and the law barred Douglass himself from doing so.

Douglass noted that "until a very little while after I went there, white and black ship-carpenters worked side by side, and no one seemed to see any impropriety in it. All hands seemed to be very well satisfied."[11] Free Black men had participated in Baltimore's caulking trade in unusually high numbers for decades. In 1838, the year Douglass fled Baltimore to escape slavery, Black shipyard workers established the Caulkers Association, a trade union that was able to secure high wages and stable employment for nearly three decades. Black caulkers may have formed the union in response to racial labor insecurity like the 1836 strike Douglass witnessed. Or the growing power of Black labor in an industry so central to Baltimore's economy may have provoked anti-Black forms of organizing among white laborers.

Douglass himself saw the hand of slavery at work. Reflecting on the strike and his subsequent assault in his 1855 autobiography, he wrote, "the white man is robbed by the slave system, of the just results of his labor, because he is flung into competition with a class of laborers who work without wages." Urban slaveowners who hired out enslaved people's labor to shipyards depressed wages for white workers because the possibility of being replaced by enslaved labor hung over negotiations between employers and workers. "The slaveholders," Douglass wrote, "with a craftiness peculiar to themselves, by encouraging the enmity of the poor, laboring white man against the blacks, succeeds in making the said white man almost as much a slave as the black slave himself."[12] To Douglass's mind, white labor, whether out of deference to slaveowners' power or by falling victim to their cunning manipulation, blamed Black people both enslaved and free for their economic struggles rather than the institution of slavery itself. No matter whether the Caulker's Association was a cause or effect of the racial violence Douglass experienced on the shipyards, the timing of the association's formation—just as Douglass escaped to the North—meant that he did not witness firsthand the security the union brought to Baltimore's free Black shipyard workers.

Douglass fared little better in New Bedford, Massachusetts, where he began his life in freedom. He chose to settle in New Bedford, because, like Baltimore, the city had an active shipbuilding industry, and a conductor of the Underground Railroad thought Douglass could find work as a caulker there. And find work he did; a member of New Bedford's antislavery society offered Douglass a job caulking one of his merchant vessels. However, upon his first day of work, Douglass was "informed that every white man would leave" if he were allowed to stay.[13] Despite having completed his apprenticeship, Douglass spent his years in New Bedford performing only unskilled labor. When he began his career as a speaker on the abolitionist circuit in 1841, Douglass was far more familiar with the ways that white workers could band together to push Black workers out of skilled employment than with how unions could forge new economic protections for Black labor.

Born to free parents in Maryland in 1835, Isaac Myers began his apprenticeship as a Baltimore caulker more than a decade after Douglass departed the city. Thanks in part to the achievements of the Caulker's Association, when Myers entered the trade around 1851, conditions were especially favorable to Black labor. But white workers' jealousy would not be staved off indefinitely. In a series of incidents in 1858 and 1859, white mobs attacked Black caulkers and attempted to intimidate shipyard owners into hiring white caulkers, pushing some Black workers out of the industry. But because of these white caulker's poor workmanship and inexperience, as well as the strength of the Caulker's Association, these assaults were largely unsuccessful in fully displacing Black labor. However, the Civil War shifted the balance of power in Maryland in favor of white labor. Baltimore's white workers found enthusiastic allies in the state's Unionists, who opposed secession and thus avoided the disenfranchisement faced by many former Confederates immediately following the war. In 1865, white workers throughout Baltimore's shipbuilding industry went on strike to oppose Black competition, and, with the support of the city's political establishment, the strike resulted in more than a thousand Black workers being fired, including Myers.[14] He responded by spearheading the creation of a cooperative union that hoped to avoid white racial animus by purchasing its own shipyard and railway. Fashioned as the Colored Caulkers Trade Union Society, the cooperative issued stock to raise funds, and Black Baltimoreans responded enthusiastically by buying enough stock to secure a further loan. In February 1866, the cooperative founded the Chesapeake Marine Railway and Dry Dock Company, and soon employed hundreds of Black workers.[15]

Bolstered by the early success of the company, Myers encouraged Black workers in other industries throughout Maryland to organize their own cooperatives. In 1869, he presided over the Convention of Colored Mechanics, "which was called for the purpose of organizing the colored mechanics and tradesmen of the city and State into societies or trades-unions, such as are adopted by white mechanics throughout the country." The convention was held at the Douglass Institute, a physical meeting space for Baltimore's Black community. The location was apt; although Myers had never met the Institute's namesake, Douglass was one of the Colored Caulkers Trade Union Society's early investors. While Myers and Douglass had not yet been introduced, the convention's location presaged the abiding influence Myers's early labor organizing would have upon Douglass's thinking about race, labor, and capital in the 1870s. By all accounts the convention was a success, with "the hall well filled, and the various branches of mechanism represented."¹⁶

While the stated purpose of the convention was to build support for a series of Black trade unions modeled after white organizations, the aims of Myers and the other Black labor organizers in attendance differed in significant ways from those of white labor reformers, and these differences would put Black and white labor at odds in the coming decades. Most importantly, the organizers of the convention did not seek conflict with either capitalists or white laborers. In cases where the power of capital or racism was so overwhelming that Black workers could not negotiate fair terms for their labor, members of the convention advocated the formation of workers' cooperatives, creating a parallel labor market and ensuring high wages "without the resort to strikes." The convention also asserted its support for absolute racial equality in its unions and cooperatives, resolving that "no person shall be proscribed from membership on account of his race, color, or nationality."¹⁷ And, like the vast majority of Black political organizations during Reconstruction, members of the convention were utterly loyal to the Republican Party. Each of these beliefs was out of step with white labor, whose activism in this period was defined by widespread strikes, a willingness to exclude Black and Chinese workers to appease white reactionaries, and experimentation with political affiliations outside of the two-party system. Despite such ideological differences, Myers and the rest of the convention resolved to send five delegates to the 1869 annual meeting of the National Labor Union, the first nationwide federation of trade unions, which held its inaugural meeting in Baltimore three years earlier.

Although he delivered an impassioned speech advocating unity between white and Black laborers, Myers was unable to persuade the National Labor Union to fully incorporate Black unions into its national membership.¹⁸ But Myers was undeterred. Even before sending a delegation to the National Labor Union, he had planned for a meeting of Black representatives to be held in Washington, DC, at the end of the year for the purpose of creating a national umbrella organization that would house local cooperative unions in each state. This gathering, the Colored National Labor Convention, took place over five days in December 1869 and resulted in the formation of the Colored National Labor Union, the first national Black labor organization to be established after emancipation.[19] Nearly 250 delegates hailing from 21 states and the District of Columbia expressed their intention to attend the Colored National Labor Convention, and more than 100 actually did. The delegates were both Black and white. While the majority were men, about a dozen women attended, and one of the convention's chief areas of concern was women's labor, with delegates voting to affirm that none should be excluded from cooperative unions "on account of sex or color."[20]

Although the convention's focus was Black laborers, a population made up overwhelmingly of the formerly enslaved, delegates themselves tended to be either skilled tradesmen, reformers who were active in the abolitionist movement, or Black public officials newly elected to Reconstruction governments in the South. Most were born free or had achieved freedom before the Civil War. Among the most prominent delegates included all three of Douglass's sons; John Mercer Langston, abolitionist and inaugural dean of Howard University School of Law; Mary Ann Shadd Cary, a prominent newspaper editor and the first Black woman publisher in the United States; Joseph Hayne Rainey, the nation's first Black congressman; and George Downing, one of the country's most successful Black businessmen and conductor on the Underground Railroad.[21] Although few delegates were so well-off that they did not count themselves as part of the laboring class, their experiences were far removed from that of the typical freedperson. The ideas and resolutions that emerged from the convention, then, reveal more about how questions of labor and economic security shaped Black political thought during Reconstruction than they do about the aims of the majority of Black workers.

The Colored National Labor Union shared the same goals, principles, and ideology of the Convention of Colored Mechanics that had convened in Maryland earlier that year. The organization's prospectus was grounded in the position that laborers, first and foremost, should organize to protect their interests against the domination of capital, which was itself highly organized. It advised "first, to immediately organize, because labor can only protect itself when organized; that is, by being organized, thoroughly, you have the command of capital. You receive better pay for your labor. You learn where and how to invest your labor to better advantage. You learn the value of the capital invested with your labor—how to respect that capital, and make that capital respect your labor . . . In a world without organization, you stand in danger of being exterminated."[22] The second principle of the prospectus was that the strategy of such organization would be to form labor cooperatives rather than engage in strikes or other means of withholding labor. Like the Chesapeake Marine Railway and Dry Dock Company Myers organized, these cooperatives would be owned by workers, funded by the savings of workers themselves and through the investment of local Black communities and white Republican supporters, "so that, by a combination of their money and labor, they will form a capital and business that will give them an independent living."[23] The prospectus similarly advised local communities to form "building and land associations," which would pool the resources of a community and allow a man to "buy a house for what he would pay rent for one."[24] Thus, the Colored National Labor Union envisaged economic security through organization into local unions, protecting Black labor from exploitative conditions through collective ownership of productive and manufacturing enterprises, and individual ownership of housing and land.

These two principles found expression in a goal uncommon among labor organizations: "It should be the aim of every man to become a capitalist; that is, every man should try and receive *an exchange* for this labor, which by proper economy and investment, will, in the future, place him in the position of those on whom he is now dependent for a living. At least it should be your aspiration to become the owner of your own homestead, and place that homestead beyond the reach of want and poverty."[25] Black reformers utilized the term *capitalist* in eclectic ways; to them, it did not mean a wealthy corporate master but simply one who was not economically dependent on another and owned the means of production for whatever trade he was engaged in. In other words, the injunction to be a capitalist was not a celebration of wealth but a rejection of dependence, the desire to live a life not marred by the economic insecurity that had, to this point, characterized most Black life, even if free. The idea that every Black worker might become a capitalist signaled the belief that Black history was in motion; after a half-century struggle against an institution that at times seemed unassailable, it expressed a hope that class positions were not static categories and that no identity would be structurally opposed to another—after all, if a chattel could become a man, then what was so unbelievable about an unskilled worker becoming economically independent? The very fact that Black labor organizations were necessary was evidence that the power of capital, concentrated in the hands of former slaveowners, was hostile to emancipation and that the work of protecting Black labor was an extension of the work of abolition. In 1869, Black reformers could still feel confident that the momentum of Reconstruction would carry them to victory.

The ideology of the Colored National Labor Union resembled a republicanism inflected by the legacies of exclusion that had long shaped Black life in the United States.[26] This republicanism—not to be confused with the philosophy of the Republican Party—was premised on the ideal of collective self-governance among an educated and politically empowered citizenry. Key to such governance was the ability to freely exercise one's own will and political judgment, a form of independence that could only be guaranteed by economic self-sufficiency, usually achieved through land ownership. Republicanism also required the absence of any form of dependency that would render its citizens unable to fulfill their primary duty—acting in the common interest of the republic. Slavery was a paradigmatic form of such dependence, but so, too, was working for a wage. Subject to the will of an owner or employer, large populations of enslaved and wage laborers were threats to republican ideals.[27] Republicanism was the animating ideology of the American Revolution and the early republic, but the rise of industrial capitalism largely foreclosed the possibility of economic independence for American workers.[28] Over the course of the nineteenth century the dependent wage labor that was once the greatest threat to republican liberty became reinscribed as the very epitome of freedom through the favorable comparison of consent-based free labor contracts to the coercive violence of slavery.[29] Crucially, during this period businessmen and Republicans increasingly adopted an ideology of liberal capitalism, premised on nonintervention in market and labor relations, while labor organizations embraced socialism and trade unionism. Black political thinkers of the postwar era imagined a different path to freedom, one that could be achieved through the active participation of a state dedicated to political equality, education, and access to land.[30]

Many speakers at the Colored National Labor Convention translated republican principles of universal equality into the idiom of Black history and concrete political goals. In the convention's opening address, Downing asserted that the labor of enslaved people, which contributed to building the wealth of the nation, and the blood of free Black people, which contributed to defending the

Union, gave Black Americans a "double entitlement" to the land. These twin contributions formed the basis for his belief that Black people "should be secured in the soil."[31] Downing presented Black labor's right to the soil as a racial right grounded in the specific history of slavery and the Civil War. He invoked this history to reinforce the notion that Black people had earned the rights and responsibilities granted by the Reconstruction Amendments, and sought to find common cause between Black and white labor. Similarly, in his address Langston argued that the Colored National Labor Union should not discriminate on the basis of race, sex, or nationality. He invited immigrant and native-born white laborers, "so long ill-taught and advised that his true interest is gained by hatred and abuse of the laborer of African descent, as well as the Chinaman . . . to join us in our movement, and thus aid in the protection and conservation of their and our interests."[32] For Langston, a commitment to combating discrimination was necessary for a successful labor movement, lest the capitalist class take advantage of racial antagonism to further its own ends.

Shadd Cary, who established herself as a newspaper editor in Ontario after her family fled to Canada in the wake of the Fugitive Slave Act of 1850 before returning to the United States during the Civil War, spoke about the importance of women's participation in the Colored National Labor Union. She noted that Black women faced even more discrimination and had fewer employment opportunities than Black men, and thus, their uplift was central to the struggle for Black labor. Shadd Cary encouraged women to take leading roles in developing a subsistence agriculture economy, as many freedwomen possessed extensive agricultural knowledge.[33] She urged Black women, "bring to the pursuits of freedom the knowledge of husbandry learned when in bondage, and make it magnify and beautify your present improved condition."[34] Shadd Cary concluded her address by stressing "the importance of removing all barriers to the full recognition and success of woman as an important industrial and moral agent in the great field of human activities and responsibilities."³⁵ She proposed a resolution that the Colored National Labor Union not repeat the mistakes of white labor unions by excluding women, and that Black women should be included in the Union's efforts to organize worker cooperatives. Shadd Cary's resolution was adopted by the delegates, and she was elected as a member of the Union's eight-member executive committee, signaling the organization's willingness to acknowledge the significance of gendered work to the Black labor movement.³⁶

Other delegates focused on how securing justice for Black labor could eliminate the remnants of slavery. George Boyer Vashon, an abolitionist, attorney, and the first Black professor at Howard University, presented a report on the importance of education to protecting the interests of Black labor. Invoking the ideals of republican independence, Vashon argued that a laborer must be "free in all his acts, thoughts, and volitions." Without an education and independent mind, the laborer could not in fact "be counted among a portion of the country's labor; but must be classified as a part of its capital," nothing more than a machine that could be directed according to the will of his employer, much like a steam engine, a cotton gin—or a slave. Vashon described emancipation as a kind of property regulation; he reasoned that if the promise of emancipation was "in effect a conversion of capital into labor," then the transformation would only be complete when freedpeople were no longer subject to the deadening effects of wage labor.³⁷ Vashon saw education as a necessary tool for separating the desires of labor from the will of its employer. Rainey, too, rejected the idea that freedpeople should pursue the path of wage labor in his address. He argued that it was of the utmost importance for formerly enslaved people to become landowners, "so that they would not be obliged to build up another southern aristocracy" with their labor.³⁸ In other words, land was necessary to ensure that a new slaveocracy did not develop. Vashon and Rainey placed slavery and emancipation into the history of capital and labor. In doing so, they suggested that emancipation was not only the end of slavery, but the beginning of labor reform. Labor emerged as central to the history of Black progress.

Despite the enthusiasm among both Black reformers and their white allies for supporting Black labor organizing, the Colored National Labor Convention was in dire financial straits from the start, unable to fully cover costs for the 1869 convention. Although the dozens of delegates left with the intention of organizing labor cooperatives in their home states, there is little evidence of them successfully doing so. The Colored National Labor Union held one more national convention, thirteen months after the first, in January 1871. Existing records do not specify the size of the convention, but this was the last known national meeting. The 1871 gathering framed the goals of the Black labor movement in ways that were nearly identical to the first convention, with differences being primarily in tone and a more pointed partisan criticism. For example, the delegates adopted a resolution against free trade—a policy supported by Democrats—because it would promote further American investment in European markets, where low-wage labor abounded, foreclosing the development of Southern manufacturing and all but ensuring that labor had no bargaining power in the South. Delegates also further sharpened distinctions between their own labor movement, envisioned as protecting the interests of all labor without distinction on the basis of race, gender, or national origins, and the white-led labor movement, which delegates associated with the Democratic Party and the Confederacy.[39]

Although the Colored National Labor Union was too short lived to make good on its ambitions, it shaped the tenor of Reconstruction-era Black economic thought in important ways. At the 1871 convention, Douglass was elected president, and his ascendance to leadership of the organization represented an ongoing commitment to questions of labor, economic rights, and the relationship between race and capital in his writing. He assumed editorship of the newspaper that published and circulated the proceedings of the 1869 convention, renaming it the *New National Era*. Until it ceased publication in 1874, the *New National Era* circulated the republican ideology convention delegates had debated to a wide readership, making labor and capital central to the paper's analysis of how to make Black freedom meaningful.

RECONSTRUCTING BLACK LABOR

In the first years of the 1870s, Douglass had reason to think that the completion of his life's work was within reach. The fetters of slavery had been cast off and the sense of inexorable progress that had sustained him during the antebellum decades was bearing fruit. As editor of the *New National Era*, Douglass developed arguments about race, labor, and capital intended to secure the future of his people. Douglass's hopefulness about this future was anchored by his faith in emancipation as a radical break from the past. But neither Douglass nor the nation could cast off the past so easily. The history of slavery and debates among abolitionists and their detractors provided much of the context for Douglass's writing on the challenges facing Black labor during Reconstruction, even when it was ill-suited for providing insight into the uncertain future of Black freedom. This tension made Douglass an unconventional theorist of postwar capitalism; he was in turn both insightful and narrow-minded, both critical of capital and faithful that alone among the nations of the world, the United States could avoid class conflict. For example, Douglass was an unapologetic booster for Republican Reconstruction policy. "The Republican Party is the ship, all else is the sea," he told an audience in 1872.[40] He was loath to criticize the party of antislavery, emancipation, and equal rights, even as it turned away from its commitment to racial justice over the course of the 1870s. Douglass's support for the Republican Party was a first principle of his thought on labor and capital, and thus his analysis precluded casting Republicans or their policies as stumbling blocks to Black economic progress. Likewise, in his writings against free trade, Douglass often noted that the policy was a favorite of slaveholders. His skepticism of trade unions and alliances with white labor organizations was due in no small part to their association with Democrats and that party's historical hostility to antislavery. Throughout the early 1870s, Douglass maintained that the Republican Party was the only stalwart defender of workers' rights, and that the most dire threats to labor were the Democratic Party, whose politicians' and labor unions' support for workers he believed to be disingenuous, and free trade, which would degrade American labor to European standards.

Yet just as often Douglass invoked the legacies of slavery and abolition to demand economic rights and indict forms of freedom that were anything but. For Douglass, "the abolition of slavery, of property in man" was the "first grand step" in "the labor question."[41] By conceptualizing labor reform efforts as an extension of the work of abolition, Douglass asserted that emancipation was not accomplished in a single moment, but tenuous and in need of constant defense. His belief that the question of emancipation was necessarily a question of labor troubled from the start any immutable break between slavery and freedom.

In the early years of Reconstruction, Douglass's support for labor and his loyalty to the Republican Party were overlapping. "There is, there has been, and there can be, but one real workingman's party in this country," he wrote. "That is the party of equal rights and progress, known as the Republican party." For Douglass, Republicans' position on formal equality for all, rather than any particular advocacy on behalf of the laborer, was the source of their status as the workingman's party. Douglass defended this type of universalism against the pursuit of particular interests, arguing that "there is no justice or safety in any organization which seeks to specifically promote the interests of any one class of citizens at the expense of others," for that would ultimately "create such divisions that anarchy and violence would sooner or later become inevitable."[42] Democratic claims to advancing the interests of labor rang supremely hollow to Douglass, who believed that, by definition, the Democrats' long proslavery past made them the enemy of labor. He had long insisted that "their avowed creed was that *'capital should own labor,'* that *'slavery was the normal condition of laboring men whether white or Black,'* and that white Northern laborers, whom they had not been able as yet to reduce to chattel slavery, 'were the mud-sills of society.'"[43] For Douglass, the labor advocacy of Democrats was inextricably bound up with white supremacy, both for its support of slavery and its push to exclude Black labor from trades. His understanding of the labor movement was a history of its sacrifice of Black equality to advocate for its own particular interests.

Douglass also believed that unions and strikes, hallmarks of white labor organizing, often interfered with individual rights of workers and the rights of capitalists. While Douglass understood that workers needed to be in a strong position to equalize the power between capital and labor, and that in the past capital may have crushed labor and consigned it to interminable poverty, he insisted that present conditions, particularly in the United States, were far less dire.[44] In theory labor could indeed be disadvantaged in the face of capital, but, to Douglass's mind, in the United States—in contradistinction to Europe—"whatever wrongs workingmen may suffer, they possess the power to remedy" through their political enfranchisement and legal rights.[45]

Given his belief in a kind of American labor exceptionalism, Douglass's critique of capital was at its most powerful when he looked to its operation in Europe and the West Indies. The United States had long been interested in extending its political influence and territorial control to the Caribbean, and as president, Ulysses S. Grant organized a Commission of Inquiry to investigate the viability of annexing Santo Domingo in 1871. Although the nation's interests were primarily commercial and military, Grant also suggested that American control of Santo Domingo might provide a refuge for freedpeople who sought to escape the racism and violence of the South. He appointed Douglass as a commissioner to punctuate the idea of annexation as a benefit for Black Americans. On the return to the United States, the commission's ship experienced mechanical problems and stopped in Jamaica for repairs, which provided Douglass with the opportunity to tour the island and to observe the condition of Black people who had been emancipated for nearly half a century.[46]

Douglass saw many obstacles to Black labor's success. "The old slavemasters of that island did not (although they were paid for their human property) accept emancipation with much better grace than do our United States slaveholders accept the triumph of freedom," Douglass wrote. "They did not, it is true, organize Ku-Klux bodies to murder at midnight as we do; but they went to work with something like satanic ingenuity to make freedom to the emancipated as bitter and as burdensome as possible. No longer able to hold the negroes as slaves to individuals, they sought to make them the bond slaves of society, by throwing every possible obstacle in the way of their acquiring wealth and intelligence."[47] Douglass also considered for the first time East Indian coolie labor recruited to the British West Indies to provide white planters with an easily subjugated labor force that would diminish the ability of Black people to negotiate for better wages.[48] Reporting on his trip in the *New National Era*, Douglass noted that coolies had "expressions which might be worn by convicts serving out a sentence in a penal colony," and was perhaps reminded of his first exposure to Irish workers a quarter century earlier. "This Coolie trade—this cheap labor trade, as now called and carried on—is marked by all the horrible and infernal characteristics of the slave trade." He continued, "There is nothing in the details of the African slave trade, either in the manner of procuring its victims or of treatment of them in transit, more revolting and shocking to the sense of decency, justice, and humanity than are seen in this foul, harrowing, sickening, and deadening Coolie trade." Douglass recognized that the neutral, neat language of free buying and selling of labor sanitized a trade that looked like slavery by another name.[49]

In the following issue of the *New National Era* Douglass followed up his remarks on the coolie trade with a more expansive critique of cheap labor. "How vast and bottomless is the abyss of meanness, cruelty, and crime sometimes concealed under fair-seeming phrases," he wrote. "Cheap labor . . . seems harmless enough, sounds well to the ear, and looks well upon paper," but in actuality it meant "that the capitalist shall be able to command all the laborers he wants, at prices only enough to keep the laborer above the point of starvation. It means ease and luxury to the rich, wretchedness and misery to the poor." Douglass could only describe the economic calculations that led to the grinding down of coolie laborers by invoking the language of slavery, a juxtaposition that Douglass became increasingly comfortable with in the 1870s. "The African slave trade with all its train of horrors, was instituted and carried on to supply the opulent landholding inhabitants of this country with cheap labor; and the same lust for gain . . . which originated that infernal traffic, discloses itself in the modern cry for cheap labor and the fair seeming schemes for supplying the demand."[50] Douglass was unequivocal that the call for cheap labor upheld the interests of the powerful and degraded labor. In addition to being full-throated defenses of labor against capital, these editorials made the claim that slavery itself was the result of the search for cheap labor. Douglass further argued that the current methods of procuring cheap labor so closely resembled slavery that it was difficult to see any progress at all. Crucially, Douglass associated cheap labor in both the time of slavery and the post-emancipation era as indicative of the power of capitalists to control labor utterly. He could see with perfect clarity the negative effects of capitalism in the post-slavery societies of the West Indies, but the heady successes of emancipation in the United States were too recent, and the worst violence against freedpeople and the aims of Reconstruction too far in the future, for Douglass to give up his faith in the ability of Black Americans to chart a different path. In other words, his *general* criticism of capital's oppression of labor was tempered by his *particular* faith in American institutions.

Douglass turned a similarly critical eye to the relationship between capital and labor in Europe, and frequently described white European laborers as degraded and utterly oppressed by the power of capitalists. Yet this analysis often functioned as a foil in Douglass's writing, invoked only to distinguish it from the much more dynamic class categories in the United States, where, to his mind, poverty was not immutable but merely temporary. These comparisons seemed driven by Douglass's determined hope as much as observed evidence—if the abiding poverty that free white European laborers experienced over generations was due to some flaw in European social and political systems that the United States did not suffer from, then such poverty could be consigned to Europe. But if capitalism itself was the problem—the type of capitalism championed by the very same Republicans who were the only thing standing between four million emancipated people and the overthrow of Reconstruction—then what hope did freedpeople have for escaping poverty even as they claimed their freedom? Thus he was left only with hope that the exceptionalism of the United States would lead to the swift uplift of freedpeople in ways that would have been impossible in Europe.

These tensions produced writing on labor that was often at odds with itself. When Douglass narrated the history and experiences of European laborers, he frequently described their condition as nearly enslaved, and European capitalism as similar to the Southern plantocracy. In these moments, Douglass made sweeping and incisive claims about the intimate relationship between capitalism and slavery. In one article, for example, Douglass analogized the conditions of enslaved labor and English agricultural workers. "In no respect is their condition different from the late slave of the plantation South save that they cannot be bought and sold at auction," Douglass wrote. "The Anglo-Saxon farm laborer can no more read and write than could the slaves on Southern plantations; he has no voice whatever in the Government, and is wholly subject to the will of his employer who may give what he pleases for his work, which is never sufficient to provide a decent meal for the laborer and his family."[51] This was an electrifying critique; Douglass was suggesting that even in the absence of the chattelization that exemplified Atlantic slavery, total subjection to the will of an employer and exclusion from the ability to contest such subjection through education or political participation were tantamount to slavery. In the same breath, Douglass described a form of putatively free labor that shared important characteristics with slavery, while at the same time denying such types of free labor could exist in the United States. Because Douglass understood white American workers to have full political rights and access to education, he refused to see their condition as similar to that of European workers even if they experienced similar forms of abuse from employers. In fact, Douglass saw the United States as a potential avenue of escape: "As the slaves of the South longed for Canada, so do the Anglo-Saxon slaves of England turn to the United States as a place of refuge from an oppression that they cannot overthrow."[52]

Another implication, not fully articulated, was that the relationship between labor and capital was not merely economic, and could not be diagnosed as if it were. These English farmers, like Black laborers, were vulnerable and exploited not only because of low wages and poor working conditions, but due to political and civic ostracism and lack of education. Although slavery had been forever legally abolished in the United States, freedpeople's continued freedom in the South would be predicated upon the success of Reconstruction, for white Southerners wished for all the things characterizing labor enslavement in Douglass's analysis of England.

But in the early 1870s, a future in which the opportunity for freedpeople's uplift would be foreclosed through political exclusion and labor domination seemed remote to Douglass. In only a handful of years, the South's first Black politicians had gone from being enslaved to serving in Congress. It was unthinkable that the condition of Black labor would remain static in the way it had for European labor. Problems of American labor, Black and white, Southern and Northern, would surely find solutions in American political institutions—for it was those institutions that had overturned slavery. Further, any actions on the part of laborers that threatened those institutions, such as strikes, riots, or full-scale socialist revolution, carried for Douglass a threat not dissimilar from Confederate secession, a reminder of the dangers of rejecting the authority of a legitimate government. While Douglass understood the work of uplifting Black labor as the continuation of the work of abolition and the best way to make freedom meaningful, he simultaneously associated attempts to undermine the laws or sovereignty of the U.S. government with the Confederacy and reactionary white supremacy, rather than with social movements or abolitionism. These competing views dominated Douglass's writing on white labor struggles in the United States during this period.

The Panic of 1873 exemplified how these tensions shaped Douglass's response to labor organizing. In April 1873, Douglass offered a scathing criticism of railroad monopolies, describing them as "almost literally dictators of the laws" and, by charging "exorbitant" prices to ship wheat and corn to market, oppressors of Midwestern farmers. "The ability thus to extort with impunity from the hard earnings of farmers, and to perpetuate these glaring outrages, is the result, as we have stated, of the combinations they have formed among themselves." He noted that this concentration of power was entirely legal, since Congress had given in to the railroads' every demand.[53] But six months later, Douglass's tone changed radically. Since the end of the Civil War, the United States had experienced a railroad construction boom, driven far more by speculation and easy credit than actual demand, which created a financial bubble. European capital was behind much of this investment, and in May 1873, the Vienna stock market crashed, triggering a banking crisis in Europe, which in turn contributed to the bankruptcy of Jay Cooke and Company, an American investment bank heavily involved in railroad financing, in September, bringing the panic to U.S shores.[54] In his previous article, Douglass supported the idea that farmers might create their own combinations to counter the power of railroad monopolies. By October, Douglass placed no small share of the blame for the panic on those same organizations. He took special aim at the *Chicago Tribune* newspaper, which he described as "the leading and noisiest Liberal organ of the Northwest." Douglass accused the paper of attempting "to influence the minds of Western farmers against the railroads of the country, and to bring about the panic which has involved so many of them, and so many of the enterprising businessmen of the country, in common ruin. It has waged a bitter and relentless war upon railroads as dangerous monopolies, the power of which must be utterly destroyed."[55]

Douglass seemed to have forgotten that just months earlier, he, too, had described railroads as dangerous monopolies. In a sharp about-face, his new position offered more sympathy for railroads than farmers. This change of heart was not because of a sudden shift in Douglass's economic values, but because the antagonisms of the Civil War and fears about the fragility of Reconstruction took hold of his mind. When Douglass described the *Tribune* as a "Liberal" paper, he did not mean that it was insufficiently conservative, but that it had supported the insurgent Liberal Republican Party in the 1872 election, a breakaway party that challenged Radical Republicans and ran Douglass's longtime nemesis Horace Greeley for president, supported free trade policies, and threatened Republican power—meaning it threatened Reconstruction.[56] Douglass could not abide such a challenge, and he used any tools at his disposal to impugn its legitimacy. Douglass heard an echo of the proslavery workingmen of his youth, and, conflating the panic itself with the Liberal Republican defection a year earlier, he wrote of the economic crisis, "this whole thing is the result of efforts by such demagogues as the *Tribune* men to create an excitement among farmers which might result in a combination that could be used for destroying the supremacy of the Republican Party and throwing the control of the Government once more into the hands of the Democracy, for that can be its only political result."[57] In defending his party, Douglass blunted the force of his economic critique.

Douglass's tendency to see the violent disruptions of secession in every organizing strategy that challenged political authority and to suspect white labor of wittingly or unwittingly serving the cause of Republican overthrow could warp the precise meaning of his oft-repeated claim that he sympathized with and supported labor. As the effects of the Panic of 1873 swept through American industry, "the discharge of workmen by certain manufacturing establishments"—mass layoffs—was the predictable result. Douglass noted that most unions refused to "accept lower wages or make any terms with employers," but wrote approvingly of an ironworkers' union in Pittsburgh that temporarily accepted half pay for its members in order to keep the factory they worked at afloat amid the economic crisis. "This exhibition of the old-fashioned good feeling once existing has nearly died out, and the conduct of these Pittsburgh workingmen, in such wide contrast with the members of the Unions generally, is all the more noble," he wrote.[58] He saw the concession on the part of the ironworkers as an expression of republicanism's highest ideal—striving toward the common good. To defend one's narrow class interest amid a larger crisis was to abrogate one of citizenship's primary duties. Douglass refused to see the relationship between capital and white American labor as principally one predicated upon class struggle, and could thus characterize a voluntary reduction of wages as "old-fashioned good feeling," a compromise that allowed the factory to remain open and workers to keep their jobs, rather than as submission to the power of capital.[59]

Douglass had a similarly contentious relationship to communism. He frequently denounced it, yet often demonstrated an incomplete understanding of its principles. He was critical of what he called "collectivism," a force that, to Douglass, interfered with individual rights. He also opposed extreme "leveling" and its implied forced economic equality, believing instead that ambition—particularly Black ambition—should get its due. In March 1871, amidst a military loss against Prussia and the transition from Second Empire to Third Republic, radicals took control of Paris for two months, instituting both progressive reforms and political violence against symbols of the old order. Reports of violence committed by the Paris Commune reaffirmed Douglass's rejection of communist principles, but so, too, did American reactions to the Commune. Some white Southerners saw the revolution as a just uprising against an oppressive government, evoking the cause of the Confederacy. And, some

Republicans compared communards to Black officeholders in the South, both, in their minds, unequal to the task of political rule.[60] In an April editorial, Douglass compared French republicanism unfavorably to its American cousin for how it went beyond extending equal rights and opportunities to all, instead slipping into communism. That term, for Douglass, signified class hatred, violence, and making "war on property." He argued that French republican-communists wrongly "think wealth and poverty merely the result of a perverse state of society," in other words the inevitable result of entrenched, static class positions. Such a notion flew in the face of Douglass's belief in the role of individual agency in determining one's fate. Committed to merit, Douglass was opposed to the notion that labor should be compensated "not according to its intrinsic value to the world, but according to the time spent over it," and claimed that total economic equality would disregard individual differences in aptitude and ambition.[61]

Such images of chaotic and misguided upheaval were surely on Douglass's mind when, several weeks later, he reported on a miners' strike in Pennsylvania. He described the strike as a kind of "tyranny," a "kindred subject" to the "unrepublican spirit of communism" that characterized the Paris Commune. Grudgingly, Douglass admitted that the miners had a right to strike, and acknowledged that their union was a form of "necessary self-protection and self-defense against oppression on the part of their employers," but he condemned their attempts to use physical force to prevent others from working, actions which he described as "in flagrant contradiction with the principles of equal rights and liberty." He further condemned violence against strikebreakers and insisted that capital's domination of labor was not the result of any inherent tension or inequality between the two, but of distorted political institutions. "We think that real pauperism, wherever it is found, can always be traced back to faulty political institutions; first of all, to monarchism with all the evils and wrongs attending it." Under such institutions, it was no surprise to Douglass that labor in Europe was long "reduced to abject degradation and poverty." Even where monarchy had been replaced with republicanism, it could not "undo the consequences of the accumulated wrongs perpetrated through many centuries." In his criticism of European labor relations Douglass offered a theory of how the wrongs of the past accumulate and sediment into the present, yet his faith in American exceptionalism prevented him from applying this theory to either the South or to white American labor. Reiterating his logic for rejecting the necessity of the Pittsburgh miners' strike, Douglass wrote, "real pauperism among us is indigenous only in those States where liberty and equality have been mere mockeries until lately; where the Black man was debarred by law from acquiring knowledge and wealth, and the white man who owned no slaves was the obedient tool and servant of the master of the whip. The American laborer in the Northern States, grown up under free institutions, with the proud consciousness of his equality to any one in the country, is never a helpless pauper."[62] Through the strength of American republicanism, freedpeople would avoid the fate of European labor, who remained oppressed long after conditions of political equality pertained. And, thanks to the "free institutions" Douglass referred to, white labor always had better options than to strike.

The Reconstruction South was, in effect, a laboratory for Douglass's theories of labor. So long as the future of freedpeople looked bright, his investment in Republicans and republicanism remained intact. And because Northern laborers had never been enslaved either in fact or by political institutions—at least, according to Douglass—they were categorically different from European workingmen and had even less reason than French republicans to engage in violence. Later that summer, the Paris Commune and the threat of such activism to the stability of the United States was still on Douglass's mind. He repeated his claim that French republicans were "contaminated" by communism, its leaders as bad as the worst men of the French Empire and set on instituting mob rule.[63] And when a strike in Washington, DC, remained peaceful, Douglass's relief was nearly palpable. He warned readers to not be "forgetful that we might have the same here on a smaller scale," for there was "a terrible gulf between capital and labor constantly liable to tempests and whirlwinds" that could buffet even American republican institutions, no matter how much more stable than French institutions they seemed to Douglass. In what had become a common refrain in the pages of the *New National Era*, Douglass expressed his deepest sympathies for the "perpetual struggle" of labor. But "it can never be well to take the law into our own hands and undertake to prevent other men from working. No such despotism and anarchy can be safely tolerated for an hour," he insisted.[64]

Douglass, of course, was not the sole arbiter of what constituted "communism." Despite drawing a sharp distinction between Black cooperatives and the communards of Paris, one reader of the *New National Era*, who signed his letters with the initials R. T. G., accused Douglass himself of communist tendencies. He asked of the Colored National Labor Union, "is it merely another name for Communism . . . under another form?" Turning Douglass's own critiques of communism against him, R. T. G. went on, "Does it propose to make labor the equal of capital . . . or is it merely a colored offshoot of the notorious *Internationale*, which now has its branches throughout the world; which rules Paris under the name of La Commune, and proposes to overthrow stable government in England, and eventually to give us a mobocracy in America?" R. T. G. was convinced that communism was a plot to get "ten hours' pay for eight hours' work" so that laborers might be free to spend more time "in the beer shops, or at the varieties, or in witnessing prize fights." Yet R. T. G. was no mere reactionary. He did not wish to make a life of hard labor more bearable, but for Black people to rise above physical labor altogether by aspiring to the professional and intellectual classes. R. T. G. railed against Republicans for not doing more to seize Confederate land and redistribute it to freedpeople immediately after the war, which he saw as their best chance for avoiding wage labor. Yet Republicans opposed such redistribution precisely because it reeked of socialism and would not inculcate the formerly enslaved with the proper labor discipline required to thrive under capitalism. What constituted communism was a shifting target indeed.[65]

Douglass would sometimes praise activities that others plausibly described as communism or trade unionism, even as he continued to criticize those things as abstract concepts. In the fall and winter of 1873, Douglass reprinted two stories about groups of Black farmers in South Carolina who collectively purchased land, thereby being able to afford more and better land than they would have been able to if they acted alone. In both reprints, the original authors described what the farmers did as "a sort of communism." Douglass even titled one of the articles in which he reported on this phenomenon "Colored Communism." Yet Douglass resisted such a designation, favoring more moderate language and insisting that it was "in reality a form of cooperative association."[66] Similarly, in a particularly scathing editorial the following year, Douglass wrote, "On more than one occasion we have attempted to convince workingmen of the absolute injury to their interests of the labor unions of the country, and also their oppressions and tyrannical course toward fellow workmen, as well as to their employers."[67] William V. Turner, who described himself as State Agent of the Alabama Labor Union, felt compelled to respond, writing, "I think that the assertion is rather broad when you speak so disparagingly of *all* Labor Unions without any exception whatever." He went on to explain that in Alabama, "the laboring men are almost entirely colored," and thus were given little opportunity to gain an education. Unions, then, protected against "those that would take advantage of their ignorance" and were "intended to do that for the laboring masses that they are not, as individuals, capable of doing for themselves."[68] Douglass, for his part, was humbled, responding that "such labor unions as described by our correspondent in Alabama, W. V. Turner, cannot be objectionable."[69]

Although Douglass considered American republicanism writ large as the bulwark guarding against the chaos of communism and the degradation of American workers, when it came to specifics, he invariably used the example of protective tariffs. He considered a policy of free trade to be the greatest threat to American labor, and he saw poverty wages in Europe as evidence that if exposed to European competition, the relatively high wages of American labor would be undercut, and the comparatively privileged quality of life these laborers experienced would plummet. Douglass's faith, then, that all American workers could achieve economic security and experience generational upward mobility without resorting to violence was grounded in the notion that the market should be managed so as to create advantageous conditions for labor. Absent such management, the ghosts of slavery would haunt the lives of workingmen regardless of race. For Douglass, limiting the exposure of American labor to foreign competition through conscious policy decisions was a more effective means of protection than measures directly targeting the capitalist class—international tariffs, not unions, socialism, or outright redistribution, emerged as the solution to domestic inequality. These questions were a matter of special concern to the freedpeople of the South, for Douglass saw the future of the South in manufacturing, not merely agriculture. He wrote, "though the South grows more than half the cotton the world consumes, they have always been poor and dependent, because they have always sent it to England or the North to be manufactured."[70] Without protectionism, the South's industrial production would never have the opportunity to grow and thrive, since both manufacturing infrastructure and cheap labor were abundantly available in Europe.[71] No wonder, then, that writing of free trade, Douglass asked, "What more fatal blow than this could be struck against the interests of our workingmen?"[72]

Slavery was never far from Douglass's mind when he attacked free trade. He associated free trade with slaveowning politicians' antebellum economic policy, and even four decades after South Carolina threatened to secede over the highly protectionist Tariff of 1828, attributed support for free trade to slaveholding ideology. Referring to John Calhoun, who led South Carolina's opposition to the tariff, Douglass wrote, "the teachings of Calhoun and his 'revenue reform' disciples have so thoroughly poisoned the people's minds . . . that a large portion of the people are still the blind and obstinate believers in the beauties and benefits of free trade."[73] According to Douglass, opposition to protection "was stimulated by slavery, and should have died with it."[74] Douglass frequently warned that being exposed to competition from European labor would reduce American workers to the degraded conditions of their European counterparts—conditions that Douglass did not hesitate to compare to slavery. "The French workman is little more than a slave, bound for life to one mill, unable to emigrate, and powerless to improve his social condition." Britain fared better, but only marginally. There, Douglass wrote, "women are found in the mills, doing men's work . . . and even little children toil for a few pennies, to help keep the family above the swelling ranks of pauperism."[75] Opposition to free trade was at the center of Douglass's theory of the uplift of labor. This, too, was a lesson learned from slavery; Douglass saw antebellum white workers as oppressed not by their position as laborers per se but by exposure to competition from enslaved labor, which drove down the price of free white labor.

Douglass's optimism could not survive the violent overthrow of Reconstruction intact. Even as Douglass remained a Republican loyalist, he abandoned his notion that American institutions—at least as they operated in the South—could sustain Black laboring people as violence against freedpeople continued into the 1880s. In the 1870s, Douglass had developed critiques of European and West Indian capitalism informed by histories of slavery. By the 1880s, these critiques helped him make sense of the South as well, and Douglass began to theorize how racial capitalism distorted the ability of capital and labor to operate in idealized harmony in the post-Reconstruction South.

SLAVES TO CAPITAL

By 1874, white counterrevolutionary violence against freedpeople shook the conviction that had underwritten Douglass's thought on labor and economic justice during the early years of Reconstruction.[76] For all that emancipation did, it could not "eradicate the false theory that Black men have no rights entitled to the respect of white men. That theory outlived the war, and finds expression in the lynchings of negroes all of the South upon the slightest provocation, and oftener with no provocation whatever." Douglass's faith was by no means shattered, but for the remaining two decades of his career, his optimism about the potential of Black people to realize the widest promises of emancipation was tempered by frequent declamations about the brutal, violent realities of the post-Reconstruction period. "It is the firm conviction of the white people of the South that those who are laborers should be the property of the land owners or aristocratic element of the South," he lamented. They shared this desire with their slaveholder forebears. The white poor were not spared such attitudes, but despite the contempt in which wealthy white Southerners held their poor counterparts, Southern elites were expert in transforming whiteness itself into a psychological wage, and demanding violence against freedpeople as its price.[77] For Douglass, perpetrating and falling victim to such violence were related but racially distinct manifestations of the notion that "laborers are inferior beings and can have no rights worthy of respect."[78] The rest of the century would provide ample opportunities for Douglass to be proved correct.

Douglass gradually came to see the organization of the Southern economy, the management of white labor under racial capitalism, and white working-class violence and racism as tools that produced an afterlife of slavery. Writing for the *North American Review* in 1881, Douglass claimed that the freedman "may not now be bought and sold like a beast in the market, but he is the trammeled victim of prejudice, well calculated to repress his manly ambition, paralyze his energies, and make him a dejected and spiritless man." The simplicity of the word "prejudice" belied the expansive and often complex ways in which the term circulated. It did sometimes refer to individual whites harboring racist ideas about Black people, but more often prejudice referred to the calculus of justifications for denying freedpeople legally mandated rights and committing violent atrocities upon Black bodies. Prejudice was, in effect, an adjutant to slavery itself rather than a mere feeling. "The workshop denies him work, the inn denies him shelter; the ballot-box a fair vote, and the jury-box a fair trial. He has ceased to be the slave of an individual, but has in some sense become the slave of society," Douglass concluded. Ever-popular ideas about Black indolence and criminality, Douglass argued, were the result of psychic and physical violence that prevented Black people from participating in political and economic life, rendering them enslaved to a society shaped by white supremacist beliefs about Blackness. Prejudice, then, was not a matter of individual attitudes, but an afterlife of slavery unto itself, rendering Black life subject to the whims not of one master or household, but to all of white society.[79] Douglass had used the phrase "slave of society" to describe the constricted forms of freedom Black people experienced in the North as early as the 1840s. The phrase found new purchase in the post-Reconstruction decades, and Douglass began to wrestle with the idea that the language of slavery was necessary to properly describe the counterrevolution white Southerners mounted in opposition to emancipation.

Addressing a group of Black men in Kentucky in 1883, Douglass showed how his thinking on labor had developed over the course of the previous decade.[80] He began familiarly enough, asserting that the cause of Black laborers in the South was "one with the labor classes all over the world," and supporting cooperative unions. What came next defied everything Douglass had written about free labor in the United States over the past four decades. He declared that Black labor cooperatives were necessary because "experience demonstrates that there may be slavery of wages only a little less galling and crushing in its effects than chattel slavery, and that this slavery of wages must go down with the other." The vitality of emancipation could not outpace the necromantic reach of slavery. "Though we have had war, reconstruction and abolition as a nation, we still linger in the shadow and blight of an extinct institution," Douglass lamented. "Though the colored man is no longer subject to be bought and sold, he is still surrounded by an adverse sentiment which fetters all his movements."[81] These fetters went beyond sentiment to bind in material ways, for "the man who has it in his power to say to a man, you must work the land for me for such wages as I choose to give, has a power of slavery over him as real, if not as complete, as he who compels toil under the lash. All that a man hath will he give for his life."[82] Douglass approached something like a socialist critique filtered through the particular history of Southern slavery.

Douglass was particularly distressed by the fact that owners of labor shifted the blame for these slave-like conditions from their exploitative practices to cultural and mental deficiencies of Black laborers. Douglass pointed to the especially disturbing testimony of a grandson of the secessionist firebrand John Calhoun before the Senate Committee of Labor and Education. The younger Calhoun blamed the low condition of Black labor on a failure to seize the opportunities emancipation offered. Douglass retorted that "his testimony proclaims him the grandson of the man whose name he bears," because "the blame which belongs to his own class he shifts from them to the shoulders of labor."[83] In other words, racist ideas offered an alibi for racial exploitation under Southern capitalism both before emancipation and after. Douglass refused to indict the ambitions of freedpeople, telling his audience, "the trouble is not that the colored people of the South are indolent, but that no matter how hard or how persistent may be their industry, they get barely enough for their labor to support life at the very low point at which we find them."[84] Douglass also refused to accept racist ideas about Black criminality, which were increasingly circulating as justifications for lynching, as inherent or a result of unpreparedness for freedom.[85] Instead, he attributed the supposed low morals among freedpeople as a social construction borne from being beholden to capital. "The power of life and death held over labor which says you shall work for me on my own terms or starve, is a source of crime, as well as poverty," he wrote.[86] Douglass asked, "How happens it that the land-owner is becoming richer and the laborer poorer?" There was no ambiguity in his answer, and no reluctance to fully indict the power of capital: "This sharp contrast of wealth and poverty . . . can only exist in one way, and from one cause, and that is by one getting more than its proper share of the reward of industry, and the other side getting less, and that in some way labor has been defrauded or otherwise denied its due portion."[87] Douglass lamented the fact that emancipation provided freedpeople with rights and constitutional protections, but no material resources in which to ground the meaning of their freedom.

Douglass used two addresses commemorating the twenty-fourth and twenty-sixth anniversaries of emancipation in Washington, DC, later in the decade to further develop this line of thinking.[88] In the first speech, delivered in 1886, Douglass began on a note that registered the failed hopes of the 1870s. He described the emancipatory work of the Republican Party as "most sadly incomplete" and lamented to his audience that "we are yet, as a people, only half free."[89] Although, Douglass admitted, some individuals had achieved great success, "the mass have had their liberty coupled with hardships which tend strongly to keep them a dwarfed and miserable class."[90] Douglass blamed this low condition on what he called the "landlord system" that prevailed in the South, which included both sharecropping and tenant farming. Sharecropping required laborers to give a portion of their crop to the landowner as rent, often leaving them in perpetual debt, while tenant farmers paid rent in cash and had more autonomy, although both systems kept Black farmers economically dependent. He accused former slaveowners of conspiring to prevent Black people from buying land, forcing them instead to rent land from the very people who had once enslaved them. The exorbitant rental prices left them "poorer at the end of the year than at the beginning." Douglass compared the landlord system in the South unfavorably to that of Ireland, which was bad enough that it had "conducted that country to the jaws of ruin."[91] The bitterest part, for Douglass, was that freedpeople were "forced to be poor, and laughed at for their destitution."[92] Whereas in the previous decade, Douglass denounced European labor's uprisings and the violence of socialist upheaval, now he warned, "the American people have this lesson to learn: That where justice is denied, where poverty is enforced, where ignorance prevails, and where any one class is made to feel that society is an organized conspiracy to oppress, rob, and degrade them, neither persons nor property will be safe."[93] Douglass suggested that the overturning of Reconstruction would destabilize society itself, undermining the very foundations of law, order, and governance. The turn away from racial and economic inequality would have consequences that extended beyond the formerly enslaved.

Two years later, Douglass's message was even more dire. It seemed as though the worst effects of capitalism were working in full force to diminish the meaning of freedom in the South. The landlord system denied any opportunity for economic security, leaving freedpeople destitute and unable to save. It was the means by which "the same class that once extorted his labor under the lash now gets his labor by a mean, sneaking, and fraudulent device."[94] Douglass described the landlord system as "a disgrace and a scandal to American civilization." It was this very civilization that was supposed to ensure a mutually beneficial relationship between labor and capital. White Southerners' counterrevolutionary violence and forms of racial labor control exposed freedpeople to a type of capitalism Douglass had believed could not pertain to free laborers in the United States—that is, a type of capitalism he often described as virtually indistinguishable from slavery. Here, too, Douglass asserted that the laws upholding the landlord system "sound to me like the grating hinges of a slave prison."[95] This address was the most complete and forceful expression of Douglass's disgust with the failure of Reconstruction. Douglass had by this point dedicated half a century to the pursuit of Black freedom; too often that project had seemed impossible, and Douglass's work was sustained not by the likelihood of success but by his all-consuming faith that abolition could remake the world. To see that work coming undone before his eyes stretched the limits of even Douglass's seemingly boundless facility of language to the point that the present reached back to the past. Thus his conclusion that the Black laborer, "though he is nominally free he is actually a slave," and "is worse off, in many respects, than when he was a slave."[96] And so, thinking of a people who had escaped the horrors of slavery only to be crushed by poverty and racial violence, Douglass turned to his audience declared, "I here and now denounce his so-called emancipation as a stupendous fraud—a fraud upon him, a fraud upon the world."[97]

CONCLUSION

While Douglass never fully abandoned his faith in American political institutions, he did revise his understanding of how economic forces could subvert the rights those institutions promised. By the end of his life, Douglass often spoke of freedom as having been severed from the economic means necessary to sustain it. Douglass's speeches and writings from the 1880s and 1890s, then, marked a radical turn in his thought, though one forged within the limits of his lifelong commitments. He never embraced socialism or labor radicalism wholesale, remaining wary of movements that threatened political order. Yet his own analysis grew increasingly compatible with those traditions. His claim that wage labor, in its most exploitative form, could become a kind of slavery was an acknowledgment of racial capitalism's capacity to warp the contours of freedom.

Douglass's insistence that the condition of freedpeople in the 1890s could be "worse than in the time of slavery" is an interruption of progressive historical time. His formulation suggests that the injustices of the past do not merely cast echoes into the present, slowly fading over time. Nor do they linger statically—they can amplify (be *worse than*). If what came after was potentially worse than slavery, Black reformers could not be sure that the march away from slavery was inevitably a march toward freedom. By asking his audience to imagine a freedom so low that it was more terrible than slavery, Douglass challenged them to think of the fight against slavery as but one part of a larger struggle to disentangle Black freedom from racial capitalism.

4

ABOLITIONISM IS ANOTHER TERM FOR COMMUNISM

Abolition Democracy Against Racial Capitalism

T. Thomas Fortune and Ida B. Wells were among the most prominent Black newspaper editors and writers of the late nineteenth century. Heirs to the most subversive strains in Frederick Douglass's thought, they anticipated many of Du Bois's arguments in *Black Reconstruction* regarding capitalism, labor organizing, and backlash against Black economic development by nearly half a century. Like Du Bois, they theorized the economic forces animating Black dispossession in the wake of Reconstruction; both understood post-Reconstruction violence and repression as part of a contest over the South's economic order. They made politics economic by arguing that disenfranchisement and political repression were tools of economic domination that maintained labor exploitation and upheld capitalist interests. And they made economics political, advocating collective action to interrupt the circuits of capital that made white supremacy profitable.

This approach to the investigation of Black life, characterized by skepticism toward the idea that political freedom could exist without economic justice, found its most striking expression in an editorial Fortune wrote for his newspaper the *New York Globe* in 1884. After revolutionary socialists assassinated Emperor Alexander II of Russia in 1881, the Black press published articles contrasting the violent nature of political change in Europe to the democratic institutions governing politics in the United States. In one such article, the editor of the *Detroit Plaindealer* described "Russian Nihilism," broadly used at the time to mean *socialism*, as "a parasite which is sucking the lifeblood of the people," and railed against the use of "anarchy" and "assassination" as weapons against tyranny or tools of social reform. Fortune responded with an editorial of his own, writing that he had "scarcely ever seen so much error crammed into one paragraph" as he had in the *Plaindealer* piece. He contended that it was the tsar, not the Nihilists, who was the true parasite of Russia, and that when the power of "thrones and armies" united to oppress the people, "anarchy for the time is the only power which can relieve the distresses of the people." Fortune then wrote that if old political orders had to crumble and rulers assassinated to free their people from the shackles of oppression, "let the thrones topple and the bloody tyrants die." Fortune's endorsement of anarchy and political violence was nearly unheard of among Black newspaper editors. Such violence likely reminded them of the assaults they had suffered at the hands of white vigilantes, and most condemned it in the same way that Douglass had denounced the Paris Commune. But even more singular in nineteenth-century Black political thought was the comparison Fortune made next. He wrote, "we are with the people. Nihilism in Russia, Communism in Germany, and in France, Irish contention in Great Britain and Abolitionism (another term for Communism) in the United States, are only synonyms for resistance by the people to the tyranny and corruption of the Government,—whether it be imperial, monarchical or constitutional government."[1]

Fortune reimagined abolition as a revolutionary and unfinished project that challenged property rights and class hierarchy in South. His comparison between abolitionism and communism was based on the notion that abolition was a subversion of property rights in the name of justice, but one that was not taken far enough. Allowed to mature without the interference of Southern vigilantism or Northern free labor ideologies, slave emancipation might have remade the South according to principles resembling European communism. Fortune intimated that demands on Southern capitalists and landowners were an extension of the kernel of communism embedded in the premise of abolition and the land redistribution that might have followed—what Du Bois later termed "abolition-democracy." It made abolition an economic issue rather than one of simple humanity. For Fortune, the disease for which slavery, wage labor, and monarchy were symptoms was inequality; the cure was economic enfranchisement. Such enfranchisement went by different names in different places—"Nihilism," "Communism," "contention," "Abolitionism"—but were bound by a commitment to toppling the political forces that abetted poverty among the laboring masses. Prefiguring how Du Bois would insert the enslaved people of the South into a global history of labor struggles, recasting the slave as "the Black worker," Fortune interpreted the abolitionist movement as one whose goal was to end the economic dispossession of slavery, not merely its abrogation of rights. Abolition, then, was not a movement that had completed its purpose with the end of slavery, but rather one whose full potential was strangled through the conspiracy between Southern revanchism and Northern industry.

While technically of the same generation as Du Bois, the careers of Fortune and Wells were waning by the time Du Bois's began its meteoric rise at the turn of the twentieth century. Although the two were born enslaved, Fortune in 1856 and Wells in 1862, their backgrounds were nearly as different from one another as both were from Du Bois's. Fortune's father, Emmanuel, was a delegate to the Florida Constitutional Convention of 1868 and thereafter served as a congressman in Jacksonville. Because of his father's prominence during Reconstruction, Fortune had the opportunity to work as a page in the state senate, and several Black luminaries of the age visited his childhood home. By the time he was eighteen, Fortune had left Florida for Howard University in Washington, DC, where he studied journalism and entered into the social orbit of two of the nation's most prominent Black figures, Frederick Douglass and John Mercer Langston. By age twenty-three, he had moved to New York and soon became editor of the *New York Globe*, a paper that would change names twice within a handful of years, first to the *Freeman* and then the *Age*, and rise to prominence as one of the nation's most important Black organs.[2]

Wells spent her childhood in rural Mississippi. Although her father trained as a carpenter while enslaved and earned a good living after emancipation, Wells had a difficult upbringing. When she was still an adolescent, her parents and one of her brothers died of yellow fever. As the eldest child, Wells took responsibility for raising her six remaining siblings. She interrupted her own education to teach at a rural school. Several years later, Wells moved fifty miles away to Memphis for a better-paying teaching position, leaving her siblings with their grandmother during the week and returning each weekend. She was eventually fired for criticizing the school, and began to write full-time in 1886. Within three years, Wells was editor and part owner of the *Memphis Free Speech* newspaper. Wells was confident and publicly assertive in a way that few women of her race and region could afford to be, and her rural upbringing and outspoken nature meant that even as her writing earned widespread recognition (Douglass once said that his own work on lynching was "feeble" in comparison), Wells was not as natural a fit among the Black elite as Fortune.[3]

Mutual admiration brought Fortune and Wells into one another's orbit. Fortune's position as a leading Black newspaper editor and radical, iconoclastic thinker was fully established by the mid-1880s, and Wells read his work as she built her own career in journalism. Both Fortune and Wells were skeptical of the unconditional faith the abolitionist generation placed in the Republican Party, and the two met in person in 1888 at a Democratic Party conference in Indianapolis. Although they harbored no illusions about working with Southern Democrats, the architects and perpetrators of anti-Black racial violence throughout the region, they believed that if Black people courted the Northern branch of the party, both Democrats and Republicans might be forced to speak out against the ongoing Black disenfranchisement in the South. Reflecting on their meeting, Fortune described Wells as "smart as a steel trap," the equal to any male journalist, and he began publishing her work in the *Age*.[4] In 1892, Wells published a particularly incendiary editorial in the *Free Speech* on the topic of interracial intimacy, and immediately faced death threats.[5] Days after the editorial appeared, while Wells was traveling in New York, a white mob descended upon the offices of the *Free Speech*, destroying its printing presses and the building itself. Friends warned Wells not to return to Memphis, and she never did. Fortune offered Wells a job at the *Age* and opened his home to her, and the two worked together closely for the next three years.

This chapter charts the development of Fortune's and Wells's economic thought, which was characterized by an abiding skepticism about Black integration into the post-Reconstruction South, even under terms of political equality. Fortune produced his most important writing on these topics in the 1880s, beginning with the publication of a long treatise on race, land, and labor, and elaborated upon in editorials for the *Age*. Fortune's intellectual project was to situate the Black South alongside the labor conflicts unfolding across the nation in the late nineteenth century, with the aim of recasting the primary struggle in the South as one between labor and capital rather than between Black and white. Fortune did not see the possibility of Black ascension to the Southern elite as progress, for it would merely diversify the class of capitalists that was exploiting labor of all races. Wells, in turn, found success as the nation's foremost writer on lynching in the 1890s. Her work revealed how these killings were not merely excessive punishments for criminal acts, but rather functioned principally as a tool for economic domination and racial plunder. She recognized that no matter the effort or concessions Black people made, they could never gain entry into middle-class Southern respectability, for preventing that entry was what animated the entire culture. For both thinkers, Black subjugation in the post-Reconstruction South was not a failure of political inclusion alone, but the result of a racial capitalist order that made economic exclusion and exploitation its foundation.

LABOR AND CAPITAL IN BLACK AND WHITE

Fortune was part of the first generation of Black writers in the South to grow up free. It was the crushing defeat of Reconstruction rather than the success of the abolitionist crusade that formed the crucible for his intellectual development. Thus Fortune could see what emancipation and the Republican Party had left undone far more clearly than what they had accomplished. Despite publishing one of the most widely read Black newspapers of the late nineteenth century, few of Fortune's most radical ideas were taken up by his contemporaries. Unlike Douglass, Fortune was not bound to the party by any sense of loyalty, and he searched restlessly for opportunities to build Black political and economic power outside Republican circuits. In his yearning to find new paths forward for the race, Fortune could be ideologically dilettante, and while his deep interest in land reform and labor organizing became less pronounced by the late 1880s, Fortune's work was the most sustained engagement with land and labor in the entirety of nineteenth-century Black thought.

Fortune once asserted that there must be something wrong with capitalism if it spurred "nihilism in Russia, socialism in Germany, communism in France and agrarianism in Ireland," and expected a similar movement to take hold in the United States. He offered as evidence the nation's own recent history, suggesting that "the people of the United States turned socialists for a moment when they abolished slavery and readjusted, by statutory enactment, the relations of master and servant."[6] The history of slavery and emancipation provided Fortune with a way of thinking about the South alongside the social movements of Europe and of imagining Black freedom as part of a global class struggle.

Fortune's most significant work, *Black and White: Land, Labor, and Politics in the South*, was a microcosm of these tensions and contradictions. Published in 1884, *Black and White* was the first Black-authored book devoted to economic, class, and labor analysis. Fortune's aim in writing *Black and White* was to convince his readers of two points. First, that the source of poverty and inequality in the United States, and throughout the world, was land monopoly, the concentration of the majority of land in the hands of a wealthy minority. Second, and consequently, the terrain of struggle in the South was not "racial or political in character," pitting Black against white or Republican against Democrat, but essentially economic—a struggle between labor and capital. In other words, Fortune sought to integrate the post-Reconstruction South into a larger narrative of labor's dispossession globally.[7] He argued that Black Southerners were not oppressed simply because they were disenfranchised and terrorized by racial violence, but because they were the proletarian class of that region.

These were claims wholly out of step with his contemporaries, and in framing the plight of the Black poor in the South as a generalized struggle between labor and capital, Fortune did not fully capture how the threat of violent death hung over Black life in the South in ways that were highly racialized and regionally specific. Yet in his insistence that Black laborers were a proletariat oppressed by the same forces that sought to crush all labor, Fortune attempted to make the Black South legible as a potential ally to the labor movements sweeping across the United States and Europe in the 1880s. This was a major revision to Black economic thought. By writing about freedpeople as *poor laborers* rather than *Black Southerners*, Fortune hoped that all working people in the South might find solidarity with one another and with laborers outside the South. Fortune's foregrounding of class was not a repudiation of the ways that race was central to how Black workers navigated the terrain of labor, but a rejection of the belief that racial inclusion and political equality alone could protect them from economic exploitation. Fortune saw the tension between capital and labor was both inevitable and inherent. He understood the racial violence of the South to be a local form of capital's universal oppression of labor; although race was the justification for such violence, for Fortune, focusing too much on its racial character obscured the fundamentally capitalist social relations it enforced.

Fortune structured his book in two parts. The first half of *Black and White* recounted the history of slavery, emancipation, and Reconstruction, and offered a platform through which Fortune could argue that the limitations of emancipation policy had continued to enable Black economic exploitation even two decades after the end of the war. The second half argued that the problems Black people faced in the South were inevitable within a capitalist system, and that the only hope for improvement was for Black Southern labor to ally itself with labor everywhere lest it be trapped in a new, industrial wage slavery.

Fortune was deeply pessimistic about the progress Black Southerners had made in the two decades since emancipation, going so far as to argue that the problems that led to the Civil War "are to-day as far from solutions as if no shot had been fired upon Fort Sumter." He claimed that "the giant form of the slave-master" still loomed large to "oppress the unorganized proletariat—the common people, the laboring class." He blamed both the South and the North for this state of affairs. He considered the Republicans' amnesty policy toward Confederates to be sheer folly, mocking the presumption that former Confederates and freedpeople could live together as equals. Fortune decried the notion that Southern whites would ever accept their loss and the terms of slave emancipation without being "subjected to that severe governmental control which their treason merited," and he was equally skeptical that freedpeople could simply assume the duties and responsibilities of citizenship without money or "mental resources." Emancipation was doomed to fail for the unequal way that freedpeople were set in opposition to former Confederates, which amounted to putting the former "more absolutely in the power" of the latter than under slavery. "And, so, having made the people free, and equal before the law, and given them the ballot with which to settle their disputes," Fortune wrote, Republicans "left the people to live in peace if they could, and to cut each other's throats if they could not. That they should have proceeded to cut each other's throats was as natural as it is for day to follow night."[8]

Fortune feared that the failure of Reconstruction and Republican abandonment had left Black Southerners vulnerable to a new form of industrial wage slavery. "It was not sufficient that the Federal government should expend its blood and treasure to unfetter the limbs of four millions of people," he wrote. Under Democratic rule, only the letter of emancipation remained, nothing of the spirit; the legal protections and political rights accompanying emancipation in the form of the Fourteenth and Fifteenth Amendments had been all but rescinded, and even at the height of their power Republicans had never been interested in pursuing Black economic rights. Without further protections, Black people were faced with "a slavery more odious, more galling, than mere chattel slavery." Fortune's notion of a "more odious, more galling" slavery may have been inspired by a speech Douglass delivered the previous year, in which he said, "there may be slavery of wages only a little less galling and crushing in its effects than chattel slavery."⁹ But while Douglass used such language to foreground the continued racial vulnerability of Black labor in a way that set it apart from the relative privilege he believed white labor enjoyed, Fortune's words echoed those of antebellum land reformers who cautioned that abolition would merely consign formerly enslaved people into the same wage slavery to which white laborers were subjected. He was convinced that freedom meant worse economic oppression than under slavery, and he argued that freedpeople were "more absolutely under the control of the Southern whites; they are more systematically robbed of their labor."¹⁰

Anticipating readers' skepticism of such a claim, Fortune turned to Europe for an analogy. The disposition of the tsar, Fortune wrote, was irrelevant, for he was the head of an autocracy that produced widespread poverty regardless of his pleasantness as an individual. Replacing the ruler would not solve the structural problem; it was the political system itself that had to change. Similarly, in Ireland, landlords were not the problem in its entirety but merely a symptom; the problem was a system of land monopoly that made renting out land both possible and profitable. The same was true of the South—slavery was only a symptom of the larger economic system that dispossessed Black labor. "To tell a man he is free when he has neither money nor the opportunity to make it, is simply to mock him," Fortune wrote. "To tell him he has no master when he cannot live except by permission of the man who, under favorable conditions, monopolizes all the land, is to deal in the most tantalizing contradiction of terms." Abolishing slavery rid the South of the symptom but not the illness, and Fortune concluded that freedom without economic security and without independence from the power of wealthy landowners was a mockery.¹¹

Fortune continued to explore this line of reasoning throughout the first half of *Black and White*, working through new ways of situating the South in relationship to the rest of the nation. Like many abolitionists, he adopted the argument that it was the desire of capital to own all labor regardless of race, and took up the idea that the abolition of chattel slavery merely emancipated freedpeople into a propertyless laboring class condemned to toil for the wealthy, citing the work of the anti-monopolist political economist Henry George to support his position. In *Social Problems*, published in 1883, George argued that the essence of slavery was the theft of labor, and that chattel slavery was not the most extreme and advanced form of this phenomenon but the most primitive; to truly rob people of their labor on a vast, industrial scale would require a more sophisticated form of enslavement than individual ownership. Thus, Fortune argued, "When the American Government conferred upon the Black man the boon of freedom and the burden of the franchise, it added four million men to the already vast army of men who appear to be specially created to labor for the enrichment of vast corporations." George's analysis helped Fortune make sense of the post-emancipation South, and in turn, Fortune offered a corrective to George's work by insisting that the South must be considered as a site of modern labor struggle.[12]

Black abolitionists rarely questioned the soundness of American institutions as they pertained to white people. So powerful was slavery's gravitational force that it could warp even a society founded upon the protection of white freedom, as when Douglass argued that competition with enslaved labor caused the depression of wages for free white labor in the South.[13] In other words, Black abolitionists thought of slavery as a social ill so profound that nearly all others could be traced back to it. Fortune was not so convinced, and as the Republican Party evolved from a radical reformist party focused on civil rights and Reconstruction to a more conservative, pro-business party emphasizing tariffs, economic development, and administrative reform, Fortune questioned the older abolitionist reasoning. "When a society fosters as much crime and destitution as ours, with ample resources to meet the actual necessities of every one, there must be something radically wrong, not in the society but in the foundation upon which society is reared," he wrote. Fortune argued that corporate monopoly over railroads, telegraphs, and manufacturing created a society forced to "submit to the humiliation of being ruled by them," as was "largely the case at the present time" regardless of whether white supremacy reigned or not. The particular failure of the federal government to protect the rights of freedpeople in the South was, to Fortune, a reflection of a broader federal abandonment of its citizens to the domination of capital. Fortune claimed that a government powerful enough to transform slaves into "free men and citizens" was powerful enough "to insure the enjoyment of the freedom conferred," to make that freedom meaningful. And if it chose not to, it "would make its conferring of freedom and citizenship absurd in the extreme, a mere trick of the demagogue to ease the popular conscience."[14] The failure to empower freedpeople to claim their own destinies was a part of the same larger failure to empower common people against industrial monopolies.

Fortune ended the first half of *Black and White* with the assertion that Black workers were even more ensnared by the power of capital than in the time of slavery, with little chance of salvation from a government whose policies enriched the capitalist class, be it Southern plantation owners or Northern railroad barons. Yet Fortune saw hope for the future if labor could unite against capital. The second half of *Black and White* was intended to "incontestably demonstrate that *the condition of the Black and the white laborer is the same, and that consequently their cause is common.*"[15] Fortune made his case with a structural critique of capitalism and by arguing for the importance of Black and white working people in the South coming together to fight land monopoly.

Fortune began this section by articulating his basic theory of capital: "Capital can produce nothing." All natural resources and other forms of capital would lie fallow and inert without the power of labor to activate it, and thus capital was subordinate to labor, for capital would be worthless without labor. Yet capital reaped by far the greater share of rewards for production, essentially stealing from labor, for the capitalist "not only exacts an unjust proportion of the laborer's hire, but takes more than he justly should as interest upon his capital and as reward for his own time and labor." This dynamic constituted the basic problem of capitalism. Fortune concluded that millionaires were "enemies of society" not simply because they were rich, but because their riches were gained by foul means and wielded to oppress.[16] Altering these conditions was difficult because they broke no laws; in fact, Fortune argued that it was "through the operation of law that mankind is ground to powder." Capital's extraction of wealth from labor was called "law and order" and protected by various police forces, and any society that could only be held together through such use of force was surely unjust.

Fortune's argument reflected the sharp rise in labor unrest in the decade before the publication of *Black and White* as industrialization accelerated and workers protested low wages, long hours, and dangerous working conditions. In response, both private employers and government authorities often met organized labor with violence and repression. Rutherford Hayes deployed federal troops to suppress the Great Railroad Strike of 1877, the first strike to organize workers across state lines, using violent clashes between workers and strikebreakers, police, and private security as justification. This deployment marked a precedent for federal intervention on behalf of corporate power. Local police and state militias frequently broke strikes and protected strikebreakers, while courts issued injunctions against unions. Railroads and steel companies used private security forces to intimidate and attack labor organizers. This period revealed a growing alignment between government and industrial capitalists, with political leaders often justifying repression in the name of maintaining order and protecting commerce.[17]

Fortune asserted that it was through the operation of the law that the power of capital increased and the gap of inequality widened. In his assessment of the relationship between capital and labor, wealth, and legal protections, Fortune drew from the work of white labor radicals, but he also sustained and extended Black abolitionist engagements with those ideas. "Already it is almost impossible to obtain any legislation, in State or Federal legislatures, to ameliorate the condition of the laboring classes. Capital has placed its tyrant grip upon the throat of the Goddess of Liberty," he wrote. "The power of railroad and telegraph corporations, and associated capital invested in monopolies which oppress the many, while ministering to the wealth, the comfort and the luxury of the few, has become omnipotent in halls of legislation, courts of justice, and even in the Executive Chambers of great States, so that the poor, the oppressed and the defrauded appeal in vain for justice."[18] Fortune's description of a federal government corrupted by the forces of monopoly capital echoed the abolitionist critique of slaveholders' capture of national politics to sustain their own wealth earlier in the century. He drew these two struggles together through the claim that "the people of the United States turned socialists for a moment when they abolished slavery and readjusted, by statutory enactment, the relations of master and servant."[19] In this history Fortune saw one capital's most spectacular, if fleeting, defeats; it was evidence that the interests of Southern labor were aligned with those of all other regions.

Fortune endeavored to show that the tenets of socialist thought were the best tool for understanding the condition of Black labor in the South. Doing so allowed him to argue that the region was a crucial battleground of the labor struggle, and that Black Southerners were not merely former slaves but allies in waiting for the global proletariat. Fortune was concerned that racial antagonism in the South would inhibit such forms of solidarity. When the white South wielded the law as a weapon against Black people to criminalize and punish them, it not only harmed Black people and made white Southerners contemptuous of them, it also promoted white criminality by making white people feel above the law, as though the sole purpose of legal consequences was to enforce racial dominance. Fortune concluded that so long as the South had a reputation for "mob law" and racial violence pervaded, the South "cannot hope to encourage the investment of large capital in the development of her industries."[20] Thus, for political and economic reasons, it was in the interest of all Southerners to foster racial egalitarianism, and Fortune encouraged the South to spend less on prisons, guns, and propping up white supremacy, and more on schools, equity, and the interests of common people.

If overcoming racial differences was a precondition for working people to have any chance in the struggle against capital in the South, Fortune believed that the nature of capitalism itself could abet this process, arguing that the "political disorders" and "race-wars" that plagued Black life were expected, but temporary, outcomes of Reconstruction policy.[21] While Fortune condemned without reservation the "death and terror" white men sowed throughout the South to undermine Black political power, he did not find it surprising given his view that the Black vote propped up corrupt Reconstruction governments that perpetuated "organized robbery on the part of the white adventurers, who have become infamous under the expressive term 'carpet-baggers.'" Fortune argued that such terror would not last, and that race-based political violence would disappear once a small Black elite emerged, washing away concerns about race in the face of this elite's "bank-account" and "important money interests."[22] For Fortune, the notion that wealth accumulation would lead to the erosion of race prejudice was not a goal, but a warning. He envisaged Black wealth as the consolidation of a dangerous class power that would enrich Black individuals but "pauperize Black and white labor." In Fortune's prediction for the

South's future, "the intelligent, the ambitious and the wealthy men of both races will eventually rule over their less fortunate fellow-citizens without invidious regard to race or previous condition." Thus, the working people of the South would similarly have to abandon race prejudice in defense of class interests. While Fortune was curiously silent on the ways that racial violence enabled Black economic domination, his provocations offered a cautionary tale about political inclusion without economic equality.[23]

Just as antebellum land reformers pushed Black abolitionists to sharpen their economic critiques of slavery, critics of land monopoly provided the context for Fortune's diagnosis of Black poverty. In the 1880s, the productive capacity of the South was overwhelmingly rural, and thus Fortune was concerned with the concentration of agricultural capital rather than industrial or financial capital. He feared that land monopoly would reproduce the two greatest evils of slavery, namely "the creation of vast landed estates, and the pauperization and debasement of labor."[24] Fortune's argument that "individual ownership in the land is a transgression of the common right of man, and a usurpation which produces nearly, if not all, the evils which result upon our civilization" was largely drawn from the work of Henry George. After establishing his arguments about land monopoly as the cause of Southern poverty, Fortune rehearsed a global history of misfortune caused by the same. "The great French Revolution would have never occurred but for the monopoly of land, which reduced the proletariat to "vassalage, more grinding than slavery itself," he wrote. The cause of Russian Nihilism was "the outgrowth of monopoly in land and the consequent enslavement of the people by the aristocracy." Something similar pertained in Britain, where the nobility and capitalists extracted rents from tenants, and beyond Europe, Fortune argued, the "British land shark" was responsible for an array of crimes, for he had "reduced the people of India to a state worse than death; and his iron grip has been placed upon the uncounted millions of African soil; the Islands of the sea squirm in his grasp; the West India Islands are his prostrate prey."[25] The world over, land monopoly was capital's method of dispossessing labor. Fortune abandoned a degree of investment in the particular racial histories of the South and the United States in order to connect the region and the nation to this larger imagined history of class struggle, in the hope of building the ideological basis for an interracial labor strategy for the present.

Having tethered the fate of Black labor in the South to both white labor and the assemblage of peoples Du Bois would refer to as "that basic majority of workers who are yellow, brown, and black," in the last section of *Black and White* Fortune returned to the history of emancipation in the South.[26] The Union "took the slave and left the thing which gave birth to *chattel slavery*," Fortune wrote, "and which is now fast giving birth to *industrial slavery*; a slavery more excruciating in its exactions, more irresponsible in its machinations than that other slavery" into which Fortune himself was born. This new industrial slavery was worse than what came before because there was no legal requirement nor financial incentive to value the life of a worker in any way, and no disincentive to working laborers to death. Under such a system, the landowner "forges wealth and death at one and the same time," which was only possible because workers could not themselves own land and were thus a captive labor force.[27] By advocating for an interracial labor coalition with the aim of breaking up plantations and distributing the land to common people so that they could escape wage labor, Fortune articulated a vision of Black freedom predicated upon the downfall of both white supremacy and the power of capital. He brought slavery into the history of labor rather than cast it out, motivated by his faith that working people would soon realize that they all shared a "common cause" and a "common enemy," for "the rich, be they Black or be they white, will be found upon the same side; and the poor, be they Black or be they white, will be found on the same side." Fortune left his readers with the final message: "the future struggle in the South will be, not between white men and Black men, but between capital and labor, landlord and tenant."[28]

THE *AGE* OF THE *FREEMAN*

In the pages of the *New York Freeman* and later the *New York Age*, Fortune tested the ideas he laid out in *Black and White* against the current events of the 1880s, most notable among them the dramatic rise and fall of the Knights of Labor. Fortune's theory of history was that of perpetually unfolding class struggle. He found industrial society, "based as it is upon feudal conditions," to be "an outrageous engine of torture and an odious tyranny," for the laws of society were structured to elevate the few over the many. Fortune argued that from the feudal period to the present, the purpose of the law had been to protect the interests of capitalists and land owners, giving them the necessary tools to repress labor. He recast the major political milestones of the previous century—the French, Haitian, and American Revolutions—as in fact victories of the proletarian masses against an aristocratic and landowning elite. "At bottom in each case bread and butter was the main issue. So it has always been." The nineteenth-century labor struggle, then, was merely the latest iteration of a much older struggle of "the capitalist, land owner and hereditary aristocracy against the larger masses of society—the untitled, disinherited proletariat of the world."[29] For Fortune, capitalism had wholly corrupted political institutions, transforming the momentous achievement of formal legal equality Black people won during Reconstruction into a sham. But in the Knights of Labor Fortune saw a vehicle of interracial labor solidarity that could fight back.

Fortune considered the most viable prospect for Black workers in the South to be participation in national labor organizations, particularly the Knights of Labor. Fortune was not alone in this impression; he regularly reprinted laudatory articles about the organization from other Black newspapers. The *Chicago Observer* wrote, "the Knights of Labor have shown themselves to be true to their colored brother, and henceforth colored men will feel that labor begets a fraternity that will in time usurp the power of political and sectional prejudice." The *Detroit Plaindealer* declared the Knights of Labor "the most potent factor ever yet entered into our American life to secure full justice to the Afro-American." In the South, where white labor organizing was less prevalent, the Knights earned equally strong praise from the Black press. Referring to the Knights' stand against racism, the *Wilmington Chronicle* wrote, "Every colored man ought to treat the order with greater respect and consideration as it has shown itself courageous enough to face a strong popular prejudice," while the *Salisbury Star of Zion* declared, "whatever may be said in criticism or denunciation of the Knights of Labor, the fact remains that they are doing more to blot out color prejudice and recognize the equality of manhood in all the races than any organization in existence."[30] The Knights enjoyed widespread support from Black communities, and Fortune felt confident that its chapters across the country supported Black labor.

Founded in 1869 and growing significantly under the leadership of Terence Powderly in the 1880s, the Knights of Labor sought to unify American workers under the umbrella of a single organization. Unlike many trade unions that represented only skilled workers, the Knights in theory sought to include all labor, including women and Black workers, even as their inclusivity had limitations in practice. Their goals included the eight-hour workday, equal pay for equal work, the abolition of child and convict labor, and the promotion of cooperative ownership of businesses.[31]

Fortune was especially eager to report on instances in which the Knights of Labor worked with Black Southern workers to strike for higher wages. A Louisville, Kentucky, correspondent for the *Freeman* reported in March of 1886 that the Knights were recruiting heavily among the city's Black residents in anticipation of a looming strike.[32] Several months later, Fortune covered a strike of Black Knights of Labor members in Arkansas who worked on a large plantation, noting that the local white population evacuated out of fear for their safety and that "frantic appeals were made to the county and State authorities to put down the strikers, before any violence was shown." He argued that it was ironic that white Southerners would call on the forces of law and order to protect them when they feared a Black uprising but had no problem abandoning the law and engaging in vigilante or mob violence when it suited them. Despite the racialization of the strike response, Fortune framed the racial conflict as an expression of economic inequality, an "industrial" rather than "political" matter, arguing that "nowhere else in the world can there be found a more odious, unjust and tyrannical landlord system than that which obtains in the South" and that "there is more direct and indirect robbery of the colored laborers of the South than is practiced anywhere else on earth."[33] These labor problems required economic solutions, and the Knights were poised to provide them.

Fortune implicitly juxtaposed the success of the Knights of Labor in organizing interracial coalitions of workers across the country against the failures of the Republican Party to do the same during Reconstruction. In doing so, the Knights had seemed to dismantle the practical barriers to making the vision Fortune articulated in *Black and White* a reality. Before the Knights' nationwide rise in popularity, Fortune was not sanguine about the prospects for bringing Black and white labor together, particularly in the South, and feared that labor was "hopelessly arrayed against itself." In response to a report that during a strike of Black coal-wheelers in New Orleans, white strikebreakers were brought in to take their jobs, Fortune did not see an example of racial prejudice so much as one of how the very nature of capitalism militated against the possibility of true labor solidarity. Fortune acknowledged that since laborers were dependent on work for subsistence, they could not always stand in solidarity with other laborers and labor movements, since doing so would threaten an already precarious livelihood. "Being dependent upon the labor of the day for fuel and food the laboring man is as absolutely the slave of his employer as was formerly the Black slave of the South," he wrote. "Concert action is utterly out of the case."[34] This already difficult problem was often exacerbated in racialized ways, as with the example of white strikebreakers, or when white labor refused to admit Black workers to unions.

Fortune believed the key to the Knights' vastly expanding membership beginning in 1885 was their broad embrace of all types of laborers. He had so much faith that labor organizing, rather than political agitation, was the path to Black freedom in the South that he cautioned Black readers against taking opportunities for immediate economic gains that threatened long-term labor solidarity. "We cannot afford to stand off from or to antagonize the army under whose banners we labor in the common lot of toil," he wrote. "All we can do is to fall into line on the right or left, and which side it shall be will depend entirely upon whether we are a capitalist or a laborer."[35] Fortune vehemently opposed the sentiment expressed in another New York newspaper that Black workers could improve their lot by taking the place of white Third Avenue Railroad Company workers, who went on strike in April 1886. He urged Black labor not to "antagonize" white workers by strikebreaking and warned that such a strategy would be shortsighted for two reasons. The first was that Black and white laborers were "inseparably yoked together" by their exploitation at the hands of capital, and Black labor could not take action against the interests of white labor without ultimately harming itself. The second was that such an action would harm the goodwill that had been building between Black workers and labor organizations. Fortune saw these strategic questions as of the utmost historical significance. "We venture to say that no class of our population has been more systematically wronged, outraged, and robbed than the colored laborer. Capital from the earliest period of American history has crushed out his life and thrown his mutilated carcass to the vulture crows," he wrote. Yet that long history of suffering was on the verge of changing, and Fortune predicted that "the hour is at hand when the wage workers of all races are organizing for the purpose of forcing a more reasonable distribution of the products of labor." To work against the interests of labor at such a crucial junction would be disastrous, and for Fortune, the choice of whether to stand with labor was no choice at all, for "the Black man who arrays himself against labor would be like a Black man before the war taking sides with the pro-slavery as against the anti-slavery advocates."[36]

It took a coalition of Black and white abolitionists to overthrow slavery, and Fortune believed it would take a similar coalition to improve the conditions of the majority-Black Southern workforce. He wrote, "nothing short of a potentiality like the Knights of Labor can ever force Southern capitalists to give their wage workers a fair percentage on the results of their labor. If there is any power on earth which can make the white Southern employers of labor face the music it is organized white and Black labor, with the labor power of the Nation to sustain it."[37] And yet, jobless Black workers could not fill their bellies with ideology and hope. Fortune keenly understood how white supremacy had made Black labor the most abject in the nation, but not how it acted as a barrier to unflinching Black support for white strikers. These competing impulses had no easy resolution, and the difficulty was compounded by the fact that white advocates of Black strikebreaking were sometimes invested in perpetual Black degradation. Southern observers not only encouraged strikebreaking, but also discouraged Black labor organizing. An editorial in the *Southern Leader* newspaper argued that Black labor was only desirable because it commanded lower wages than white labor, and if Black laborers demanded equal wages, they would find themselves unemployable. For this reason, the editor argued, joining the Knights of Labor would be disastrous for Black laborers, since the Knights demanded equal pay for all members.

Perhaps sensing that in the racial environment of the South such logic might appeal to Black readers, Fortune offered up a different possibility—a vision of class solidarity that would lead to racial solidarity and a credible challenge to the power of capital. Fortune refused to let the unequal bargaining position of Black labor relative to white undercut his dedication to solidarity and interracial labor cooperation. "If the inequality in the relative wages paid Black and white laborers is to be rectified it is to be accomplished by an understanding with white laborers and a union of forces to compel the equalization," he wrote.[38] The notion that membership in the Knights of Labor hurt Black workers by removing the one thing that made them desirable to employers—their lower cost—seemed to Fortune as self-defeating as the idea that Black workers should take advantage of strikebreaking to gain entry into the labor market. Both conceded the animating, unalterable force of race prejudice and in doing so refused to take seriously the possibility of interracial labor solidarity. Holding on to this idealistic vision in the face of opportunities for short-term gain was the central piece of Fortune's vision for Black advancement. To accept that racial inequality made Black and white workers incompatible partners in organizing was to hand capitalists all the power; to Fortune, such logic meant that there was no way out of the cycle of Black labor being used to undercut white labor, keeping white wages low and Black wages even lower.

Fortune grasped for any evidence he could find that his strategy could bear real fruit. He offered one example brought to his attention by Isaac Myers in which a group of Black and white laborers in Baltimore went to a pub together. The staff refused to serve the Black members, prompting the group to block the entrance so "business at this end was literally cut off." Their strategy was successful; the pub relented and served the Black patrons. Fortune was especially heartened because he believed that "color prejudice is nowhere in the Union more firmly entrenched and rampant than in Baltimore."[39] In the same city where both Douglass and Myers experienced firsthand how white labor could embrace racism to crush Black economic aspirations, Fortune saw hope for a different outcome.

Fortune thus often found himself in the nearly impossible position of having to argue both that Black Southern labor was the most degraded in the nation and thus must be central to any organized labor strategy, and that some strategies for ameliorating Black workers' conditions in the short term—most notably strikebreaking—should be considered off-limits because they were self-defeating in the long term. For help in balancing these two ideas, Fortune sometimes looked to white labor radicals for support and inspiration. In one such example, Fortune republished an editorial authored by John Swinton, a newspaper editor and labor radical who, alongside Henry George, was a major influence on *Black and White*. The editorial offered a nuanced analysis of the relationship between Black and white labor. Swinton acknowledged that Black labor was so exploited in the South that it was tantamount to slavery, and was thus sympathetic to Black Southerners who were lured North to break strikes or drive down the wages of white labor. Swinton argued that the racism of the North and South worked in tandem to degrade all labor, and that the systematic dispossession of Black Southern labor provided the avenue for the dispossession of white Northern labor. When Southern capitalists kept Black labor in a condition that resembled slavery, Northern capitalists could entice Black strikebreakers from the South with wages "disgustingly inadequate for white workingmen" because even such wages were more than they could earn in the South. Swinton concluded that "while every effort must be made to assert the rights of the colored laborers of the South, they should be loudly warned against being used as tools to break down the white labor of the North."[40] In the same issue, Fortune defended Swinton's article by reiterating that Black strikebreakers who went North at the urging of labor recruiters gained only temporary benefits, at the expense of the common interests that all laborers shared. Yet Fortune did not place the blame entirely on Black strikebreakers. He wrote, "it is a work of self protection for the labor organizations of the North to educate the colored laborers of the South on the true conditions of the labor problem in the North." And, in recognition that laborers of any race could be tempted to engage in strikebreaking, Fortune wryly assured his readers, "we have no doubt *John Swinton's Paper* will read a severe lesson to those white New York laborers who went to Virginia last week to take the places of dissatisfied colored stevedores. This conduct of the white men is as reprehensible as the conduct of the colored men."[41] Fortune aimed to build an interracial labor coalition, but he was careful not to adopt assumptions about the inferiority or unpreparedness of Black labor to be equal partners in this alliance.

The labor solidarity that Fortune's writing cultivated was a fragile thing, its foundation constantly under threat by the daily realities of racial violence and the depths of Black dispossession. The relationship between Black labor and the Knights was not always harmonious, and racial tensions at a national meeting in 1886 caused a major blow to Fortune's faith in the organization. The Knights held their national convention in Richmond, Virgina, that year, hoping to show Southern chapters that they understood the importance of labor in the region. The stakes of the convention were high, as the

Knights had recently suffered their greatest defeat thus far. The previous spring, the Great Southwest Railroad Strike, in which more than 200,000 workers struck against the Union Pacific and Mississippi Pacific Railroads, ended in utter defeat.[42] Fortune came to the conclusion that "not only has the strike failed to remedy the flimsy grievance complained of, but has also failed to demonstrate that the Knights of Labor as a potentiality can successfully cope with organized capital."[43] In Richmond, the Knights hoped simply to settle the question of whether leadership of the organization would be concentrated in a central body or local chapters would have autonomy. Yet the Southern press and many Southern Knights themselves forced the question of race to the foreground. The fact that Black delegates from outside the South were lodging and socializing with white delegates raised the specter of "social equality." A term with ambiguous and overlapping meaning, social equality justified Black disenfranchisement, economic exclusion, and political violence through the logic that such actions were necessary to prevent Black Southerners from mixing in public and intimate ways with whites, and drew on older antebellum fears of interracial sexual contact.

Despite Fortune's praise of the organization's interracial foundation, the Knights did not have an official stance on social equality. Northern and Midwestern chapters were indeed unusually open to the notion of absolute racial equality, as Fortune had reported. Southern branches were often less so, and they also had leeway to exclude Black members without facing censure or expulsion. Northern delegates, Black and white, understood that the presence of Black Knights at a Southern convention would provoke the ire of Richmond's white population, but many refused to concede to local prejudice on principle. Assembly 49, a New York chapter, went further, openly challenging Southern racial conventions by suggesting that a Black delegate, Frank Ferrell, should introduce the convention's opening speaker, Virginia Governor Fitzhugh Lee. Terrence

Powderly, leader of the Knights, did not wish to openly endorse either Northern equality or Southern discrimination, so he demurred by offering that he himself be introduced by Ferrell. Assembly 49 agreed, but in his introductory remarks Ferrell rankled white Southern audience members by insisting that one of the goals of the Knights was "the abolition of those distinctions which are maintained by class, by creed, by color, and by nationality . . . Here we stand as brethren and equals."[44] Members of Assembly 49 were also openly vocal about the fact that they refused segregated sleeping accommodations, and Black and white members attended the theater together on two occasions, creating a scandal in the Richmond press and among some white Southern Knights. The press—probably correctly—claimed that Assembly 49 was intentionally testing how far they could push against Virginia's segregation laws, and whether they could force Southern Knights to adopt more explicit policies on racial equality.

As it turned out, they could not. The Richmond chapter spoke out against Assembly 49 and social equality in the press, forcing the Knights to directly confront the differing racial politics of Northern and Southern chapters in a way it had carefully avoided up to this point. Powderly issued a tepid statement to the press, asserting that while the rights of citizenship and the brotherhood of labor "recognize no lines of race, creed, politics, or color," social equality was an individual matter, not something that could be forced through law or policy.[45] Powderly's triangulation failed, and he lost the respect of many Northerners who had previously praised the Knights' racial egalitarianism. Southern Knights felt that Powderly made too many concessions to social equality, and responded to his statement with one of their own, which asserted the principles of segregation and white supremacy. Amidst threats that Southern chapters would split from the Knights and form their own organization, the convention adopted a resolution nearly identical to Powderly's earlier statement:

the Knights of Labor would recognize the "civil and political equality of all men," and make no racial distinctions "in the broad field of labor," but would not "interfere or disrupt the social relations which may exist between different races in any part of the country."[46] Fortune was incensed at what he saw as a cowardly capitulation to Southern white supremacy. Although the incident broke Fortune's faith in the Knights—he rarely wrote about them afterward—he saw its failure to stand its ground as part of a larger pattern of national acquiescence to white supremacy, from the Dred Scott decision to the Compromise of 1877. The outcome of the convention seemed to confirm to Fortune that the race and class politics of the South had national implications, both for how capital was organized and organized against. "The Labor Convention was compelled to do in this matter as the white knight of the South dictated," he wrote. "Northern sentiment however just has always crawled before and fawned upon the domineering sentiment of the South, however unjust and insolent."[47]

However, the Knights' failure to protect Black members was not merely the result of voluntary conciliation toward the racial attitudes of the South, but also of reactionary racial terror meant to break the influence of organized labor. Fortune struggled to fully reconcile himself to the reality that this violence was the primary deterrent to Black and interracial labor organizing in the South. The Thibodaux Massacre of 1887 was the most consequential example of how the Knights were unable to protect Black workers from the intersection of anti-labor and racial violence after Reconstruction. Black sugar cane workers in Louisiana had pressed for higher wages since the mid-1870s, even organizing strikes in 1874 and 1880; both failed. In 1887, cane workers enlisted the Knights' aid in challenging planter power and organized themselves into several local chapters. Processing sugar cane was highly time-sensitive, and the Louisiana Knights thought they could time their demand for higher wages with the cane harvest to exert maximum pressure on their employers. They miscalculated. Planters refused to negotiate, fired the Knights, and ordered them off the plantations where they worked and lived. Instead of leaving, workers went on strike in early November, and the governor of Louisiana, a planter himself, authorized white militias to forcibly evict strikers. In this initial clash, the militias killed four Black workers. As the strike continued, evicted workers gathered in the town of Thibodeaux. Tensions continued to rise and news of the strike appeared in the national press; intermittent violence broke out between strikers and militia, and it was in this context that a parish judge placed Thibodeaux under martial law. Whites barricaded Black workers inside the town, and when strikers shot and injured two white guards, white militias unleashed a fury of violence, storming through the town and killing sixty Black people.[48] "The same injustice and oppression which have been inflicted upon the inoffensive colored people from the dawn of their freedom still follow close and fast upon their heels," Fortune wrote in response.[49] The massacre ended the ambitions of the Knights in the South.

Although Fortune's disappointment with the Knights suggested that their political imagination was overly limited compared to his own, Fortune himself increasingly embraced racial exclusions after 1886—he merely drew his lines differently than Southern members of the Knights. Fortune's description of an egalitarian North accommodating a white supremacist South did not capture the full complexity of the Knights' racial politics, which could be exclusionary even in the North. The Knights disallowed Chinese laborers from joining the organization, and while they embraced Black Americans, if unevenly at times, they also embraced nativist ideas. That is to say, the Knights could overlook Black laborers' racial difference because they recognized a shared nationality. Like Myers and other Black labor organizers during Reconstruction, the Knights conceived of the category of "labor" using the idiom of republicanism, which valorized the "citizenship, democratic participation, and social status" of workers. It provided tools to critique exploitation and exclusion, but also cast those without these qualities outside the category of productive laborer, such as slaves and many immigrants.[50]

Fortune's writing increasingly reflected these biases after 1886. Americans, both Black and white, associated European radicalism with political violence, and Black writers were no less likely than their white counterparts to condemn anarchism and communism as incompatible with the nonviolent principles of American democracy. Indeed, part of their horror at the anti-Black violence endemic to the South was that they often understood it as a deviation from, rather than emblematic of, those principles. Fortune was never fully at ease with the idea of political violence, but neither did he reject radical movements that utilized such violence out of hand. He sometimes framed anarchism as a form of self-defense, arguing that the conditions that inspired it were worse than the anarchists' tactics. "The labor classes all over the world are arraying themselves against the tyrannous exactions of corporate and capitalistic edacity, and society can only hope to protect itself from the desperation and violence of the myriad toilers by curbing the rapacity of the capitalistic few, he wrote."[51] Similarly, while Fortune condemned the violent actions of anarchist "Continental agitators," he could not help but acknowledge that such actions had "the effect to quicken the conscience of Kings and Parliaments and the public, and thus hasten a solution of questions which have appealed for centuries for consideration and honest adjudication."[52]

Yet in an 1886 editorial titled "Chinamen and Anarchists," Fortune criticized anarchist immigrants from Europe, claiming that they "abuse the liberties of our Constitution." He argued in favor of restricting European immigration due to how such immigration competed with American labor, using the Knights' and other white labor organizations' broad support of the 1882 Chinese Exclusion

Act, which barred virtually all immigration from China, as justification. Fortune noted that when white labor spoke out against Chinese labor, it did so using the logic of protecting American workers from a group considered foreign. To not call for similar limitations on European labor would reveal antipathy toward Chinese migration as a racist appeal rather than a genuine concern for domestic labor. Yet ascribing the idea of foreign threat to immigrant labor pushed against Fortune's broad, idealistic claims about labor struggles the world over. He advocated domestic unity among Black and white workers and situated U.S. labor in relation to global class struggles, but came to use the foil of nativism to do so.[53]

In the late 1880s, Fortune and his correspondents embraced restrictions on Italian labor migrants while also condemning the precarious conditions under which they worked. Like the Chinese, Italian laborers did not fit easily into the South's binary racial logic. Planters saw them as a cheap, pliable labor force, not racial equals. Italian migrants were subject to racialized associations with disease, crime, and poverty, and they experienced nativist violence.[54] Fortune prefaced one editorial on what he called Italian migrant "slaves" in the South with a generalized indictment of post-emancipation labor regimes. He compared how the concentration of property ownership, whether landed or industrial, allowed employers to trap labor in slavery-like conditions, and argued that the aims, interests, and methods of employers varied little between Europe and the U.S. North and South. "The industrial systems of every civilized country are based upon what amounts practically to slave labor. That is to say, the laborer receives so small a share of the earnings that enter into the problem of wealth production and the conditions that hedge about his employment are such that it all amounts practically to industrial slavery." It hardly surprised Fortune, then, that Italian laborers found themselves subjected to such conditions.

Fortune's theory of labor organizing outlined in *Black and White* should have allowed him to translate these similar forms of oppression into a call for solidarity with Italian labor, but in the end it did not. He was approaching the conclusion that differing experiences of racialization could offer incentives against solidarity. Fortune argued that Northern capitalists operating in the South sought out Italian migrants to undercut the Black labor, which was not "as cheap, servile and subservient as they desired." Yet when Southern planters treated Italian migrants in ways that recalled chattel slavery, they could appeal to the Italian government and expect a degree of sympathy from the press; Fortune bristled at the fact that Black Southerners had no such advocacy.[55] Fortune was concerned with Italian immigration to the South because in it he saw a plot to starve Black labor of work, in order to more effectively break and subjugate it. "If the experiment of Italian labor being tried in the Mississippi Valley should prove satisfactory, there is not much doubt that a very serious menace would at once present itself to Afro-American labor there," he wrote.[56] Fortune was faced with a political and intellectual problem: How could he work toward interracial labor solidarity when capitalists operating in the South were systematically excluding Black labor by using Italian migrants? Despite his desire to unify all labor around a common cause, Fortune resolved the difficulty of transforming the racial realities of the South by embracing nativism, making the same concession generations of white laborers had when they excluded Black workers.

Fortune's writing in the 1880s was the most sustained articulation of Black economic thought produced to that point. In his columns for the *New York Freeman* and later the *New York Age*, Fortune argued that Black people in the post-Reconstruction South were not merely victims of political exclusion but the region's proletariat—oppressed through their economic position as laborers and sharecroppers. He framed disenfranchisement, segregation, and racial terror not only as violations of civil rights, but as mechanisms to preserve land monopoly and protect capital's hold over labor. In Fortune's view, the fundamental problem was not race prejudice alone but an economic system that could only function by making Black labor cheap and disposable. Even as Fortune adapted deracinated critiques of property in land to the specific conditions of the South, framing Black labor as an ally to labor struggles around the globe, he struggled to understand why race fractured the possibility for class solidarity. He predicted that a growing class of Black capitalists would diminish racial violence and lead to a struggle between a multiracial working class on one side, a multiracial capitalist class on the other. Wells did not situate her work within a radical economic tradition in the same way Fortune did, but she understood far more keenly than her mentor that the white South would not abide Black economic success.

RACIAL VIOLENCE AS ECONOMIC DISPOSSESSION

If Fortune positioned Black labor within a global struggle between capital and labor, Wells illuminated the means by which that economic order was preserved. Fortune envisioned interracial labor solidarity as the basis for Black advancement, while Wells revealed how white supremacy preemptively stemmed such possibilities through violence, targeting not only political resistance but also economic self-sufficiency. Her investigations into lynching demonstrated that racial terror was not simply a reaction to Black criminality or political agitation, but a calculated enforcement of economic dispossession, punishing attempts at autonomy and success in order to uphold the racial hierarchies on which Southern capitalism depended.

From her earliest published work, much of which appeared in Fortune's papers, Wells explored economic issues. She defended the *New York Freeman* against charges of disloyalty to the Republican Party, arguing that as editor, Fortune rightly held the interests of the race above those of any party, and, like Fortune, she believed both parties had contributed to stripping Black Southerners of their rights and subjecting them to white violence.[57] Wells was skeptical that the pursuit of wealth offered a path forward for Black people, reminding her readers, "all of us can not be millionaires, orators, lawyers, doctors; what then must become of the minority, the middle and lower classes that are found in all races?"[58] She argued that labor should be a source of pride for women, rejecting the idea that freedom from labor made women more feminine or noble.[59] And, so long as white supremacy reigned, she considered the work of abolition to be incomplete.[60] Wells began to sharpen this inchoate economic framework when she turned her attention to lynching in the early 1890s.

In March 1892, three Black businessmen—Thomas Moss, a close friend of Wells, and his partners, Will Stewart and Calvin McDowell—were lynched in Memphis, Tennessee, in what became known as the Curve lynchings. The men operated the People's Grocery, a cooperative enterprise that had begun to draw business away from a nearby white-owned store, Barrett's Grocery. The rivalry escalated into outright conflict when William Barrett, the store owner, found a thin excuse to assault Stewart and McDowell. When they defended themselves, Barrett returned to the grocery the next day with a small mob intent on taking revenge. Stewart and McDowell fired on the mob, injuring two men. The group dispersed, but Stewart, McDowell, and Moss were arrested and held at the county jail. Four nights later, a mob of dozens stormed the jail and executed the three grocers, shooting them in a nearby rail yard. Although the men had not been convicted of any crime, and were in fact respected members of the community, local newspapers and officials portrayed the event as the end result of a race riot. The killings occurred at a time when Memphis was trying to present itself as a modern, economically stable city, but also during a period of growing efforts to limit Black political power through disenfranchisement laws.⁶¹ Moss's killing had a transformative effect upon Wells. Like many Black professionals, Wells did not previously question the idea that most victims of lynching were criminals. The punishment for their crimes might be overly harsh and even transgress the rule of law, but the culpability of the victim was not in question. And such violence would certainly never be meted upon law-abiding Black people so long as they refrained from taking an overt interest in politics, a heinous crime in the minds of Southern whites. But Moss was neither a criminal nor political. He simply sought economic stability through hard work.⁶²

Between 1880 and 1900, lynching became a widespread and brutal method of racial terror, primarily in the Southern United States. Following the end of Reconstruction, white supremacists sought to reassert dominance over Black people through violence and intimidation. During this period, thousands of Black men and women were lynched, often under false accusations of crimes such as rape or theft. These acts were frequently public spectacles, attended by large crowds, and used to reinforce racial hierarchies. The rise of lynching coincided with the establishment of Jim Crow laws, which codified racial segregation and disenfranchised Black citizens. The lack of legal consequences for perpetrators, who were often protected by local law enforcement and juries, underscored the complicity of the justice system. White mobs operated with impunity, and newspapers often justified the violence.⁶³

After the Curve lynchings, Wells began to suspect that whites lynched Black people not for any desperate, criminal actions they took because of their poverty, but to prevent Black success and reinforce the racial, social, and economic hierarchies of white supremacy.

Barrett, the white grocery owner, was jealous of Moss's successful business and set into motion a series of events that ended with Moss's assassination. This lynching did not comport with the narrative that emancipation had allowed Black people's inherent criminality to run rampant, necessitating lynching as both deterrent and justice. After emancipation, white Southerners increasingly associated Black freedom with lawlessness, using the courts and police to discipline formerly enslaved people and portray them as inherently criminal to justify political repression. Laws against vagrancy, loitering, idleness, and petty theft could target Black people selectively, thereby criminalizing and racializing behaviors that were either normal or necessary for survival in a post-slavery economy.[64] Wells was the first to contend that lynching did not punish Black poverty, but rather economic mobility. To justify the murder of Moss and his partners, the white press impugned their character, claiming that they ran a "low dive" and thus, must have been criminals. In reality, it was Barrett whose business practices were questionable; he had numerous citations for violating liquor laws and conducted illegal activity out of his store.[65]

Armed with a newfound suspicion about the stated justifications for lynching, Wells began to investigate as many cases of lynching as she could. Her editorship of the *Memphis Free Speech* gave her a platform to circulate her findings. It also set her up for a potentially deadly conflict with Memphis's white residents. Two months into her new crusade, Wells published an editorial in which she argued that the rape of white women by Black men—the crime that justified the frequency and brutality of lynching in white and Black minds alike—was largely a fiction.[66] Wells claimed that the charge of rape was a "threadbare lie" used to deny the reality that Black men and white women engaged in consensual sexual relationships.[67] The response was swift. The editor of the *Daily Commercial,* one of the most prominent newspapers in Memphis, wrote, "the fact that a

Black scoundrel is allowed to live and utter such loathsome and repulsive calumnies is a volume of evidence as to the wonderful patience of Southern whites. But we have had enough of it. There are some things that the Southern white man will not tolerate."[68] Wells was in New York when her editorial was published, and advised by friends that it was too dangerous to return. They were right. Wells reported that after she published her editorial, "threats of lynching were freely indulged, not by the lawless element upon which the deviltry of the South is usually saddled—but by the leading business men, in their leading business centre."[69] After an unsuccessful attempt at lynching Wells's business partner, a group of white vigilantes attacked and destroyed the offices of the *Free Speech*. Wells never returned to Memphis. And, she recalled, "creditors took possession of the office and sold the outfit, and the *Free Speech* was as if it had never been."[70] The destruction of the *Free Speech* at once silenced Black objections to violence and struck a blow to its proprietors' economic security.

From the experience of Moss's murder and the destruction of the *Free Speech*, Wells concluded that lynching was not a response to Black criminality but to Black progress. Her first significant analysis of lynching was a pamphlet titled *Southern Horrors: Lynch Law in All Its Phases*. Building upon an article she had previously published in the *New York Age*, Fortune published the pamphlet as well, which featured an introduction by Frederick Douglass. Wells argued that lynching was a tool to maintain white supremacy in the face of emancipation and growing Black self-determination. She explained that some Black people believed sacrificing their political rights would stop the violence endemic to the post-Reconstruction South, and, once Black people had progressed enough morally and economically to satisfy Southern whites, they could gradually and peacefully take their place as equal citizens. The reality, Wells contended, was that whites believed "this is a white man's country and the white man must rule." Any form of Black progress or uplift whatsoever was a threat to white supremacy, and as Black people invested in "general education and financial strength," the "mob spirit has grown," rather than diminished.

Even when Black people removed themselves from politics and acquiesced to disenfranchisement, whites invented a new justification for their continued violence—the defense of white women against sexual violence perpetrated by Black men. This new narrative about defending white women from Black rapists served several overlapping purposes. First, it quelled Black resistance to lynching, as many Black people, particularly Black elites, were so disgusted by the crime of rape that they did not object to lynching as its consequence. Second, it further entrenched the idea that Black people were criminal, morally unprepared for full citizenship among white people. Third, consenting to lynching as an acceptable punishment for the worst of crimes made it more acceptable to lynch for any crime whatsoever, or no crime at all, as "when drunken or criminal white toughs feel like hanging an Afro-American on any pretext." Wells argued that lynching was acceptable in the largest, most "civilized" cities and by the leading men of the South, permeating the entirety of Southern society.[71] White elites, though rarely part of lynch mobs, sanctioned violence to eliminate economically successful Black competitors and to prevent interracial labor solidarity, and provided ideological justification through their influence over courts, newspapers, and politics. Poor and working-class whites, often the active participants, used lynching to assert racial superiority amid economic insecurity, understanding Black advancement as a threat to their fragile status. The white middle and professional class, though more passive, reinforced the system through silence and institutional complicity, helping normalize racial violence in the name of order and tradition.

Wells concluded *Southern Horrors* with a call for organized economic resistance. She reasoned that the South depended on Black labor and Northern capital; if Black people withheld their labor, capital would soon dry up, and "the Afro-American is thus the backbone of the South." Because "the white man's dollar is his god," Wells argued that armed with this fact, which was also a kind of power, Black Southerners would be able to put economic pressure on whites and "effect a bloodless revolution" by refusing to work in response to incidents of lynching and other forms of violence and political repression. Wells offered the People's Grocery lynchings as an example. After the murder of Moss and his partners, Black people left Memphis in large numbers, "bringing about great stagnation in every branch of business." Those who did not leave refused to ride the street cars. The effect was so great that the company superintendent unsuccessfully appealed to the *Free Speech*, urging the paper to convince Black people to ride the cars again. When the *Free Speech* refused, "other business men became alarmed over the situation," and they needed only the excuse of Wells's incendiary editorial on white women's consensual relationships with Black men for them to destroy the organ. "Memphis is fast losing her Black population, who proclaim as they go that there is no protection for the life and property of any Afro-American citizen in Memphis who is not a slave," Wells wrote.[72]

Wells was also inspired by the Black response in Louisville to a segregated railroad law passed in Kentucky just months before Wells published *Southern Horrors*.[73] Black citizens abandoned the state's railroads, having previously used them in very large numbers. Wells quoted a Kentucky newspaper that estimated reduced Black ridership would cost the railroads $1 million in revenue for 1892, the year the segregation law was passed.[74] She surmised that if Black leaders organized statewide boycotts of railroads in response to segregated car laws, there would be no need for political activism or lawsuits, as the economic effect would be so impactful that railroad corporations themselves would advocate for the repeal of Jim Crow laws.

Conversely, if no such boycotts were organized, corporations would easily be able to fund challenges to any lawsuit Black activists brought against Jim Crow. In short, Wells advocated putting economic pressure on corporations as a central strategy for Black reformers who wished to challenge not only the denial of their rights, but also the impunity of white lynch law, which Wells described as a "relic of barbarism and slavery." Successful activism would begin by recognizing, then exercising, the power Black people held as the labor base of the South. "The appeal to the white man's pocket has been ever more effectual than all the appeals ever made to his conscience," Wells concluded.[75]

In her analysis of the Memphis and Louisville streetcar boycotts, Wells positioned Black economic behavior as a form of political power. In the wake of diminished political rights, Wells grounded her vision of resistance in the material realities of the post-Reconstruction South. By targeting profit, she exposed a key contradiction in Southern racial capitalism: the economic dependence on Black labor and Black consumers coexisted with the political imperative to exclude and subjugate them. Wells thus reframed the struggle against white supremacy as a contest over who could control the flow of capital, suggesting that economic withdrawal could be as potent assertion of rights and influence.

After the publication of *Southern Horrors*, Wells searched for further evidence that boycotts would be effective weapons against lynching and segregation laws. For Wells, Black Southerners' overlapping status as disenfranchised citizens, targets of extreme violence, and laborers who were rebuilding the region meant that the only power they had to exercise was economic in nature. Economic questions were necessarily political questions. In an article for the *New York Age*, she reported on a congregation of one of Atlanta's largest Black churches that voted to refuse to ride in segregated street cars. Their refusal had demonstrable economic impact on the streetcar company—$700 for the month of October 1892, according to the *Atlanta Journal.* After taking note of the financial loss ("now that the white man's pocket is feeling it," in Wells's words), the *Journal* condemned the "unjust treatment of colored passengers." It had never done so before. "If they keep on losing money, the whites will be the first to petition the legislature for the repeal of any such law," she opined. Wells's conviction that Black people must hang on to this power so that they might collectively direct it explains her advice to Black readers in the same article: "When he has a dollar in his pocket and many more in the bank, he can move from injustice and oppression and no one to say him nay . . . A wasteful and spendthrift race or individual is always poor, is always the slave of the man who has money and will never be in a position to dictate to parties, or demand race rights." Wells admonished those who spent their meager earnings "for car rides, for cigars, for drinks, for bootblacks, for foolishness of all sorts" because she saw such choices as a cavalier abandonment of one of the few tools of resistance Black people possessed—boycotts and labor withdrawals could not be implemented effectively without some level of personal economic discipline, even as the People's Grocery lynchings proved to Wells beyond any doubt that such discipline could not in and of itself transform the broader conditions of Black life.[76]

Wells further developed her ideas about the relationship between Black labor exploitation and economic protest in a speech before the National Press Association, a Black journalists' organization, that was published in the *AME Zion Church Quarterly* in January 1893. She began by recounting how "honest, hardworking, land owning men and women of the race have been hung, shot, whipped and driven out of communities in Texas and Arkansas for no greater crime than that of too much prosperity." Even worse, upstanding victims were posthumously branded as criminals in order to justify the violence that took their lives. And while successful members of the race lived under threat of lynching, most Black people were conscripted into "the vast army who make the industrial wealth of the South," kept in contented ignorance by white landlords. The Black laborer, she noted, "makes the money of the South, but has never been taught that a husbanding of resources will cease to enrich gigantic corporations at his own expense. Intelligently directed, by exercise of this power alone, the race can do much to bring about a change in race condition. The sudden withdrawal of the labor force of any one community, paralyzes the industry of that community." Such forms of paralysis could be so shocking to whites that it might spur them to abandon their support for white supremacist politics out of economic interest. In the context of pervasive racial violence, this was Black people's most potent political strategy—to subvert the circuits of profit that transformed Black labor into white wealth, amounting to a "bloodless revolution." Personal thrift was central to this strategy and would do more for the race than pursuing a legal strategy of suing segregated railroads and streetcar companies, for how could Black people withhold labor, or move to a new city, or boycott a vital service without a modicum of savings?[77]

Wells transformed economic thrift into an argument for collective labor action very different from those made by Fortune and other labor reformers. She recognized that while capitalism and white supremacy were mutually reinforcing systems, the two could have divergent interests. By exploiting that divergence and applying pressure to the source of capitalists' profits, Wells hoped Black collective action would force capital to disinvest in some of the most overt forms of Southern white supremacy. She confronted racial capitalism as it actually existed in the South, which meant recognizing that neither capital nor labor had singular, simplistic interests. Thus even as Wells expressed less of an overt interest in labor politics than Fortune, she was no less a theorist of subverting the structures of capitalism and white supremacy that shaped the limits of Black freedom at the close of the century.

The next several years were the most active in Wells's career. She remained in New York after the *Free Speech* was destroyed, and continued to write for Fortune's *New York Age* and other prominent Black newspapers. In 1893, Wells traveled to England to spread the truth about lynching to the British public before spending the summer in Chicago for the World's Columbian Exposition, which she used as an opportunity to educate foreign visitors about lynching and Jim Crow legislation. In a pamphlet titled *The Reason Why the Colored American Is Not in the World's Columbian Exposition*, Wells, along with Douglass, Irvine Garland Penn, and Ferdinand Barnett, expounded on specific dimensions of Jim Crow policies and practices.[78] After the Exposition, Wells settled in Chicago permanently, eventually marrying Barnett, an attorney and fellow journalist, in 1895. And she continued to publish writing that made landmark contributions to the study of lynching.

Wells published her most comprehensive study of lynching, *A Red Record*, in 1895. In addition to furnishing additional examples of Wells's argument that lynching was not a response to Black criminality but a tool for maintaining white supremacy, *A Red Record* made important methodological innovations to the study of Black life. Throughout the nineteenth century, Black women derived their authority in a male-dominated community of reformers by approaching social ills from the position of caretakers of morality, faith, and restraint. Wells did not accept such limitations. In particular, she sought to make arguments grounded in empirical, statistical evidence. Thus, she personally investigated the circumstances of as many lynchings as she was able, and hired detectives to investigate some of those she could not. *A Red Record* was the culmination of this work; it compiled all known lynchings in which a Black person was killed between 1892 and 1894. In addition to these statistics, Wells offered detailed accounts of a handful of especially egregious cases to illuminate the economic foundations of the violence that hung over Black life in the South.

One such case was the February 1892 lynching of Hamp Biscoe and his family in Arkansas. Biscoe was able to purchase a plot of land through a policy known as preemption, by which settlers and squatters on federal land could acquire the land at a price set by the government, usually very low.[79] After Biscoe had cultivated his land for more than half a decade, the white man who originally facilitated the land sale—or so he claimed, at least—demanded $100 from Biscoe for his services. Biscoe refused, but the white man sued him and won. Unable to pay the fee, Biscoe was forced to sell his land to cover the debt. It is unclear if Biscoe remained on the land as a tenant farmer, or rented another nearby plot, but the "suit, judgment and subsequent legal proceedings" left their mark on Biscoe, and thereafter he became paranoid about being dispossessed of his farm a second time, and refused to allow anyone, Black or white, neighbor or stranger, onto his land.[80]

The chain of events that ended with Biscoe's death began a week before the lynching. A white neighbor, Venable, crossed Biscoe's land without permission, and Biscoe shouted at him and made threats. Venable sought a warrant for Biscoe's arrest, and returned with John Ford, a constable. Biscoe warned Ford that he would resist arrest, and when Ford persisted, Biscoe shot him, grazing him with the bullet. Ford returned fire, incapacitating Biscoe. Two other white men, hearing the gunfire, came upon the scene and arrested Biscoe, his pregnant wife, their thirteen-year-old son, and infant child. The men detained the Biscoes in a small structure nearby, and set two Black men to guard them. That evening, a mob of a dozen or more white men set upon the makeshift jail and ordered the guards to leave. They did, and went to a nearby church to find help. These men had come to lynch the Biscoes, not just for the crime of injuring a white man, but also to steal from them. The men knew Biscoe's wife had a large sum of cash on her person, since she had been seen with it earlier in the day. When the men approached, she "began to cry and said, 'You intend to kill us to get our money.'"[81] The men shot and killed Biscoe and his wife, and took $220—nearly a year and half of wages for the average farm worker in Arkansas—from her body.[82] Their son was fatally wounded, but survived long enough to tell the guards what had happened once they returned. The infant escaped with just a wound on the lip. In the end, Biscoe's fear that he would once again have his livelihood stolen came true. Like the People's Grocery lynchings, Wells's account of the Biscoes' fate offered an example of how racial violence worked in tandem with economic dispossession, rendering Black success as criminality, and white perfidy as meting out justice.

The murder of Allen Butler was another example of the connection between lynching and economic domination. Butler was a wealthy Black man who was respected even by the whites in his Indiana community. He was so well-off, in fact, that he could afford to employ a white servant. Butler's son was romantically involved with the servant, and she became pregnant. There was an uproar when her condition became public, and rumors circulated that Butler had arranged for an abortion. Warrants were issued for the arrest of both Butler and his son. Butler posted bail for himself, but not his son. Incensed by the son's actions and the elder Butler's rumored deception, a white mob planned to lynch them that night. But the distance between the county jail and Butler's residence was too great to accomplish both murders, so the mob satisfied themselves by hanging Butler. His body was found the next morning. Butler rose above his place and employed a white servant. His economic mobility and his son's flouting of the color line embodied white people's fears that Black rights would lead to social equality, which in turn would lead to widespread miscegenation. As Wells had predicted in her earliest anti-lynching writing, Black economic success could provoke, rather than prevent, racial violence.[83]

Wells's contribution to Black economic thought came from her reframing of racial violence as a form of economic dispossession. She argued that lynching was not merely a reaction to crime or political agitation, but a tool to undermine Black economic advancement and preserve the racial hierarchies that undergirded Southern capitalism. In her analysis, economic self-sufficiency among Black people engendered white hostility because it destabilized the social and material foundations of white dominance. Her advocacy for boycotts and labor withdrawal strategies reflected a belief that economic behavior could be wielded as political power in the absence of formal rights. This approach offered an alternative to legal redress or party allegiance, suggesting instead that disrupting profit was a viable form of resistance. Wells thus made a case for understanding white supremacist violence as a form of economic control.

CONCLUSION

By the early 1890s, Fortune's career moved away from his early emphasis on labor organizing and toward a political project centered on racial justice and civil rights. Even as the urgency of political repression came to dominate his writing, he remained engaged with the problem of labor, but increasingly viewed racial solidarity, not interracial class solidarity, as the more feasible foundation for political organizing in the South. The failure of groups like the Knights of Labor to sustain multiracial coalitions further deepened Fortune's disillusionment, and he turned his efforts toward building independent Black institutions. In 1890, he founded the National Afro-American League, an organization that advocated for legal equality, political independence, and race solidarity. During this period, Fortune developed a complex and often uneasy alliance with Booker T. Washington, serving as his ghostwriter, adviser, and public supporter despite clear ideological differences. While Washington emphasized accommodation and economic advancement through vocational training, Fortune remained committed to immediate civil and political rights. In 1898, he revived the earlier League as the National Afro-American Council, the first nationwide civil rights organization. Although the group eventually faltered under internal conflicts and Washington's growing influence, it served as a model for the National Association for the Advancement of Colored Peoples (NAACP). In his later years, Fortune remained active as a journalist and race advocate, contributing to various Black newspapers and ultimately supporting Marcus Garvey's Universal Negro Improvement Association.

After 1895, Wells continued her work as a journalist while navigating parenthood and family life. Residing in Chicago with her husband, Ferdinand Barnett, she remained engaged in political activism. In addition to her anti-lynching work, Wells became increasingly involved in organizing Black women's clubs and suffrage groups. She challenged segregationist practices within the suffrage movement and participated in national demonstrations, insisting on visibility for Black women in public life. In 1909, she took part in the founding of the NAACP, although her role within the organization diminished in later years due to disagreements with its leadership. Toward the end of her life, she turned her attention to documenting her experiences in an autobiography and made an unsuccessful bid for the Illinois State Senate. Through these efforts, she sustained a lifelong commitment to racial justice, political enfranchisement, and social reform.

The economic thought of Fortune and Wells offer examples of how Black reformers considered questions of labor and capital between the time of the abolitionist generation and the rise of Black engagements with formal socialism and anticolonial Marxism in the twentieth century. They elevated economic issues to the highest importance; rather than framing Black poverty and dispossession as consequences of disenfranchisement, they theorized economic domination as the foundation of racial subjugation. Both thinkers rejected the view that political rights alone could secure Black freedom. Fortune theorized Black Southerners as a dispossessed proletariat whose exploitation aligned them with global labor struggles; he insisted that the true terrain of conflict in the South was between labor and capital, not simply between Black and white. Wells, in turn, exposed how white supremacy violently enforced economic subordination by targeting Black prosperity and autonomy. While Fortune envisioned interracial labor solidarity as a corrective to capitalist exploitation, Wells demonstrated how racial violence preemptively foreclosed such solidarity. Together, their work reframes abolition not as a completed legal project but as an ongoing struggle against the economic and social structures that replaced slavery. By linking racial domination to broader systems of labor extraction and monopoly, they anticipated later critiques of racial capitalism, understanding the failures of Reconstruction and the shape of Black life in its aftermath as the results of an economic logic that underwrote labor repression and racial terror.

EPILOGUE
Unending Histories

Historians have focused, understandably, on the narratives of the abolition of slavery—on a story of endings," Kris Manjapra writes. Certainly, the British, American, and French planters of the late eighteenth century whose enslaved property made them among the world's richest people did not expect that within a matter of decades, the system that created their vast wealth would be a thing of the past. To reject the idea that the abolition of slavery constituted some kind of ending would be to dismiss the collective achievement of abolitionism, surely one of the most consequential social movements in world history. And yet the fact remains that in every instance "emancipations conserved and then reactivated the racial caste system of slavery, putting it to new uses that still structure the disequilibrium of life chances in our present societies." Thus Manjapra argues that the "history of slavery and emancipation is not a story of endings, but of unendings."[1]

Throughout the nineteenth century, Black abolitionist and postslavery thinkers criticized forms of freedom that relegated free Black people to menial labor and permitted whites to dispossess them of their property; attempted to forge alliances with white labor organizations to act as a united front against the power of slaveholding and industrial capital; demanded land redistribution and economic security in the wake of the Civil War; and revealed the profit motive behind the white supremacist violence that engulfed the South in the century's final decades. These thinkers, in other words, began to describe the ways racial capitalism constrained free Black life and articulated versions of what Du Bois would come to call abolition democracy—that elusive union between expansive participatory democracy and redistributive political economy secured by an egalitarian state. "Abolitionists expanded how people understood human rights," Kellie Carter Jackson has argued in a recent reflection on the place of abolitionist thought within the field of Black intellectual history. "Reforms in the realms of, but not limited to, labor, gender, criminality, capital, citizenship, empire, and nation all owe a debt to the efforts and tactics that abolitionists championed."[2] Yet for everything Black abolitionist thought bequeathed to the future, it could not disentangle the project of emancipation from that of racial capitalism.

By the end of the century, the states of the former Confederacy had enshrined legalized segregation in all aspects of social and institutional life, and erected barriers to voting that functionally erased Black enfranchisement. Paired with these forms of political domination was a labor regime that relegated the majority of Black Southerners to exploitative forms of tenant farming such as sharecropping. The threat of convict leasing—which condemned victims to work conditions so precarious that it was essentially a death sentence—and lynching hung over any who dared to challenge this new order in the post-Reconstruction South. In the North, the forces of capital that had once supported the Union now gazed westward, turning the power of the federal government away from the protection of freedpeople and toward the suppression of labor and genocidal campaigns against Indigenous sovereignty, amassing fortunes and concentrating national wealth in the process. The malign partnership between South and North worked "to destroy the possibility of democracy in the South, and thereby make the transition from democracy to plutocracy all the easier and more inevitable."[3] The failure of abolition democracy in the nineteenth century, then, had profound implications for Black struggles in the twentieth.

The transition from democracy to plutocracy that Du Bois referred to would unfold on a global scale. In the abandonment of abolition democracy, he saw the seeds of the New Imperialism and the conflagrations of the Great War. In "The African Roots of War," Du Bois argued that as white workers in the Global North demanded a greater share of national wealth, they became willing participants in the exploitation of "the darker nations of the world—Asia and Africa, South and Central America, the West Indies and the islands of the South Seas." Through imperial expansion and investment in white supremacy—in short, through racial capitalism—the white world could stem the tensions between capital and labor, preventing socialist upheaval and preserving the status quo of capitalist democracy. Du Bois observed that with the advent of the new century, "it is no longer simply the merchant prince, or the aristocratic monopoly, or even the employing class, that is exploiting the world: it is the nation; a new democratic nation composed of united capital and labor."[4] Du Bois insisted that it was competition among imperial powers for territory, rather than intra-European geopolitics, at the root of the war.

A lasting peace and the prevention of future wars would require more than the cessation of hostilities among European powers; those powers would have to "extend the democratic ideal to the yellow, brown, and black peoples" and abandon "the doctrine of forcible economic expansion over subject peoples."[5] Du Bois argued that it would be the "the twenty-five million grandchildren of the European slave trade," especially the "ten million black folk of the United States" who were "now writhing desperately for freedom" who were best suited to the work of overthrowing this emergent world order. Du Bois imagined they would achieve this goal by pursuing the same tenets that were at the heart of abolition democracy—that is, land, education, and self-governance. In doing so these dispossessed millions would bring about a "world-salvation."[6]

The Black thinkers who challenged regimes of racial capitalism in the twentieth century revitalized the aspect of abolition democracy that sought to compel state power in defense of both political equality and economic redistribution. Just as the concept of racial capitalism exposes the continuities that bridge the gap between slavery and freedom, the language of abolition democracy reveals Black economic thought of the nineteenth century as a precursor to the more explicitly socialist and anticolonial Black thought of the twentieth. Despite crucial distinctions between the Black thought of these periods, *The Lowest Freedom* has shown that Black abolitionist and post-slavery thinkers understood their freedom to be less meaningful under conditions of land dispossession and labor exploitation, which were the very conditions that would propel the radical anticolonial revolutions of the twentieth century.

The history of emancipation is not one of clean breaks or definitive victories. Rather, it is a history of transformation—of how the end of slavery gave way to new modes of exploitation, and how Black thinkers, in response, reconceptualized freedom as a project fundamentally tied to economic justice. Their work exposed the false dichotomy between slavery and freedom and insisted that meaningful liberation would require not only the abolition of legal bondage but also the dismantling of the systems of racial capitalism that reproduced its effects. Theirs was a vision of freedom that refused to separate political rights from material conditions, and that demanded a democracy rooted in both recognition *and* redistribution.

This history, then, culminates in an imperative. If the nineteenth century's experiments in abolition democracy reveal how racial capitalism reasserted itself through new forms of domination, they also offer a blueprint—partial, aspirational, and unfinished—for how

Black thinkers sought to imagine freedom beyond its narrow legal and political definitions. Their insistence on the centrality of land, labor rights, and economic autonomy to any meaningful conception of freedom prefigured the demands of future liberation movements. In charting the limits of emancipation, they also traced the outlines of a more expansive, egalitarian order. This was a freedom rooted not only in civil rights but in the power to transform the material conditions of life itself.

To read the nineteenth-century Black intellectual tradition through the lens of racial capitalism is to see not only the limits of emancipation, but the clarity with which Black thinkers grasped those limits in their own time. The thinkers at the heart of *The Lowest Freedom* refused to accept a freedom of the "lowest kind," and in so doing, they left future generations with a framework for confronting the unending histories of racial capitalism with the unyielding promise of abolition democracy.

NOTES

INTRODUCTION

1. W.E.B. Du Bois, *Black Reconstruction in America, 1860–1880*, intro. David Levering Lewis (Free Press, 1992), 182.
2. Du Bois, *Black Reconstruction*, 55, 16, 391.
3. Du Bois, *Black Reconstruction*, 727.
4. Du Bois, *Black Reconstruction*, 707.
5. Du Bois, *Black Reconstruction*, 187.
6. Du Bois, *Black Reconstruction*, 30.
7. Jennifer Schuessler, "Emory University Acquires W.E.B. Du Bois's Copy of Rare Early Abolitionist Appeal," *New York Times*, March 7, 2016. On Du Bois's encounter with Douglass, see Herbert Aptheker, "Du Bois on Douglass: 1895," *Journal of Negro History* 49, no. 4 (1964): 267. On his relationship to Fortune and Wells, see David Levering Lewis, *W.E.B. Du Bois, 1868–1919: Biography of a Race* (Henry Holt, 1993).
8. I am indebted to Britt Rusert, Tamara Nopper, and three anonymous reviewers at Columbia University Press for this language.
9. Brandon R. Byrd, "The Rise of African American Intellectual History," *Modern Intellectual History* 18 (2021): 863. Once marginalized, Black intellectual history has seen a resurgence, particularly since the first meeting of the African American Intellectual History Society in 2016. See Keisha N. Blain, Christopher Cameron, and Ashley D. Farmer, eds., *New Perspectives on the Black Intellectual Tradition* (Northwestern University Press, 2018), http://www.jstor.org/stable/j.ctv7tq4rv; Brandon R. Byrd, Leslie

M. Alexander, and Russell Rickford, eds., *Ideas in Unexpected Places: Reimagining Black Intellectual History* (Northwestern University Press, 2022), https://doi.org/10.2307/j.ctv2ckjpp9; Derrick P. Alridge, Cornelius L. Bynum, and James B. Stewart, eds., *The Black Intellectual Tradition: African American Thought in the Twentieth Century* (University of Illinois Press, 2021), http://www.jstor.org/stable/10.5406/j.ctv1vo9oqz; Adolph L. Reed, and Kenneth W. Warren, *Renewing Black Intellectual History: The Ideological and Material Foundations of African American Thought* (Paradigm Publishers, 2010); Mia Bay and Farah Jasmine Griffin, eds., *Toward an Intellectual History of Black Women* (University of North Carolina Press, 2015); and Brian D. Behnken, Gregory D. Smithers, and Simon Wendt, eds., *Black Intellectual Thought in Modern America: A Historical Perspective* (University Press of Mississippi, 2017), https://doi.org/10.2307/j.ctv5jxnoq.

10. Manisha Sinha, *The Slave's Cause: A History of Abolition* (Yale University Press, 2016); Sean Griffin, *The Root and the Branch: Working-Class Reform and Antislavery, 1790–1860* (University of Pennsylvania Press, 2024); Jacqueline Jones, *No Right to an Honest Living: The Struggles of Boston's Black Workers in the Civil War Era* (Basic Books, 2023); Jesse Olsavsky, *The Most Absolute Abolition: Runaways, Vigilance Committees, and the Rise of Revolutionary Abolitionism, 1835–1861* (Louisiana State University Press, 2022); Joe William Trotter, *Workers on Arrival: Black Labor in the Making of America* (University of California Press, 2019), https://doi.org/10.1525/9780520971172; Rudi Batzell, *Organizing Workers in the Shadow of Slavery: Global Inequality, Racial Boundaries, and the Rise of Unions in American and British Capitalism, 1870–1929* (University of Chicago Press, 2025); Roberto Saba, *American Mirror: The United States and Brazil in the Age of Emancipation* (Princeton University Press, 2021); and Zach Sell, *Trouble of the World: Slavery and Empire in the Age of Capital* (University of North Carolina Press, 2021).

11. Frederick Cooper, Thomas C. Holt, and Rebecca J. Scott, *Beyond Slavery: Explorations of Race, Labor, and Citizenship in Postemancipation Societies* (University of North Carolina Press, 2000) is a landmark study that addresses these forms of coercion in a wide geographical scope. The literature is extensive. On the colonial and early American North, representative works include Jared Ross Hardesty, *Unfreedom: Slavery and Dependence in Eighteenth-Century Boston* (New York University Press, 2016); and Sarah L. H. Gronningsater, *The Rising Generation: Gradual Abolition, Black Legal Culture, and the Making of National Freedom* (University of

Pennsylvania Press, 2024), https://doi.org/10.9783/9781512826326. On the post-Reconstruction South, see David W. Blight and Jim Downs, *Beyond Freedom: Disrupting the History of Emancipation* (University of Georgia Press, 2017); Moon-Ho Jung, *Coolies and Cane: Race, Labor, and Sugar in the Age of Emancipation* (Johns Hopkins University Press, 2006); Mathew J. Mancini, *One Dies, Get Another: Convict Leasing in the American South, 1866–1928* (University of South Carolina Press, 1996); and Sarah Haley, *No Mercy Here: Gender, Punishment, and the Making of Jim Crow Modernity* (University of North Carolina Press, 2016). On the American West, see Stacey L. Smith, *Freedom's Frontier: California and the Struggle over Unfree Labor, Emancipation, and Reconstruction* (University of North Carolina Press, 2013); and Gunther Peck, *Reinventing Free Labor: Padrones and Immigrant Workers in the North American West, 1880–1930* (Cambridge University Press, 2000). Douglas A. Blackmon, *Slavery by Another Name: The Re-Enslavement of Black People in America from the Civil War to World War II* (Doubleday, 2008) extends these histories well into the twentieth century.

12. Thomas C. Holt, *The Problem of Freedom: Race, Labor, and Politics in Jamaica and Britain, 1832–1938* (Johns Hopkins University Press, 1992); Saidiya V. Hartman, *Scenes of Subjection: Terror, Slavery, and Self-Making in Nineteenth Century America* (Oxford University Press, 1997); Rinaldo Walcott, *The Long Emancipation: Moving Toward Black Freedom* (Duke University Press, 2021), https://doi.org/10.1515/9781478021360; Kris Manjapra, *Black Ghost of Empire: The Long Death of Slavery and the Failure of Emancipation*, First Scribner hardcover edition (Scribner, 2022); Lisa Lowe, *The Intimacies of Four Continents* (Duke University Press, 2015); Christina Elizabeth Sharpe, *In the Wake: On Blackness and Being* (Duke University Press, 2016); Ian Baucom, *Specters of the Atlantic: Finance Capital, Slavery, and the Philosophy of History* (Duke University Press, 2005), https://doi.org/10.1515/9780822387022; and Chandan Reddy, *Freedom with Violence: Race, Sexuality, and the US State* (Duke University Press, 2011).
13. Holt, *Problem of Freedom*, xxii.
14. Hartman, *Scenes of Subjection*, 6, 119.
15. Walcott, *Long Emancipation*, 105.
16. On freedom's disappointment as generative for scholars of African American history, see Britt Rusert, "Disappointment in the Archives of Black Freedom," *Social Text* 125 (2015): 19–33.
17. Chapters 2 and 3 describe several examples of Douglass's use of the term.

18. W. E. B. Du Bois, "The Freedmen's Bureau." *Atlantic Monthly* 87 (1901): 354–65.
19. I am indebted to Max Mishler for this formulation.
20. In *Lose Your Mother: A Journey Along the Atlantic Slave Route* (Farrar, Straus and Giroux, 2007), Saidiya Hartman describes these continuities as the "afterlife of slavery." While my analysis builds upon her theorization of slavery's afterlife, I avoid the term so as to emphasize the role of racial capitalism's innovations in the conscription of Black freedom rather than simply a desire on the part of whites to return to the time of slavery.
21. Walter Johnson, "To Remake the World: Slavery, Racial Capitalism, and Justice: How the History of Slavery Prompts Us to Rethink Our Notion of Justice," *Boston Review*, February 1, 2017, www.bostonreview.net/forum/walter-johnson-to-remake-the-world/.
22. Destin Jenkins and I elaborate upon this brief definition in *Histories of Racial Capitalism* (Columbia University Press, 2021). For other useful definitions, see Andy Clarno, *Neoliberal Apartheid: Palestine/Israel and South Africa After 1994* (University of Chicago Press, 2017); and Jodi Melamed, "Racial Capitalism," *Critical Ethnic Studies* 1, no. 1 (2015): 76–85, https://doi.org/10.5749/jcritethnstud.1.1.0076.
23. For more on race as an ideological justification for accepting the economic inequality of capitalism as necessary and natural, see Nikhil Pal Singh, "Black Marxism and the Antinomies of Racial Capitalism," in *After Marx: Literature, Theory, and Value in the Twenty-First Century*, ed. Colleen Lye and Christopher Nealon (Cambridge University Press, 2022), 23–39.
24. Cedric Robinson, *Black Marxism: The Making of the Black Radical Tradition* (1983; University of North Carolina Press, 2020).
25. Robinson, *Black Marxism*, 2.
26. Robinson, 2–3.
27. Herbert Hill, "The Problem of Race in American Labor History," *Reviews in American History* 24, no. 2 (1996): 189.
28. Peter James Hudson, *Bankers and Empire: How Wall Street Colonized the Caribbean* (University of Chicago Press, 2017); Destin Jenkins, *The Bonds of Inequality: Debt and the Making of the American City* (University of Chicago Press, 2021); Nathan D. B. Connolly, *A World More Concrete: Real Estate and the Remaking of Jim Crow South Florida* (University of Chicago Press, 2014); Denise Lynn, "Charisse Burden-Stelly. Black Scare/Red Scare: Theorizing Capitalist Racism in the United States," *American Historical Review* 130,

no. 1 (2025): 493–94, https://doi.org/10.1093/ahr/rhae626; Kendra D. Boyd, *Freedom Enterprise: Black Entrepreneurship and Racial Capitalism in Detroit* (University of North Carolina Press, 2025); Nikhil Singh Pal, *Race and America's Long War* (University of California Press, 2017); Jordan T. Camp, *Incarcerating the Crisis: Freedom Struggles and the Rise of the Neoliberal State* (University of California Press, 2016); Paige Glotzer, *How the Suburbs Were Segregated: Developers and the Business of Exclusionary Housing, 1890–1960* (Columbia University Press, 2020); Arun Kundnani, *What Is Antiracism? And Why It Means Anticapitalism* (Verso, 2023); Susan Koshy, Lisa Marie Cacho, Brian Jordan Jefferson, Jodi Byrd, Susan Koshy, and Lisa Marie Cacho, eds., *Colonial Racial Capitalism* (Duke University Press, 2022), https://doi.org/10.1515/9781478023371; Nancy Leong, "Racial Capitalism," *Harvard Law Review* 126, no. 8 (2013): 2151–26; Jodi Byrd et al., eds., "Economies of Dispossession: Indigeneity, Race, Capitalism," special issue, *Social Text* 36, no. 2 (2018).

29. Mingwei Huang, *Reconfiguring Racial Capitalism: South Africa in the Chinese Century* (Duke University Press, 2024), https://doi.org/10.1515/9781478059998; Darren Byler, *Terror Capitalism: Uyghur Dispossession and Masculinity in a Chinese City* (Duke University Press, 2021), https://doi.org/10.2307/j.ctv21zp29g; Harsha Walia, *Border and Rule: Global Migration, Capitalism, and the Rise of Racist Nationalism* (Haymarket Books, 2021); Neferti X. M. Tadiar, *Remaindered Life* (Duke University Press, 2022), https://doi.org/10.2307/j.ctv2j86bp5; Shannon Speed, *Incarcerated Stories: Indigenous Women Migrants and Violence in the Settler-Capitalist State* (University of North Carolina Press, 2019); Piro Rexhepi, *White Enclosures: Racial Capitalism and Coloniality Along the Balkan Route* (Duke University Press, 2022); Christopher Krupa, *A Feast of Flowers: Race, Labor, and Postcolonial Capitalism in Ecuador* (University of Pennsylvania Press, 2022); Muriam Haleh Davis, *Markets of Civilization: Islam and Racial Capitalism in Algeria* (Duke University Press, 2022); Andy Clarno, *Neoliberal Apartheid: Palestine/Israel and South Africa after 1994* (University of Chicago Press, 2017); Brenna Bhandar, *Colonial Lives of Property: Law, Land, and Racial Regimes of Ownership* (Duke University Press, 2018); and Hannah Appel, *The Licit Life of Capitalism: US Oil in Equatorial Guinea* (Duke University Press, 2019).

30. Walter Johnson, *River of Dark Dreams: Slavery and Empire in the Cotton Kingdom* (Harvard University Press, 2013); Jennifer Morgan, *Reckoning with Slavery: Gender, Kinship, and Capitalism in the Early Black Atlantic*

(Duke University Press, 2021); Justene Hill Edwards, *Unfree Markets: The Slaves' Economy and the Rise of Capitalism in South Carolina* (Columbia University Press, 2021); Sven Beckert, *Empire of Cotton: A Global History* (Knopf Doubleday Publishing Group, 2014); Seth Rockman, *Scraping By: Wage Labor, Slavery, and Survival in Early Baltimore* (Johns Hopkins University Press, 2009) and *Plantation Goods: A Material History of American Slavery* (University of Chicago Press, 2024); Sven Beckert and Seth Rockman, eds. *Slavery's Capitalism: A New History of American Economic Development* (University of Pennsylvania Press, 2016); Caitlin Rosenthal, *Accounting for Slavery: Masters and Management* (Harvard University Press, 2018); Edward E. Baptist, *The Half Has Never Been Told: Slavery and the Making of American Capitalism* (Basic Books, 2014); Joshua D. Rothman, *The Ledger and the Chain: How Domestic Slave Traders Shaped America* (Basic Books, 2021) and *Flush Times and Fever Dreams: A Story of Capitalism and Slavery in the Age of Jackson* (University of Georgia Press, 2012); Sharon Ann Murphy, *Banking on Slavery: Financing Southern Expansion in the Antebellum United States* (University of Chicago Press, 2023); Daina Ramey Berry, *The Price for Their Pound of Flesh: The Value of the Enslaved from Womb to Grave in the Building of a Nation* (Beacon Press, 2017); and Calvin Schermerhorn, *The Business of Slavery and the Rise of American Capitalism, 1815–1860* (Yale University Press, 2015).

31. On the relationship between Indigenous dispossession and slavery, see Michael J. Witgen, *Seeing Red: Indigenous Land, American Expansion, and the Political Economy of Plunder in North America* (Omohundro Institute of Early American History and Culture and University of North Carolina Press, 2022); Emilie Connolly, "Fiduciary Colonialism: Annuities and Native Dispossession in the Early United States," *American Historical Review* 127, no. 1 (2022): 223–53, https://doi.org/10.1093/ahr/rhac012; and Claudio Saunt, *Unworthy Republic: The Dispossession of Native Americans and the Road to Indian Territory*, Norton paperback edition (Norton, 2021).

32. Notable work that engages with racial capitalism beyond slavery and Southeastern Indigenous dispossession in the nineteenth century includes Manu Karuka, *Empire's Tracks: Indigenous Nations, Chinese Workers, and the Transcontinental Railroad* (University of California Press, 2019), https://doi.org/10.1525/9780520969056; Sell, *Trouble of the World*; and Batzell, *Organizing Workers in the Shadow of Slavery*.

33. Du Bois, *Black Reconstruction*, 325.
34. Du Bois, *Black Reconstruction*, 611.
35. Du Bois, *Black Reconstruction*, 240.
36. Du Bois, *Black Reconstruction*, 239.
37. Jesse Olsavsky, "The Abolitionist Tradition in the Making of W.E.B. Du Bois's Marxism and Anti-Imperialism," *Socialism and Democracy* 32, no. 3 (2018): 14–15. Contemporary use of the term *abolition democracy* can be traced to Angela Davis's twenty-first-century scholarship, beginning with *Abolition Democracy: Beyond Empire, Prisons, and Torture* (Seven Stories Press, 2005).
38. Robinson, *Black Marxism*, l–li.
39. There are surprisingly few studies of Black abolitionism that frame the movement within a longer tradition of Black radical thought. The work of Kellie Carter Jackson is a standout exception to this trend. See Jackson, *Force and Freedom: Black Abolitionists and the Politics of Violence* (University of Pennsylvania Press, 2020) and *We Refuse: A Forceful History of Black Resistance* (Seal Press, 2024). There is a body of work that situates enslaved rebellion, flight, and self-destruction as part of the Black radical tradition. See, for example, Vincent Brown, *Tacky's Revolt: The Story of an Atlantic Slave War* (Harvard University Press, 2022); Neil Roberts, *Freedom as Marronage* (University of Chicago Press, 2015); and Terri L. Snyder, *The Power to Die: Slavery and Suicide in British North America* (University of Chicago Press, 2015).

1. FREEDOM'S DREGS: BLACKNESS, INDIGENEITY, AND RACIAL CAPITALISM IN ANTEBELLUM NEW ENGLAND

1. On the relationship between slavery and dispossession, see Daniel H. Usner Jr., "American Indians on the Cotton Frontier: Changing Economic Relations with Citizens and Slaves in the Mississippi Territory," *Journal of American History* 72, no. 2 (1985): 297–317; Adam Rothman, *Slave Country: American Expansion and the Origins of the Deep South*, ((Harvard University Press, 2007); Claudio Saunt, *Unworthy Republic: The Dispossession of Native Americans and the Road to Indian Territory* (Norton, 2020); and Vivien Tejada, "Unfree Soil: Empire, Labor, and Coercion in the Upper

Mississippi River Valley, 1812–1861" (PhD diss. Duke University, 2024). See also a data visualization project, Claudia Saunt, "The Invasion of America," video, 1 minute, 27 seconds, Facing History & Ourselves, updated November 17, 2022, www.facinghistory.org/resource-library/invasion-america. On the relative value of financial assets, see David Brion Davis, "Free at Last; The Enduring Legacy of the South's Civil War Victory," *New York Times*, August 26, 2001.

2. Clayton E. Cramer, *Black Demographic Data, 1790–1860: A Sourcebook* (Greenwood Press, 1997), 66; Richard Archer, *Jim Crow North: The Struggle for Equal Rights in Antebellum New England* (Oxford University Press, 2017), 14.
3. Daniel R. Mandell, *Tribe, Race, History: Native Americans in Southern New England, 1780–1880* (Johns Hopkins University Press, 2008), xvii, 4; Jean M. O'Brien, *Firsting and Lasting: Writing Indians Out of Existence in New England* (University of Minnesota Press, 2010).
4. I draw from the following biographical sources: Peter P. Hinks, *To Awaken My Afflicted Brethren: David Walker and the Problem of Antebellum Slave Resistance* (Penn State University Press, 1997); Marilyn Richardson, ed., *Maria W. Stewart, America's First Black Woman Political Writer: Essays and Speeches* (Indiana University Press, 1987); Kristin Waters, *Maria W. Stewart and the Roots of Black Political Thought* (University Press of Mississippi, 2021); Philip F. Gura, *The Life of William Apess, Pequot* (University of North Carolina Press, 2015); and Drew Lopenzina, *Through an Indian's Looking-Glass: A Cultural Biography of William Apess, Pequot* (University of Massachusetts Press, 2017).
5. Although two Black newspapers, *Freedom's Journal* and the *Rights of All*, were extant in the 1820s, both ceased publication in 1829. The next known Black newspapers would not emerge until 1837.
6. John Ernest, *A Nation Within a Nation: Organizing African American Communities Before the Civil War* (John R. Dee, 2011), 3–53.
7. *Laws of the African Society, Instituted at Boston, Anno Domini 1796* (Boston: Printed for the Society, 1796). On the African Grand Lodge, see Stephen Kantrowitz, *More Than Freedom: Fighting for Black Citizenship in a White Republic* (Penguin, 2012), 30.
8. "Constitution of the Afric-American Female Intelligence Society of Boston," *The Liberator*, January 7, 1832.
9. Kantrowitz, *More Than Freedom*, 22.
10. Hinks, *To Awaken My Afflicted Brethren*, especially chapters 3 and 4.

11. James Turner, ed., *David Walker's Appeal, in Four Articles: Together with a Preamble, to the Coloured Citizens of the World, but in Particular, and Very Expressly, to Those of the United States of America*, Third and Last Edition, Revised and Published by David Walker, 1830 (Black Classic Press, 1993), 58.
12. Herbert Aptheker, ed., *One Continual Cry: David Walker's Appeal to the Colored Citizens of the World (1829–1830), Its Setting & Its Meaning* (Humanities Press, 1965).
13. Turner, *David Walker's Appeal*, 14–18.
14. On the distribution of the *Appeal*, see Hinks, *To Awaken My Afflicted Brethren*, chapter 5; and Sean Wilentz, ed., *David Walker's Appeal, In Four Articles; Together With A Preamble, to the Coloured Citizens of the World, but In Particular, and Very Expressly, to Those in the United States of America* (Hill and Wang, 1995), xiv–xv. On Black seamen's information networks more generally, see Julius S. Scott, *The Common Wind: Afro-American Currents in the Age of the Haitian Revolution* (Verso, 2018). On the profound influence the *Appeal* had on Black and Indigenous print culture in the first half of the nineteenth century, see Marcy J. Dinius, *The Textual Effects of David Walker's "Appeal": Print-Based Activism Against Slavery, Racism, and Discrimination, 1829–1851* (University of Pennsylvania Press, 2022).
15. Garrison estimated that three-quarters of subscribers to *The Liberator* were Black. Donald M. Jacobs, "William Lloyd Garrison's *Liberator* and Boston's Blacks, 1830–1865," *New England Quarterly* 44, no. 2 (1971): 259–77.
16. Richardson, *Maria W. Stewart*, 3–27; Douglas A. Jones, ed., *Maria W. Stewart: Essential Writings of a Nineteenth-Century Black Abolitionist* (Oxford University Press, 2024). In the last year of her life, Stewart republished her writings from the 1830s as *Meditations from the Pen of Mrs. Maria W. Stewart (Widow of the Late James W. Stewart), Now Matron of the Freedmen's Hospital, and Presented in 1832 to the First African Baptist Church and Society of Boston, Mass* (Washington: n.p., 1879).
17. On Apess's life, see Drew Lopenzina, *Through an Indian's Looking-Glass: A Cultural Biography of William Apess, Pequot* (University of Massachusetts Press, 2017); Philip F. Gura, *The Life of William Apess, Pequot* (University of North Carolina Press, 2015); and Barry O'Connell, ed., *On Our Own Ground: The Complete Writings of William Apess, a Pequot* (University of Massachusetts Press, 1992).
18. Margaret Ellen Newell, *Brethren by Nature: New England Indians, Colonists, and the Origins of American Slavery* (Cornell University Press, 2015), 15;

Daniel R. Mandell, "Shifting Boundaries of Race and Ethnicity: Indian-Black Intermarriage in Southern New England, 1760–1880," *Journal of American History* 85, no. 2 (Sep. 1998): 466–501; and Joanne Pope Melish, *Disowning Slavery: Gradual Emancipation and "Race" in New England, 1780–1860* (Cornell University Press, 1998), 37–38.

19. The federal government and state governments did not recognize Indigenous people as citizens of the United States and unevenly recognized them as citizens of their own sovereign nations, treating Native people instead as wards. In *Cherokee Nation v. Georgia* (1831), Chief Justice John Marshall coined the term "domestic dependent nations" to describe the limited recognition of Indigenous polities on the part of the United States. See also Deborah Rosen, *American Indians and State Law: Sovereignty, Race, and Citizenship, 1790–1880* (University of Nebraska Press, 2007); and Jean M. O'Brien, *Dispossession by Degrees: Indian Land and Identity in Natick, Massachusetts, 1650–1790* (Cambridge University Press, 1997).

20. For an excellent example of how to place Black and Indigenous histories side by side to illuminate historical dynamics that might otherwise be obscured, see Nicholas Guyatt, *Bind Us Apart: How Enlightened Americans Invented Racial Segregation* (Basic Books, 2016).

21. David Walker and Henry Highland Garnet, *Walker's Appeal, with a Brief Sketch of His Life, by Henry Highland Garnet, and Also Garnet's Address to the Slaves of the United States of America* (New York: J.H. Tobitt, 1848), vi.

22. Leonard Curry, *The Free Black in Urban America, 1800–1850: The Shadow of the Dream* (University of Chicago Press, 1981), 125.

23. Curry, *The Free Black in Urban America*, 135.

24. Maria Stewart, "Lecture Delivered at the Franklin Hall, Boston, September 21, 1832," in *Meditations*, 55.

25. On the hardening of ideas about race in the early nineteenth century, see Bruce Dain, *A Hideous Monster of the Mind: American Race Theory in the Early Republic* (Harvard University Press, 2003).

26. Leon F. Litwack, *North of Slavery: The Negro in the Free States, 1790–1860* (University of Chicago Press, 1961), 93–94; Archer, *Jim Crow North*, 6.

27. Mandell, *Tribe, Race, History*, 2.

28. Curry, *Free Black in Urban America*, 19–35; James Oliver Horton and Lois E. Horton, *In Hope of Liberty: Culture, Community and Protest Among Northern Free Blacks, 1700–1860* (Oxford University Press, 1997), 110–19; Litwack, *North of Slavery*, 153–61. Quotation from Thomas Hamilton, *Men and*

Manners in America, vol. 1 (Edinburgh: 1834), 104, as cited in Horton and Horton, *In Hope of Liberty*, 114.
29. Stewart, "Lecture Delivered at the Franklin Hall," 56.
30. Mandell, *Tribe, Race, History*, viii.
31. Mandell, *Tribe, Race, History*, 1–20.
32. Walker, *Walker's Appeal*, 11–12.
33. Quotation from "War of 1812, Claim of Widow for Service Pension," reproduced in Richardson, *Maria M. Stewart*, 117. On James Stewart's racial designation, see Richardson, *Maria M. Stewart*, 122n5.
34. Louise C. Hatton, "Biographical Sketch," in Stewart, *Meditations*, 8.
35. Richardson, *Maria M. Stewart*, 113–15.
36. Stewart, "Preface," in *Meditations*, n.p. (line 2).
37. Gura, *Life of William Apess*, 16–20.
38. Apess, *A Son of the Forest* (Boston: James B. Dow, 1833), 54.
39. Kim McQuiad, "William Apes, Pequot: An Indian Reformer in the Jackson Era," *Journal of New England History* 50, no. 4 (1977): 609.
40. Apess, *Son of the Forest*, 66.
41. Apess, 67.
42. Apess, 68.
43. Apess, 79.
44. Apess, 79. Although Apess identified his employer's refusal to pay him with the racialized and unfree labor of slavery, it was not a gesture of solidarity, as Apess's political commitments were still developing. In another piece of autobiographical writing, he, in masculinizing terms, distanced himself from the condition of enslavement, writing of his childhood indenture, "I never cried out, like the poor African, 'Massa, Massa—Mister, Mister'"; William Apess, *The Experiences of Five Christian Indians of the Pequod Tribe, Published by William Apes, Subsequently a Missionary of that Tribe, and author of "The Son of the Forest,"* (Boston: James B. Dow, 1833), 10.
45. Apess, *Son of the Forest*, 66.
46. "Address, Delivered Before the General Colored Association at Boston, by David Walker," *Freedom's Journal*, December 19, 1828.
47. Stewart, "Lecture Delivered at the Franklin Hall," 57.
48. Quoted in Curry, *Free Black in Urban America*, 112.
49. Horton and Horton, *In Hope of Liberty*, 108; Curry, *Free Black in Urban America*, 112–15.

50. George A. Levesque, "Black Crime and Crime Statistics in Antebellum Boston," *Australian Journal of Politics and History* 25, no. 2 (1979): 221; Litwack, *North of Slavery*, 94–96.
51. Mandell, *Tribe, Race, History*, 13, 15, 34.
52. Walker, *Walker's Appeal*, 65.
53. Walker, *Walker's Appeal*, 31.
54. Walker, *Walker's Appeal*, 65.
55. Stewart, "Lecture Delivered at the Franklin Hall," 57.
56. Stewart, "An Address Delivered at the African Masonic Hall, Boston, February 27, 1833," in *Meditations*, 66.
57. Stewart, "Lecture Delivered at the Franklin Hall," 57.
58. Stewart, "Religion and the Pure Principles of Morality," in *Meditations*, 25.
59. Stewart, "Mrs. Stewart's Farewell Address to Her Friends in the City of Boston, Delivered September 21, 1833," in *Meditations*, 79.
60. Litwack, *North of Slavery*, 98.
61. Stewart, "Address, Delivered at the African Masonic Hall," 69.
62. Walker, *Walker's Appeal*, 67.
63. Wendy Warren, *New England Bound: Slavery and Colonization in Early New England* (Livewright, 2017); and Newell, *Brethren by Nature*.
64. Bernard Bailyn, "Slavery and Population Growth in Colonial New England," in Peter Temin, ed., *Engines of Enterprise: An Economic History of New England* (Harvard University Press, 2000).
65. Jared Hardesty, *Unfreedom: Slavery and Dependence in Eighteenth-Century Boston* (New York University Press, 2016), 5.
66. Melish, *Disowning Slavery*, 8, 17–18 and quotation on p. 8.
67. Walker, *Walker's Appeal*, 72.
68. William Apes, *Indian Nullification of the Unconstitutional Laws of Massachusetts, Relative to the Marshpee Tribe: Or, the Pretended Riot Explained* (Boston: Jonathan Howe, 1835), 10.
69. William Apess, *Eulogy on King Philip, as Pronounced at the Odeon, in Federal Street, Boston, by the Rev. William Apes, an Indian* (Boston: Published by the Author, 1836), 10–11.
70. Apess, *Son of the Forest*, 67.
71. Apess, *Indian Nullification*, 79–80.
72. Apess, *Eulogy on King Philip*, 50–51.

73. William Apess, "An Indian's Looking-Glass for the White Man," in *The Experiences of Five Christian Indians of the Pequod Tribe* (Boston: James B. Dow, 1833), 58.
74. Apess, *Indian Nullification*, 103.
75. Kantrowitz, *More Than Freedom*, 22.
76. Hinks, *To Awaken My Afflicted Brethren*, 71–73.
77. Hinks, *To Awaken My Afflicted Brethren*, 84–85. Quotation from Walker and Garnet, *Walker's Appeal, With a Brief Sketch of His Life*, vi.
78. Curry, *Free Black in Urban America*, chapter 12.
79. Stewart, "Address, Delivered at the African Masonic Hall," 70.
80. Archer, *Jim Crow North*, 11–12; Curry, *Free Black in Urban America*, chapter 10.
81. Stewart, "Religion and the Pure Principles of Morality," 31.
82. Mandell, *Tribe, Race, History*, 35–37, 83.
83. Melish, *Disowning Slavery*, 127–32; Litwack, *North of Slavery*, 168–70; Archer, *Jim Crow North*, 8–9 and 14–16; Curry, *Free Black in Urban America*, 100–2 and 118; Douglas R. Egerton, "Slaves to the Marketplace: Economic Liberty and Black Rebelliousness in the Atlantic World," *Journal of the Early Republic* 26, no. 4 (2006): 629. Perhaps the most famous study of this Atlantic working class is Peter Linebaugh's *The Many-Headed Hydra: Sailors, Slaves, Commoners, and the Hidden History of the Revolutionary Atlantic* (Beacon, 2000).
84. Melish, *Disowning Slavery*, 137.
85. Mandell, *Tribe, Race, History*, 36.
86. Mandell, *Tribe, Race, History*, 141.
87. Walker, *Walker's Appeal*, 48.
88. Walker, *Walker's Appeal*, 67.
89. Ousmane K. Power-Greene, *Against Wind and Tide: The African American Struggle Against the Colonization Movement* (New York University Press, 2014), 16; Samantha Seeley, "Beyond the American Colonization Society," *History Compass* 14, no. 3 (2016): 100; David Kazanjian, *The Colonizing Trick: National Culture and Imperial Citizenship in Early America* (University of Minnesota Press, 2003), 92.
90. Ikuko Asaka, *Tropical Freedom: Climate, Settler Colonialism, and Black Exclusion in the Age of Emancipation* (Duke University Press, 2017); Eric Burin, *Slavery and the Peculiar Solution: A History of the American Colonization*

Society (University Press of Florida, 2005); P. J. Staudenraus, *The African Colonization Movement, 1816–1865* (Columbia University Press, 1961).
91. Walker, *Walker's Appeal*, 70, 49.
92. Stewart, "Address Delivered at the Masonic Hall," 70–71.
93. Stewart, "Address Delivered at the Masonic Hall," 73.
94. Nicholas Guyatt, "'The Outskirts of Our Happiness:' Race and the Lure of Colonization in the Early Republic," *Journal of American History* 95, no. 4 (2009): 986.
95. Guyatt, *Bind Us Apart*.
96. Kazanjian, *Colonizing Trick*, 94–95.
97. Power-Greene, *Against Wind and Tide*, 14.
98. Mark A. Nicholas, "Mashpee Wampanoags of Cape Cod, the Whalefishery, and Seafaring's Impact on Community Development," *American Indian Quarterly* 26, no. 2 (2002): 165–97.
99. McQuaid, "William Apes, Pequot," 614–15; "The Mashpee Indians," *Boston Daily Advocate*, quoted in Apess, *Indian Nullification*, 74.
100. Quoted in Donald M. Nielsen, "The Mashpee Indian Revolt of 1833," *New England Quarterly* 58, no. 3 (Sep. 1985), 401.
101. Mandell, *Tribe, Race, History*, 70–73, quotation on 75.
102. Mandell, *Tribe, Race, History*, 76–81.
103. Apess, *Indian Nullification*, 77–78.
104. Apess, *Indian Nullification*, 44.
105. Apess, *Indian Nullification*, 79.
106. Apess, *Indian Nullification*, 24.
107. Apess, *Indian Nullification*, 32.
108. Quoted in Mandell, *Tribe, Race, History*, 100.
109. *The Liberator*, January 25, 1834; much of the press coverage is reproduced in Apess's *Indian Nullification*.
110. Massachusetts General Court, House of Representatives No. 11, *Memorial of the Marshpee Indians: A Voice from the Marshpee Indians, Jan. 1834* (1834), 13, 8–9.
111. "But I must, really, observe that in this very city, when a man of colour dies, if he owned any real estate it most generally falls into the hands of some white person. The wife and children of the deceased may weep and lament if they please, but the estate will be kept snug enough by its white possessor"; Walker, *Walker's Appeal*, 11–12.
112. Gura, *Life of William Apes*, 114–19.

113. Lopenzina, *Through an Indian's Looking-Glass*, 244–50.
114. "The history of Manchester never happened without the history of Mississippi"; Walter Johnson, "To Remake the World: Slavery, Racial Capitalism, and Justice," in "Race Capitalism Justice," special issue, *Boston Review*, Winter 2017.

2. THE RADICAL ABOLISHMENT OF SLAVERY: ABOLITIONIST ENCOUNTERS WITH LAND AND LABOR REFORMERS

1. James McCune Smith to Robert Hamilton, *Weekly Anglo-African*, August 20, 1864, in C. Peter Ripley, ed., *The Black Abolitionist Papers*, vol. 5: *The United States, 1859–1865* (University of North Carolina Press, 2000), 299–302.
2. Frederick Douglass, "Narrative of the Life of Frederick Douglass," in *Frederick Douglass's Autobiographies*, ed. Henry Louis Gates Jr. (Library of America, 1994), 95.
3. Frederick Douglass, "My Bondage and My Freedom," in *Frederick Douglass's Autobiographies*, 358.
4. McCune Smith referred specifically to experiments early in the war that took place on the Sea Islands of South Carolina. In 1861, Union forces took control of Port Royal harbor. Most Confederates fled, abandoning their plantations and around ten thousand enslaved people. The Union confiscated the abandoned land and paid freedpeople wages to continue working it, subsequently selling them small plots. By the end of the war, this land redistribution effort had been largely thwarted through a combination of Johnson returning most confiscated land to its original owners, Republicans' desire to transform freedpeople into wage workers rather than landowning yeomen, and freedpeople's defaults on predatory loan contracts. See Willie Lee Rose, *Rehearsals for Reconstruction: The Port Royal Experiment* (University of Georgia Press, 1962).
5. McCune Smith to Hamilton, 302.
6. See Eric Foner, "The Meaning of Freedom in the Age of Emancipation," *Journal of American History* 81, no. 2 (1994): 435–60, https://doi.org/10.2307/2081167, for relevant theory and historiography.
7. Eric Foner, *Free Soil, Free Labor, Free Men: The Ideology of the Republican Party Before the Civil War*, with *a New Introductory Essay* (Oxford University Press, 1995), xi.

8. Amy Dru Stanley, *From Bondage to Contract: Wage Labor, Marriage, and the Market in the Age of Slave Emancipation* (Cambridge University Press, 1998), 21.
9. William Lloyd Garrison, "Working Men," *The Liberator*, January 1, 1831, 3.
10. For an overview, see James L. Huston, "Abolitionists, Political Economists, and Capitalism," *Journal of the Early Republic* 20, no. 3 (2000): 487–521, https://doi.org/10.2307/3125066. The classic set of debates that aligned abolitionism with capitalist ideologies is contained in Thomas Bender, ed., *The Antislavery Debate: Capitalism and Abolitionism as a Problem in Historical Interpretation* (University of California Press, 1992). Work that has explored the economic dimensions of abolitionist critique includes Gunther Peck, "Labor Abolition and the Politics of White Victimhood: Rethinking the History of Working-Class Racism," *Journal of the Early Republic* 39, no. 1 (2019): 89–98, https://doi.org/10.1353/jer.2019.0007; Sean Griffin, *The Root and the Branch: Working-Class Reform and Antislavery, 1790–1860*, (University of Pennsylvania Press, 2024); Manisha Sinha, *The Slave's Cause: A History of Abolition* (Yale University Press, 2016); and Peter Wirzbicki, *Fighting for the Higher Law: Black and White Transcendentalists Against Slavery* (University of Pennsylvania Press, 2021).
11. A notable exception is the work of Patrick Rael, who has argued that many Black Northerners embraced market values. See Rael, "The Market Revolution and Market Values in Antebellum Black Protest Thought," in *Cultural Change and the Market Revolution in America, 1789–1860*, ed. Scott Martin (Rowman and Littlefield, 2005), 13–45; and Patrick Rael, "African Americans, Slavery, and Thrift from the Revolution to the Civil War," in *Thrift and Thriving in America: Capitalism and Moral Order from the Puritans to the Present*, ed. Joshua Yates and James Davison Hunter (Oxford University Press, 2011), 183–206.
12. "Wages slavery" was in common usage in the nineteenth century and corresponds to the more contemporary "wage slavery."
13. "Aristocracy of Wealth," *Colored American*, April 1, 1837.
14. "Important to Workers," *Colored American*, August 3, 1839.
15. "Peril to the Free," *Colored American*, September 1, 1838. Pickens quotation in *Address to the Non-Slaveholders of the South: On the Social and Political Evils of Slavery* (New York: S.W. Benedict, 1843), 9.
16. Garland I. Penn and Frederick Douglass, *The Afro-American Press and Its Editors* (N.p.: Willey), 1891.

17. Theodore S. Wright, Gerrit Smith, Charles B. Ray, and James McCune Smith, An *Address to the Three Thousand Colored Citizens of New-York: Who Are the Owners of One Hundred and Twenty Thousand Acres of Land, in the State of New-York*, September 1, 1846 (New-York, n.p., 1846), 4–5. John Stauffer, *The Black Hearts of Men* (Harvard University Press, 2009) offers a comprehensive examination of Smith's engagements with Black abolitionists and is the best biographical source on Smith's life more generally.
18. Wright et al., *Address to the Three Thousand Colored Citizens*, 10.
19. Wright et al., 14–20.
20. *History of Wages in the United States from Colonial Times to 1928.* Bulletin of the Bureau of Labor Statistics No. 499 (Government Printing Office, 1934). See table G-1, "Laborers, 1840–1900."
21. James McCune Smith to Gerrit Smith, July 7, 1848. *Speak Out in Thunder Tones: Letters and Other Writings by Black Northerners, 1787–1865*, ed. Dorothy Sterling (1973; reprint, Da Capo, 1998), 205.
22. Free Black Southerners faced a double bind. In the decades after the Revolution, manumitted people's freedom could be contingent on acceding to exile from Southern states, yet the territories of the Northwest enacted strict laws limiting the ease of Black migration. Samantha Seeley, *Race, Removal, and the Right to Remain: Migration and the Making of the United States* (Omohundro Institute of Early American History and Culture and the University of North Carolina Press, 2021); Michael A. Schoeppner, "Black Migrants and Border Regulation in the Early United States, *Journal of the Civil War Era* 11, no. 3 (2021): 317–39.
23. Martin Delany, *The North Star*, July 7, 1848. Dorothy Sterling, ed., *Speak out in Thunder Tones* (Da Capo, 1998), 207.
24. Sean Griffin, *Root and the Branch*; and Reeve Huston, *Land and Freedom: Rural Society, Popular Protest, and Party Politics in* Antebellum (Oxford University Press, 2000).
25. "Wages and Chattel Slavery—The Elevation of the Working Class," *National Era*, March 25, 1846.
26. Jeremiah B. Sanderson to William C. Nell, June 19, 1842, in Peter C. Ripley, ed., *The Black Abolitionist Papers*, vol. 3: *The United States, 1830–1846* (University of North Carolina Press, 1991), 385–86.
27. Frederick Douglass to Garrison, February 26, 1846, in Philp Sheldon Foner, *The Life and Writings of Frederick Douglass*, vol. 1: *The Early Years*

(International Publishers, 1950), 138–42. Abolitionists were often temperance reformers as well, some even going so far as to describe dependence on alcohol as its own kind of slavery. See Douglass, "Temperance and Anti-Slavery, An Address Delivered in Paisley, Scotland, 30 March 1846," in John R. McKivigan et al., eds, *The Speeches of Frederick Douglass: A Critical Edition* (Yale University Press, 2018), 9–16; and Donald Yacovone, "The Transformation of the Black Temperance Movement, 1827–1854: An Interpretation," *Journal of the Early Republic* 8.3 (1988): 281–97.

28. Frederick Douglass to Maria Weston Chapman, September 10, 1843, in Foner, *Life and Writings of Frederick Douglass*, vol. 1, 111–12.
29. "Land Reform—Wages Slavery," *National Era*, March 18, 1847.
30. Griffin, *Root and the Branch*, chapter 4.
31. "Young America—Land Reform—Wages Slavery," *National Era*, March 11, 1847.
32. "Wages and Chattel Slavery," *National Era*. These debates continued into the early 1850s. See "Land and Liberty," March 2, 1848; "The Mission of Democracy No. 2," April 20, 1848; "Labor and Capital," November 9, 1848; "Novel Argument in Support of Slavery—Immigration and Wages," November 9, 1848; "Land Reform in the Senate," February 7, 1850; "Senator Clemens," March 28, 1850; "Land Reform," May 30, 1850; "The Public Lands," February 13, 1851; and "From Rhode Island," February 20, 1851, all in the *National Era*.
33. "The North Star," *Homestead Journal and Village Register*, December 22, 1847.
34. [Untitled], *North Star*, January 7, 1848.
35. [Untitled], *North Star*.
36. "An Address to the Colored People of the United States," *North Star*, September 29, 1848.
37. "Land Reform," *North Star*, February 25, 1848. "Public Lands," *North Star*, February 25, 1848.
38. "The Laboring Men," *North Star*, November 3, 1848.
39. "The Poor Whites of the South," *North Star*, March 1, 1850.
40. "The Mission of Democracy No. 2," *National Era*, April 20, 1848. Pickens's speech did not quite go so far as the correspondent implied—Pickens exalted Southern society, in which capitalists had true legal ownership over labor, in comparison with the more limited ways in which Northern capitalists could exert control over their labor.

41. "Labor and Capital," *National Era*.
42. "Land Reform," *National Era*.
43. "From Rhode Island," *National Era*.
44. "Novel Argument in Support of Slavery," *National Era*.
45. "Land Reform in the Senate," *National Era*.
46. "The Homestead Bill," *New York Times*, May 4, 1852. A version of this bill passed during the Civil War as the Homestead Act of 1862. See also Gerald Wolff, "The Slaveocracy and the Homestead Problem of 1854," *Agricultural History* 40, no. 2 (1966): 101–12.
47. "Land Reform," *Frederick Douglass' Paper*, April 1, 1852.
48. "Land Reform and Its Prospects," *Frederick Douglass' Paper*, June 3, 1852.
49. "Land Reform," *Frederick Douglass' Paper*, May 27, 1852.
50. "Capital and Labor," *Frederick Douglass' Paper*, Rochester, March 4, 1853.
51. "The Annual Meeting of the American Anti-Slavery Society," *Frederick Douglass' Paper*, May 20, 1852.
52. Michael Mahoney, "'The Great Experiment': Explaining the Advent of Indenture to the West Indies," The National Archives blog, January 26, 2021, https://blog.nationalarchives.gov.uk/the-great-experiment-explaining-the-advent-of-indenture-to-the-west-indies/.
53. On the relationship between British West Indian emancipation and American abolitionism, see Edward Bartlett Rugemer, *The Problem of Emancipation: The Caribbean Roots of the American Civil War* (Louisiana State University Press, 2008); Gale L. Kenny, *Contentious Liberties: American Abolitionists in Post-Emancipation Jamaica, 1834–1866* (University of Georgia Press, 2010); and Dexter J. Gabriel, *Jubilee's Experiment: The British West Indies and American Abolitionism* (Cambridge University Press, 2023). On how British emancipation served as inspiration to Black people throughout the Atlantic world, see J.R. Kerr-Ritchie, *Rites of August First: Emancipation Day in the Black Atlantic World* (Louisiana State University Press, 2007).
54. "A Difficulty Explained," *Colored American*, July 27, 1839.
55. [Untitled], *Colored American*, October 2, 1841.
56. [Untitled], *Colored American*, December 25, 1841.
57. Nicholas Crawford, "Sustenance and Power: Provision Grounds and Plantation Enterprise in Eighteenth- and Nineteenth-Century Jamaican Slavery," *Journal of Caribbean History* 57, no. 2 (2023): 25–54.
58. "Letter of Charles Stuart," *The Emancipator*, December 26, 1839. Emphasis original.

59. William Wells Brown to Editor, *London Times*, July 3, 1851, in Peter C. Ripley, ed., *The Black Abolitionist Papers*, vol. 1: *The British Isles, 1830–1865* (University of North Carolina Press, 1985), 283–84.
60. "Don't Come to England," *The Liberator*, July 25, 1851.
61. "Emigration of Colored People to Jamaica," *The Liberator*, October 24, 1851. Even after apprenticeship ended, coercion and state-sponsored punitive violence remained a central feature of Black wage labor in Jamaica. Diana Paton, *No Bond but the Law: Punishment, Race, and Gender in Jamaican State Formation, 1780–1870* (Duke University Press, 2004).
62. "Letter from H.H. Garnet," *Frederick Douglass' Paper*, September 2, 1853.
63. Ikuko Asaka, *Tropical Freedom: Climate, Settler Colonialism, and Black Exclusion in the Age of Emancipation* (Duke University Press, 2017), chapter 3.
64. Philip Curtin, "The British Sugar Duties and West Indian Prosperity," *Journal of Economic History* 14.2 (1954): 157–64.
65. Henry Highland Garnet to Louis Alexis Chamerovzow, October 2, 1854, in Ripley, *Black Abolitionist Papers*, vol. 1, 407–8.
66. Henry Highland Garnet to Louis Alexis Chamerovzow, October 2, 1854, in in Ripley, *Black Abolitionist Papers*, vol. 1, 409–11.
67. James McCune Smith, *Frederick Douglass' Paper*, August 8, 1856, in John Stauffer, ed., *The Works of James McCune Smith* (Oxford University Press, 2006), 152–54.
68. The British government's payment to West Indian slaveowners in 1834 was among the largest financial transactions the nation had ever undertaken to that point. Nicholas Draper, *The Price of Emancipation: Slave-Ownership, Compensation, and British Society at the End of Slavery* (Cambridge University Press, 2010).
69. James McCune Smith, *Frederick Douglass' Paper*, August 8, 1856, in Stauffer, *Works of James McCune Smith*, 152–54.
70. "West India Emancipation, Speech Delivered at Canandaigua, New York, August 4, 1857," in Philp Sheldon Foner, *Life and Writings of Frederick Douglass*, vol. 2: *Pre-Civil War Decade* (International Publishers, 1950), 426–39.
71. "The Reproach and Shame of the American Government," *New York Times*, August 3, 1858, in Philp Sheldon Foner, *Life and Writings of Frederick Douglass*, vol. 5: *Supplementary Volume, 1844–1860* (International Publishers, 1975), 394–411.

2. THE RADICAL ABOLISHMENT OF SLAVERY ⊗ 195

72. "West India Emancipation," *National Era*, November 28, 1858.
73. "West India Emancipation," *National Era*.
74. Mifflin W. Gibbs to Amor de Cosmos, *British Colonist*, October 22, 1859, in Peter C. Ripley, ed., *The Black Abolitionist Papers*, vol. 2: *Canada, 1830–1865* (University of North Carolina Press, 1986), 417.
75. "The Meetings of the Colored People," *The Liberator*, April 4, 1851.
76. "Learn Trades or Starve," *Frederick Douglass' Paper*, March 4, 1853, in Foner, *Life and Writings of Frederick Douglass*, vol. 2, 223–25.
77. "The Industrial College," *Frederick Douglass' Paper*, January 2, 1854. Emphasis original.
78. "Communications," *Frederick Douglass' Paper*, January 1, 1852.
79. "From Our Brooklyn Correspondent," *Frederick Douglass' Paper*, January 22, 1852. Emphasis original.
80. "Letter from Communipaw," *Frederick Douglass' Paper*, February 12, 1852. McCune Smith was doubtless familiar with George Downing, a Black reformer who owned a highly successful catering business that served a wealthy white clientele. Downing used his business as a stop on the Underground Railroad and was an active abolitionist. Thus, McCune Smith implied but did not fully articulate whom he referred to as "the wealthy" in this debate. On Downing, see S. A. M. Washington, *George Thomas Downing: Sketch of His Life and Times* (Milne Printery, 1910).
81. "Letter from Communipaw," *Frederick Douglass' Paper*, February 12, 1852.
82. "To 'Ethiop' and 'Observer,'" *Frederick Douglass' Paper*, April 8, 1852.
83. "It Is Not to the Rich but to the Poor That We Must Look," August 23, 1852, in Foner, *Life and Writings of Frederick Douglass*, vol. 5, 243–45.
84. "The Accumulation of Wealth," *Frederick Douglass' Paper*, November 28, 1856.
85. "Secession," *Weekly Anglo-African*, December 22, 1860.
86. "Frederick Douglass on the Crisis," *Douglass' Monthly*, June 1861.
87. "Virginia Going Backward," *The Christian Recorder*, December 21, 1861.
88. "The Work of the Future," *Douglass Monthly*, November 1862, 290–93.
89. "Frederick Douglass at the Cooper Institute," *Douglass' Monthly*, March 1863.
90. "What the Black Man Wants," in Foner, *Life and Writings of Frederick Douglass*, vol. 4: *Reconstruction and After* (International Publishers, 1955), 157–65.
91. McCune Smith to Hamilton, 300.
92. McCune Smith to Hamilton, 301.

3. A WORSE CONDITION THAN IN THE TIME OF SLAVERY: CAPITAL, LABOR, AND THE LIMITS OF EMANCIPATION

1. Frederick Douglass, *Address by Hon. Frederick Douglass, Delivered in the Metropolitan A.M.E. Church, Washington, D.C., Tuesday, January 9th, on The Lessons of the Hour: in Which He Discusses the Various Aspects of the So-Called, But Mis-Called, Negro Problem* (Baltimore: Press of Thomas and Evans, 1894), 27, www.loc.gov/item/12002894/.
2. Douglass, *Address by Hon. Frederick Douglass*, 28.
3. Confederate Vice President Alexander Stephens distilled this ideology in his 1861 Cornerstone Speech, where he declared, "The negro is not equal to the white man. . . .slavery—subordination to the superior race—is his natural and moral condition." Quoted in Keith S. Hébert, *Cornerstone of the Confederacy: Alexander Stephens and the Speech That Defined the Lost Cause* (University of Tennessee Press, 2021), 44.
4. Douglass, *Address by Hon. Frederick Douglass*, 28.
5. Saidiya V. Hartman, *Scenes of Subjection: Terror, Slavery, and Self-Making in Nineteenth-Century America* (Oxford University Press, 1997), 139.
6. Julie Saville, *The Work of Reconstruction: From Slave to Wage Laborer in South Carolina, 1860–1870* (Cambridge University Press, 1996); Edward Royce, *The Origins of Southern Sharecropping* (Temple University Press, 1993); Joseph P. Reidy, *From Slavery to Agrarian Capitalism in the Cotton Plantation South: Central Georgia, 1800–1880* (University of North Carolina Press, 1995).
7. Douglass, *Address by Hon. Frederick Douglass*, 29.
8. Douglass, 33.
9. Douglass's particular interest in Black labor and broader idiosyncrasy of thought make it difficult to categorize him according to conventional categories of "radical" vs. "liberal" postwar economic ideologies. This ambiguity is precisely the point—Douglass refused to adopt such ideologies wholesale because of their insufficient theorization of race and slavery. The economic thought he developed attempted to take a full accounting of how race, labor, and capital shaped future possibilities for Black freedom, which is a hallmark of abolition democracy.
10. Frederick Douglass, "Narrative of the Life of Frederick Douglass," in *Frederick Douglass's Autobiographies*, ed. Henry Louis Gates Jr. (Library of America, 1994), 81.

11. Douglass, "Narrative of the Life," 80–81.
12. Frederick Douglass, "My Bondage and My Freedom," in *Frederick Douglass's Autobiographies*, ed. Henry Louis Gates Jr. (Library of America, 1994), 330.
13. Douglass, "My Bondage and My Freedom," 358–59.
14. Frank Towers, "Job Busting at Baltimore Shipyards: Racial Violence in the Civil War-Era South," *Journal of Southern History* 66, no. 2 (2000): 221–56; Eric Foner, *Reconstruction: America's Unfinished Revolution*, updated ed. (Harper Perennial, 2014), 39–41; "A Biographical Sketch of Isaac Myers," *Indianapolis Freeman*, October 12, 1889, quoted in Philip S. Foner and Ronald L. Lewis, eds., *The Black Worker: A Documentary History from Colonial Times to the Present* (Temple University Press, 1989), 158–61, https://doi.org/10.2307/j.ctvn1tbr6.
15. Bettye C. Thomas, "A Nineteenth Century Black Operated Shipyard, 1866–1884: Reflections Upon Its Inception and Ownership," *Journal of Negro History* 59, no. 1 (1974): 1–12.
16. "Convention of Colored Mechanics," *Christian Recorder*, August 14, 1869.
17. "Convention of Colored Mechanics," *Christian Recorder*.
18. Foner and Lewis, *Black Worker*.
19. The organization was formally named the National Labor Union, but was frequently stylized as the Colored National Labor Union to distinguish it from the white-led entity.
20. Colored National Labor Convention, *Proceedings of the Colored National Convention Held in Washington D.C. on December 6th, 7th, 8th, 9th, and 10th, 1869* (Office of The New Era, Washington, DC, 1870), 34.
21. Colored National Labor Convention, *Proceedings of the Colored National Convention*, 37–40.
22. Colored National Labor Convention, 44.
23. Colored National Labor Convention, 45.
24. Colored National Labor Convention, 45.
25. Colored National Labor Convention, 44.
26. On the republicanism of Myers, Douglass, and the National Colored Labor Union, see Benjamin T. Lynerd, "Republican Ideology and the Black Labor Movement, 1869–1872," *Phylon* 56, no. 2 (2019): 19–36 and "Emancipation, the *Ager Publicus*, and Black Political Thought," *American Political Thought: A Journal of Ideas, Institutions, and Culture* 12, no. 1 (2023): 28–53. On republicanism as a pro-labor ideology, see Alex Gourevich, *From Slavery to*

Cooperative Commonwealth: Labor and Republican Liberty in the Nineteenth Century (Cambridge University Press, 2015).

27. Joyce Appleby, *Liberalism and Republicanism in the Historical Imagination* (Harvard University Press, 1992); Michael Hardt, "Jefferson and Democracy," *American Quarterly* 59, no. 1 (2007): 41–78, https://doi.org/10.1353/aq.2007.0026.

28. Gordon S. Wood, *The Radicalism of the American Revolution*, First Vintage Books edition (Vintage Books, 1993); Sean Wilentz, *Chants Democratic: New York City and the Rise of the American Working Class, 1788–1850*, 20th anniversary ed. (Oxford University Press, 2004).

29. Amy Dru Stanley, *From Bondage to Contract: Wage Labor, Marriage, and the Market in the Age of Slave Emancipation* (Cambridge University Press, 2010); Eric Foner, *Free Soil, Free Labor, Free Men: The Ideology of the Republican Party Before the Civil War, With a New Introductory Essay* (Oxford University Press, 1995).

30. Lynerd, "Republican Ideology"; Eric Foner, *Nothing but Freedom: Emancipation and Its Legacy* (Louisiana State University Press, 1983).

31. Colored National Labor Convention, *Proceedings of the Colored National Convention*, 3.

32. Colored National Labor Convention, 20.

33. Cultivating Black connections to the land was a central component of Shadd Cary's thought. See Eunice Toh, "Mary Ann Shadd Cary's Black Soil Ecology," in Kristin Moriah, ed., *Insensible Boundaries: Studies in Mary Ann Shadd Cary* (University of Pennsylvania Press, 2025), 77–93. While much of Shadd Cary's work after the Civil War focused on education and women's suffrage, she saw these pursuits as tied to the Black labor struggle. See her articles "Letters to the People—No. 1 Trade for Our Boys!," *New National Era*, March 21, 1872, and "Letters to the People—No. 2 Trade for Our Boys!," *New National Era*, April 11, 1872, both cited in Nneka D. Dennie, ed., *Mary Ann Shadd Cary: Essential Writings of a Nineteenth-Century Black Radical Feminist* (Oxford University Press, 2024).

34. Colored National Labor Convention, *Proceedings of the Colored National Convention.*, 22.

35. Colored National Labor Convention, 22.

36. Colored National Labor Convention, 24.

37. Colored National Labor Convention, 26. Caitlin Rosenthal makes a similar argument about emancipation as a form of property regulation in "Abolition

as Market Regulation," *Boston Review*, February 1, 2017. See also Caitlin Rosenthal, *Accounting for Slavery: Masters and Management* (Harvard University Press, 2018), 191.
38. Colored National Labor Convention, *Proceedings of the Colored National Convention*, 24.
39. Details on the 1871 convention are drawn from "National Labor Union," *New National Era*, January 19, 1871.
40. Quoted in James M. McPherson, "Grant or Greeley? The Abolitionist Dilemma in the Election of 1872," *American Historical Review* 71, no. 1 (1965): 50.
41. "The Labor Question," *New National Era*, October 12, 1871.
42. "The Workingman's Party," *New National Era*, September 5, 1870.
43. "Vital Truths for Workingmen," *New National Era*, March 14, 1872. Italics original.
44. "The Labor Question," *New National Era*, October 12, 1871.
45. "Vital Truths for Workingmen," *New National Era*.
46. David W. Blight, *Frederick Douglass: Prophet of Freedom* (Simon and Schuster, 2018), chap. 24. Although the annexation plan was part of the acceleration of U.S. imperial expansion in the late nineteenth century, for abolitionists, the question of annexation was not so straightforward. Santo Domingo had just six years earlier won a second war of independence after being recolonized by Spain, and incorporation into the United States under conditions of political, legal, and racial equality seemed to be an extension of Radical Reconstruction to many abolitionists, including Douglass. Nicholas Guyatt, "America's Conservatory: Race, Reconstruction, and the Santo Domingo Debate," *Journal of American History* 97, no. 4 (2011): 974–1000.
47. "Santo Domingo—No. 8," *New National Era*, June 15, 1871.
48. Beginning in the mid-nineteenth century, tens of thousands of Indian and Chinese indentured laborers migrated to Jamaica and worked under coercive and violent conditions. See Walton Look Lai, *Indentured Labor, Caribbean Sugar: Chinese and Indian Migrants to the British West Indies, 1838–1918* (Johns Hopkins University Press, 1993). Moon-Ho Jung has argued that the term *coolie* does not describe any singular labor system or type of laborer, but instead functioned as a "conglomeration of racial imaginings" that embodied the continuum between slavery and freedom: "encompassing and embodying the contradictory imperial imperatives of enslavement and

emancipation, the 'coolie question' compels us to explore the messy ways that racial capitalism and liberal nation-states expanded and operated hand in hand to advance and elide empire." Moon-Ho Jung, "What Is the Coolie Question?," *Labour History* 113 (2017): 3.

49. "The Coolie Trade," *New National Era*, August 10, 1871.
50. "Cheap Labor," *New National Era*, August 17, 1871.
51. "Can the Proud Anglo-Saxon Be Enslaved?," *New National Era*, April 3, 1873.
52. "Can the Proud Anglo-Saxon Be Enslaved?," *New National Era*.
53. "Dangerous Power of Railroad Monopolies," *New National Era*," April 3, 1873.
54. Richard White, *Railroaded: The Transcontinentals and the Making of Modern America* (Norton, 2011), chapter 2. The Panic of 1873 had dire political consequences for Republicans, and contributed to the abandonment of Reconstruction. See Nicolas Barreyre, "The Politics of Economic Crises: The Panic of 1873, the End of Reconstruction, and the Realignment of American Politics," *Journal of the Gilded Age and Progressive Era* 10, no. 4 (2011): 403–23.
55. "An Inconsistent Demagogue," *New National Era*, October 16, 1873.
56. Harris L. Dante, "The *Chicago Tribune*'s Lost Years, 1865–1874," *Journal of the Illinois State Historical Society* 58, no. 2 (1965): 139–64.
57. "Inconsistent Demagogue," *New National Era*. Douglass also warns about the deleterious effect the Liberal Republican Party would have on both labor and capital, in "Workingmen Betrayed in the House of Their Friends," *New National Era*, March 7, 1872, and "A Warning to Business Men!," *New National Era*, August 15, 1872.
58. "An Example Worth Imitating," *New National Era*, October 16, 1873.
59. Douglass's views on strikes were out of step with those of ordinary Black workers. In 1877, the effects of the Panic of 1873 led to the first nationwide strike, led by railroad workers. Black participation was widespread, alongside white labor in some locations and in autonomous actions in others. Although exclusion from white labor organizations and economic necessity meant that there were also a large number of Black strikebreakers, their actions were not motivated by any ideological opposition to striking or unions. See Shannon M. Smith, "'They Met Force with Force': African American Protests and Social Status in Louisville's 1877 Strike," *Register of the Kentucky Historical Society* 115, no .1 (2017): 1–37; and David Roediger,

"'Not Only the Ruling Classes to Overcome, but Also the So-Called Mob': Class, Skill and Community in the St. Louis General Strike of 1877," *Journal of Social History* 19.2 (1985): 213–39.
60. Philip M. Katz, *From Appomattox to Montmartre: Americans and the Paris Commune* (Harvard University Press, 1998); August H. Nimtz and Kyle A. Edwards, *The Communist and the Revolutionary Liberal in the Second American Revolution: Comparing Karl Marx and Frederick Douglass in Real-Time* (Brill, 2024).
61. "Adulterated Republicanism," *New National Era*, April 6, 1871.
62. "Tyranny Among Laborers," *New National Era*, April 20, 1871.
63. "The Coming Man," *New National Era*, June 22, 1871.
64. "Wisdom in the Counsels of Washington," *New National Era*, June 15, 1871.
65. "Letter from Philadelphia," *New National Era*, October 19, 1871.
66. "Colored Communism," *New National Era*, September 25, 1873; "Co-Operation Among the Colored People," *New National Era*, December 4, 1873.
67. "The Folly, Tyranny, and Wickedness of Labor Unions," *New National Era*, May 7, 1874.
68. "From Alabama," *New National Era*, May 28, 1874.
69. "Labor Union," *New National Era*, May 28, 1874.
70. "Southern Manufactures," *New National Era*, June 22, 1871.
71. Douglass argued that protection was the reason for the economic development he observed in the South, in "Results of Protection at the South," *New National Era*, November 30, 1871.
72. "More Enmity to Workingmen," *New National Era*, December 28, 1871. Douglass broadly outlines his opposition to free trade in "A High Tariff a Necessity," *New National Era*, January 5, 1871; "A Home Market," *New National Era*, November 16, 1871; and "The Real Enemies of the Workingman," *New National Era*, November 23, 1871.
73. "Benefits of Protection to Home Industry," *New National Era*, April 3, 1873.
74. "Southern Manufactures," *New National Era*, June 22, 1871.
75. "Labor in Iron-Manufactories and Workingmen," *New National Era*, December 28, 1871.
76. On this violence, see, for example, Kidada E. Williams, *I Saw Death Coming: A History of Terror and Survival in the War Against Reconstruction* (Bloomsbury, 2023); Steven Hahn, *A Nation Under Our Feet: Black Political Struggles in the Rural South from Slavery to the Great Migration* (Belknap Press, 2003); Hannah Rosen, *Terror in the Heart of Freedom: Citizenship,*

Sexual Violence, and the Meaning of Race in the Postemancipation South (University of North Carolina Press, 2009); Carole Emberton, *Beyond Redemption: Race, Violence, and the American South after the Civil War* (University of Chicago Press, 2013); and Michael W. Fitzgerald, *Splendid Failure: Postwar Reconstruction in the American South* (Ivan R. Dee, 2007).

77. Du Bois famously wrote, "It must be remembered that the white group of laborers, while they received a low wage, were compensated in part by a sort of public and psychological wage"; W. E. B. Du Bois, *Black Reconstruction in America, 1860–1880*, intro. David Levering Lewis (Free Press, 1992). See also Ella Myers, *The Gratifications of Whiteness: W. E. B. Du Bois and the Enduring Rewards of Anti-Blackness* (Oxford University Press, 2022).

78. "A Lesson to Be Taught," *New National Era*, September 10, 1874.

79. Frederick Douglass, "The Color Line," *The North American Review*, June 1881, in Philp Sheldon Foner, *The Life and Writings of Frederick Douglass*, vol. 4: *Reconstruction and After* (International Publishers, 1955), 344.

80. Frederick Douglass, *Three Addresses on the Relations Subsisting Between the White and Colored People of the United States* (Washington: Gibson Bros., Printers and Bookbinders, 1886).

81. Foner, *Life and Writings of Frederick Douglass*, vol. 4, 378.

82. Foner, 384.

83. Frederick Douglass, *Frederick Douglass: Selected Speeches and Writings*, ed. Philip S. Foner and Yuval Taylor (Chicago Review Press, 2000), 677.

84. Foner, *Life and Writings of Frederick Douglass*, vol. 4, 383.

85. Khalil Gibran Muhammad, *The Condemnation of Blackness: Race, Crime, and the Making of Modern Urban America, with a New Preface*, 2nd ed. (Harvard University Press, 2019), https://doi.org/10.4159/9780674240919.

86. Foner, *Life and Writings of Frederick Douglass*, vol. 4, 385.

87. Foner, 383.

88. Contrast to Douglass's earlier speeches celebrating the occasion, such as Frederick Douglass, "First Congregational Church," Delivered in the Congregational Church on the Twenty-First Anniversary of Emancipation, Washington, DC, Daniel Murray Pamphlet Collection, April 16, 1883, www.loc.gov/item/90898291/.

89. Frederick Douglass, "Southern Barbarism," in *Frederick Douglass: Selected Speeches and Writings*, 696.

90. Douglass, *Frederick Douglass: Selected Speeches and Writings*, 700.

91. Foner, *Life and Writings of Frederick Douglass*, vol. 4, 436.

92. Foner, 436.
93. Douglass, *Frederick Douglass: Selected Speeches and Writings*, 699.
94. "The Freedmen Rejoice Over Their Release from the Bonds of Slavery," *National Republican*, April 17, 1888, includes the full text of Douglass' address.
95. Philp Sheldon Foner, ed., *The Voice of Black America: Major Speeches by Negroes in the United States, 1797–1971* (Simon and Schuster, 1972), 529.
96. Foner, *Voice of Black America*, 526.
97. Foner, *Life and Writings of Frederick Douglass*, vol. 4, 109.

4. ABOLITIONISM IS ANOTHER TERM FOR COMMUNISM: ABOLITION DEMOCRACY AGAINST RACIAL CAPITALISM

1. "Who Is the Parasite?," *New York Globe*, February 16, 1884.
2. For biographical information, I draw from T. Thomas Fortune, *After War Times: An African American Childhood in Reconstruction-Era Florida*, ed. Daniel R. Weinfeld (University of Alabama Press, 2014); *T. Thomas Fortune, the Afro-American Agitator: A Collection of Writings, 1880–1928*, ed., Shawn Leigh Alexander. (University Press of Florida, 2008); and, *Black and White: Land, Labor, and Politics in the South*, introduction by Seth Moglen (Washington Square Press, 2007); as well as from Emma Lou Thornbrough, *T. Thomas Fortune: Militant Journalist* (University of Chicago Press, 1972).
3. Douglass's estimation of his own work appears in his introduction to Wells's first anti-lynching pamphlet; Wells, "Southern Horrors: Lynch Law in All Its Phases," in Ida B. Wells, *The Light of Truth*, ed. Mia Bay (Penguin, 2014), 59. For biographical information, I draw from Ida B. Wells, *Crusade for Justice: The Autobiography of Ida B. Wells*, ed. Alfreda Duster (University of Chicago Press, 1970); Mia Bay, *To Tell the Truth Freely: The Life of Ida B. Wells* (Hill and Wang, 2009); and Paula J. Giddings, *Ida: A Sword Among Lions: Ida B. Wells and the Campaign Against Lynching* (Amistad, 2008).
4. "Mr. Fortune on the West: Glances at Indianapolis and Chicago," *New York Age*, August 11, 1888.
5. "Exiled," *New York Age*, June 25, 1892.
6. "Communism in the United States," *New York Globe*, May 5, 1883.
7. Fortune inaugurated an intellectual project that scholars have only recently begun to fully develop. See, for example, Gary Helm Darden, "The New

Empire in the 'New South': Jim Crow in the Global Frontier of High Imperialism and Decolonization," *Southern Quarterly* 46, no. 3 (2009): 8–25; Zach Sell, *Trouble of the World: Slavery and Empire in the Age of Capital* (University of North Carolina Press, 2020); Roberto Saba, *American Mirror: The United States and Brazil in the Age of Emancipation* (Princeton University Press, 2021); and Rudi Batzell, *Organizing Workers in the Shadow of Slavery* (University of Chicago Press, 2025).

8. Fortune, *Black and White*, 59.
9. Philip S. Foner, *The Life and Writings of Frederick Douglass*, vol. 4: *Reconstruction and After* (International Publishers, 1955), 378.
10. Fortune, *Black and White*, 14.
11. Fortune, 18.
12. Fortune, 20.
13. Frederick Douglass, "My Bondage and My Freedom," in *Frederick Douglass's Autobiographies*, ed. Henry Louis Gates Jr. (Library of America, 1994), 330.
14. Fortune, *Black and White*, 23.
15. Fortune, 108.
16. Fortune, 93.
17. Chad E. Pearson, *Capital's Terrorists: Klansmen, Lawmen, and Employers in the Long Nineteenth Century* (University of North Carolina Press, 2022).
18. Fortune, *Black and White*, 108.
19. "Communism in the United States," *New York Globe*.
20. Fortune, *Black and White*, 86.
21. Fortune vastly underestimated the noneconomic motivations for Southern whites to invest in white supremacy. On these motivations, see Ella Myers, *The Gratifications of Whiteness: W.E.B. Du Bois and the Enduring Rewards of Anti-Blackness* (Oxford University Press, 2022). Fortune's bleak (and incorrect) assessment of Reconstruction policy came from the Republican refusal to consider land redistribution and economic rights for freedpeople.
22. Fortune, *Black and White*, 112.
23. Fortune, 112 and 110.
24. Fortune, 135.
25. Fortune, 148.
26. W. E. B. Du Bois, *Black Reconstruction in America, 1860–1880* (Free Press, 1992), 16.
27. Fortune, *Black and White*, 150.

28. Fortune, 153.
29. "The Question of the Hour," *New York Freeman*, May 1, 1886.
30. All quotations reprinted in "The Knights of Labor," *New York Freeman*, October 16, 1886.
31. For a general treatment, see Robert E. Weir, *Beyond Labor's Veil: The Culture of the Knights of Labor* (Penn State University Press, 1993). On the efforts of the Knights of Labor in the South, see Matthew Hild, *Greenbackers, Knights of Labor, and Populists: Farmer-Labor Insurgency in the Late-Nineteenth-Century South* (University of Georgia Press, 2007).
32. "Grievances in Kentucky," *New York Freeman*, March 20, 1886.
33. "Colored Knights of Labor in Arkansas," *New York Freeman*, July 17, 1886.
34. "Colorphobia in Labor Organizations," *New York Globe*, January 26, 1884.
35. "Labor Upheavals," *New York Freeman*, March 20, 1886.
36. "Pernicious Labor Teachings," *New York Freeman*, May 1, 1886.
37. "Pernicious Labor Teachings," *New York Freeman*.
38. "Does the Colored Laborer in the South Receive Less Wages," *New York Freeman*, October 2, 1886.
39. "A Case in Point," *New York Freeman*, May 22, 1886.
40. "Colored Men, Reflect," *New York Freeman*, December 4, 1886.
41. "White and Colored Laborers Detrimental," *New York Freeman*, December 4, 1886. Fortune referred to the Baugman Boycott in Richmond. See Joseph Carvalho III, "The Baughman Boycott and Its Effect on the Richmond, Virginia Labour Movement, 1886–1888," *Social History* 24 (1979): 409–17.
42. Richard White, *Railroaded: The Transcontinentals and the Making of Modern America* (Norton, 2011).
43. [Untitled], *New York Freeman*, April 3, 1886; "Failure of Labor," *New York Freeman*, April 10, 1886.
44. Claudia Miner, "The 1886 Convention of the Knights of Labor," *Phylon* 44, no .2 (1983): 151.
45. Miner, "1886 Convention," 154.
46. Miner, 156.
47. "The Knights of Labor Show the White Feather," *New York Freeman*, October 23, 1886.
48. John DeSantis, *The Thibodaux Massacre: Racial Violence and the 1887 Sugar Cane Labor Strike* (History Press), 2016.
49. "Outrages in Louisiana," *New York Age*, December 3, 1887.

50. Joseph Gerteis, *Class and the Color Line: Interracial Class Coalition in the Knights of Labor and the Populist Movement* (Duke University Press, 2007), 8–9.
51. "Socialistic Riot in England," *New York Freeman*, February 13, 1886.
52. "Socialistic Literature," *New York Freeman*, February 14, 1885.
53. "Chinamen and Anarchists," *New York Freeman*, May 15, 1886. On labor's support for Chinese exclusion, see Alexander Saxton, *The Indispensable Enemy: Labor and the Anti-Chinese Movement in California* (University of California Press, 1971); and Moon-Ho Jung, *Coolies and Cane: Race, Labor, and Sugar in the Age of Emancipation* (Johns Hopkins University Press, 2006).
54. Dino Cinel, "Italians in the South: The Alabama Case," *Italian Americana* 9, no. 1 (1990): 7–24; Vincenza Scarpaci, "Walking the Color Line: Italian Immigrants in Rural Louisiana, 1880–1910," in *Are Italians White? How Race Is Made in America*, ed. Jennifer Guglielmo and Salvatore Salerno (Routledge, 2003); and Charles Seguin and Sabrina Nardin, "The Lynching of Italians and the Rise of Antilynching Politics in the United States," *Social Science History* 46, no. 1 (2022): 65–91, https://doi.org/10.1017/ssh.2021.43.
55. "Italian Slaves in the South," *New York Age*, April 4, 1891.
56. "Will They Supplant Us as Laborers," *New York Age*, January 31, 1891.
57. "Stick to the Race" and "Freedom of Political Action," in Wells, *Light of Truth*.
58. "Functions of Leadership," in Wells, *Light of Truth*, 7.
59. "The Model Woman," in Wells, *Light of Truth*, 25.
60. "The Jim Crow Car," in Wells, *Light of Truth*, 31–32.
61. Wells, *Crusade for Justice*, 47–52; Lisa A. White, "The Curve Lynchings: Violence, Politics, Economics, and Race Rhetoric in 1890s Memphis," *Tennessee Historical Quarterly* 64, no. 1 (2005): 43–61.
62. Wells, "Southern Horrors," 58.
63. Michael J. Pfeifer, *Rough Justice: Lynching and American Society, 1874–1947* (University of Illinois Press, 2006).
64. Edward L. Ayers, *Vengeance and Justice: Crime and Punishment in the Nineteenth-Century American South* (Oxford University Press, 1984).
65. On Barrett's business practices, see Giddings, *Ida*.
66. During Reconstruction, the most common justification for lynching and other forms of vigilante violence was to combat Black political participation,

which whites outside of the Republican Party considered illegitimate. The collapse of Reconstruction left Black political power vastly diminished; this was the moment when the justification for lynching shifted from political repression to retribution for sexual violence. See also Martha Hodes, "The Sexualization of Reconstruction Politics," *Journal of the History of Sexuality* 3, no. 3 (1993): 402–17; and Crystal N. Feimster, *Southern Horrors: Women and the Politics of Rape and Lynching in the South* (Harvard University Press, 2009).

67. "Exiled," *New York Age*, June 25, 1892.
68. Wells, "Southern Horrors," 61.
69. Wells, 61.
70. Wells, 61.
71. Wells, 71.
72. Wells, 79. Wells overexaggerated the role of the Curve lynchings in prompting the Memphis streetcar boycott. While the lynchings intensified the boycott, it had been ongoing since early in the year to protest newly passed segregation laws in Tennessee.
73. Blair L. M. Kelley, *Right to Ride: Streetcar Boycotts and African American Citizenship in the Era of Plessy v. Ferguson* (University of North Carolina Press, 2010).
74. The estimate might have been exaggerated but is plausible. In 1890, Black people made up just under 15 percent of Kentucky's population. Kentucky railroads' net revenue in 1892 was approximately $6.4 million; see *Thirteenth Report of the Railroad Commissioners of Kentucky, for the Year 1892* (Frankfort, KY: Capital Office: E. Polk Johnson, Public Printer and Binder, 1892), 25.
75. Wells, "Southern Horrors," 79.
76. "Iola's Southern Field," *New York Age*, November 19, 1892.
77. "The Requirements of Southern Journalism," in Wells, *Light of Truth*, 91.
78. Ida B. Wells, Frederick Douglass, Irvine Garland Penn, and Ferdinand L. Barnett, *The Reason Why the Colored American Is Not in the World's Columbian Exposition: The Afro-American's Contribution to Columbian Literature*, ed. Robert W. Rydell (University of Illinois Press, 1999).
79. This purchase would likely have taken place in the early 1880s.
80. Wells, "A Red Record," in *Light of Truth*, 237.
81. Wells, 238.
82. *Money and Prices in Foreign Countries, Being a Series of Reports upon the Currency Systems of Various Nations in Their Relation to Prices of Commodities and*

Wages of Labor: Volume XIII—Part I (Government Printing Office, 1896), 262.
83. Wells, "Red Record," in *Light of Truth*, 248–49.

EPILOGUE: UNENDING HISTORIES

1. Kris Manjapra, *Black Ghost of Empire: The Long Death of Slavery and the Failure of Emancipation* (Scribner, 2022), 4–5, 9. On the end of slavery as the revitalization of a new extractive, racialized imperial world order, see Zach Sell, *Trouble in the World: Slavery and Empire in the Age of Capital* (University of North Carolina Press, 2021); Richard Huzzey, *Freedom Burning: Anti-Slavery and Empire in Victorian Britain* (Cornell University Press, 2012); and Padraic X. Scanlan, *Slave Empire: How Slavery Built Modern Britain* (Robinson, 2022).
2. Kellie Carter Jackson, "Introduction," part 2, in *Ideas in Unexpected Places: Reimagining Black Intellectual History*, ed. Brandon R. Byrd, Leslie M. Alexander, and Russell Rickford (Northwestern University Press, 2022), 62.
3. W. E. B. Du Bois, *Black Reconstruction in America, 1860–1880* (Free Press, 1992), 632.
4. W. E. B. Du Bois, "The African Roots of War (1915)," in *W.E.B. Du Bois: International Thought* ed. Adom Getachew and Jennifer Pitts (Cambridge University Press, 2022), 27.
5. Du Bois, "African Roots of War," 32, 34.
6. Du Bois, "African Roots of War," 34–35.

BIBLIOGRAPHY

Address to the Non-Slaveholders of the South: On the Social and Political Evils of Slavery. New York: S.W. Benedict, 1843.
Alridge, Derrick P., Cornelius L. Bynum, and James B. Stewart, eds. *The Black Intellectual Tradition: African American Thought in the Twentieth Century*. University of Illinois Press, 2021. www.jstor.org/stable/10.5406/j.ctv1vo9oqz.
Apess, William. *Eulogy on King Philip, as Pronounced at the Odeon, in Federal Street, Boston, by the Rev. William Apes, an Indian*. Boston, 1836.
———. *The Experiences of Five Christian Indians of the Pequod Tribe*. Boston: James B. Dow, 1833.
———. *Indian Nullification of the Unconstitutional Laws of Massachusetts, Relative to the Marshpee Tribe: Or, the Pretended Riot Explained*. Boston: Jonathan Howe, 1835.
———. *A Son of the Forest*. Boston: James B. Dow, 1833.
Appel, Hannah. *The Licit Life of Capitalism: US Oil in Equatorial Guinea*. Duke University Press, 2019.
Appleby, Joyce. *Liberalism and Republicanism in the Historical Imagination*. Harvard University Press, 1992.
Aptheker, Herbert. "Du Bois on Douglass: 1895." *Journal of Negro History* 49, no. 4 (1964): 264–68.
———, ed. *One Continual Cry: David Walker's Appeal to the Colored Citizens of the World (1829–1830), Its Setting & Its Meaning*. Humanities Press, 1965.
Archer, Richard. *Jim Crow North: The Struggle for Equal Rights in Antebellum New England*. Oxford University Press, 2017.
Asaka, Ikuko. *Tropical Freedom: Climate, Settler Colonialism, and Black Exclusion in the Age of Emancipation*. Duke University Press, 2017.

Ayers, Edward L. *Vengeance and Justice: Crime and Punishment in the Nineteenth-Century American South*. Oxford University Press, 1984.

Baptist, Edward E. *The Half Has Never Been Told: Slavery and the Making of American Capitalism*. Basic Books, 2014.

Barreyre, Nicholas. "The Politics of Economic Crises: The Panic of 1873, the End of Reconstruction, and the Realignment of American Politics." *Journal of the Gilded Age and Progressive Era* 10, no. 4 (2011): 403–23.

Batzell, Rudi. *Organizing Workers in the Shadow of Slavery: Global Inequality, Racial Boundaries, and the Rise of Unions in American and British Capitalism, 1870–1929*. University of Chicago Press, 2025.

Baucom, Ian. *Specters of the Atlantic: Finance Capital, Slavery, and the Philosophy of History*. Duke University Press, 2005. https://doi.org/10.1515/9780822387022.

Bay, Mia. *To Tell the Truth Freely: The Life of Ida B. Wells*. Hill and Wang, 2009.

Bay, Mia, and Farah Jasmine Griffin, eds. *Toward an Intellectual History of Black Women*. University of North Carolina Press, 2015.

Beckert, Sven. *Empire of Cotton: A Global History*. Knopf Doubleday, 2014.

Beckert, Sven, and Seth Rockman, eds. *Slavery's Capitalism: A New History of American Economic Development*. University of Pennsylvania Press, 2016.

Behnken, Brian D., Gregory D. Smithers, and Simon Wendt, eds. *Black Intellectual Thought in Modern America: A Historical Perspective*. University Press of Mississippi, 2017. https://doi.org/10.2307/j.ctv5jxnoq.

Bender, Thomas, ed. *The Antislavery Debate: Capitalism and Abolitionism as a Problem in Historical Interpretation*. University of California Press, 1992.

Bernstein, Samuel. "American Labor and the Paris Commune." *Science and Society* (New York, 1936) 15, no. 2 (1951): 144–62.

———. "The Impact of the Paris Commune in the United States." *Massachusetts Review* 12, no. 3 (1971): 435–46.

Berry, Daina Ramey. *The Price for Their Pound of Flesh: The Value of the Enslaved from Womb to Grave in the Building of a Nation*. Beacon Press, 2017.

Bhandar, Brenna. *Colonial Lives of Property: Law, Land, and Racial Regimes of Ownership*. Duke University Press, 2018.

Blackett, R. J. M. *Building an Antislavery Wall: Black Americans in the Atlantic Abolitionist Movement, 1830–1860*. Louisiana State University Press, 1983.

Blackmon, Douglas A. *Slavery by Another Name: The Re-Enslavement of Black People in America from the Civil War to World War II*. Doubleday, 2008.

Blain, Keisha N., Christopher Cameron, and Ashley D. Farmer, eds. *New Perspectives on the Black Intellectual Tradition*. Northwestern University Press, 2018. www.jstor.org/stable/j.ctv7tq4rv.

Blight, David W. *Frederick Douglass: Prophet of Freedom*. Simon and Schuster, 2018.

Blight, David W, and Jim Downs. *Beyond Freedom: Disrupting the History of Emancipation*. University of Georgia Press, 2017.

Boyd, Kendra D. *Freedom Enterprise: Black Entrepreneurship and Racial Capitalism in Detroit*. University of North Carolina Press, 2025.

Brooten, Bernadette J., and Jacqueline L Hazelton. *Beyond Slavery: Overcoming Its Religious and Sexual Legacies*. Palgrave Macmillan, 2010.

Brown, Vincent. *Tacky's Revolt: The Story of an Atlantic Slave War*. Harvard University Press, 2022.

Burin, Eric. *Slavery and the Peculiar Solution: A History of the American Colonization Society*. University Press of Florida, 2005.

Byler, Darren. *Terror Capitalism: Uyghur Dispossession and Masculinity in a Chinese City*. Duke University Press, 2021. https://doi.org/10.2307/j.ctv21zp29g.

Byrd, Brandon R. "The Rise of African American Intellectual History." *Modern Intellectual History* 18 (2021): 833–64.

Byrd, Brandon R., Leslie M. Alexander, and Russell Rickford, eds. *Ideas in Unexpected Places: Reimagining Black Intellectual History*. Northwestern University Press, 2022. https://doi.org/10.2307/j.ctv2ckjpp9.

Byrd, Jodi, Alyosha Goldstein, Jodi Melamed, and Chandan Reddy, eds. "Economies of Dispossession: Indigeneity, Race, Capitalism." Special issue, *Social Text* 36, no. 2 (2018).

Camp, Jordan T. *Incarcerating the Crisis: Freedom Struggles and the Rise of the Neoliberal State*. University of California Press, 2016.

Carvalho, Joseph, III. "The Baughman Boycott and Its Effect on the Richmond, Virginia Labour Movement, 1886–1888." *Social History* 24 (1979): 409–17.

Cinel, Dino. "Italians in the South: The Alabama Case." *Italian Americana* 9, no. 1 (1990): 7–24.

Clarno, Andy. *Neoliberal Apartheid: Palestine/Israel and South Africa After 1994*. University of Chicago Press, 2017.

Colored National Labor Convention. *Proceedings of the Colored National Convention Held in Washington D.C. on December 6th, 7th, 8th, 9th, and 10th, 1869*. Office of the New Era, Washington, DC, 1870.

Connolly, Emilie. "Fiduciary Colonialism: Annuities and Native Dispossession in the Early United States." *American Historical Review* 127, no. 1 (2022): 223–53, https://doi.org/10.1093/ahr/rhac012.

Connolly, Nathan D. B. *A World More Concrete: Real Estate and the Remaking of Jim Crow South Florida*. University of Chicago Press, 2014.

Cowie, Jefferson. *Freedom's Dominion: A Saga of White Resistance to Federal Power*. Basic Books, 2022.

Cramer, Clayton E. *Black Demographic Data, 1790–1860: A Sourcebook*. Greenwood Press, 1997.

Crawford, Nicholas. "Sustenance and Power: Provision Grounds and Plantation Enterprise in Eighteenth- and Nineteenth-Century Jamaican Slavery." *Journal of Caribbean History* 57, no .2 (2023): 25–54.

Cronin, James E. "Strikes and Power in Britain, 1870–1920." *International Review of Social History* 32, no. 2 (1987): 144–67.

Curtin, Philip. "The British Sugar Duties and West Indian Prosperity." *Journal of Economic History* 14, no. 2 (1954): 157–64.

Cury, Leonard. *The Free Black in Urban America, 1800–1850: The Shadow of the Dream*. University of Chicago Press, 1981.

Dain, Bruce. *A Hideous Monster of the Mind: American Race Theory in the Early Republic*. Harvard University Press, 2003.

Dante, Harris L. "The *Chicago Tribune*'s Lost Years, 1865–1874." *Journal of the Illinois State Historical Society* 58, no. 2 (1965): 139–64.

Darden, Gary Helm. "The New Empire in the 'New South': Jim Crow in the Global Frontier of High Imperialism and Decolonization." *Southern Quarterly* 46, no. 3 (2009): 8–25.

Davis, Angela. *Abolition Democracy: Beyond Empire, Prisons, and Torture*. Seven Stories Press, 2005.

Davis, David Brion. "Free at Last; The Enduring Legacy of the South's Civil War Victory." *New York Times*, August 26, 2001.

Davis, Muriam Haleh. *Markets of Civilization: Islam and Racial Capitalism in Algeria*. Duke University Press, 2022.

Dennie, Nneka D., ed. *Mary Ann Shadd Cary: Essential Writings of a Nineteenth-Century Black Radical Feminist*. Oxford University Press, 2024.

DeSantis, John. *The Thibodaux Massacre: Racial Violence and the 1887 Sugar Cane Labor Strike*. History Press, 2016.

Dinius, Marcy J. *The Textual Effects of David Walker's "Appeal": Print-Based Activism Against Slavery, Racism, and Discrimination, 1829–1851*. University of Pennsylvania Press, 2022.

Douglass, Frederick. *Address by Hon. Frederick Douglass, Delivered in the Metropolitan A.M.E. Church, Washington, D.C., Tuesday, January 9th, on The Lessons of the Hour: in Which He Discusses the Various Aspects of the So-Called, But Miscalled, Negro Problem*. Baltimore: Press of Thomas and Evans, 1894. www.loc.gov/item/12002894/.

———. "First Congregational Church." Delivered in the Congregational Church on the Twenty-First Anniversary of Emancipation, Washington, DC, Daniel Murray Pamphlet Collection, April 16, 1883. Library of Congress (website), accessed October 13, 2025. www.loc.gov/item/90898291/.

———. *My Bondage and My Freedom*. Introduction and notes by David W. Blight. Yale University Press, 2014.

———. *Narrative of the Life of Frederick Douglass: An American Slave*. Cosimo, 2008.

———. *Narrative of the Life of Frederick Douglass: With Selected Speeches*. Dover Publications, 2024.

———. *Selected Writings and Speeches*. Broadview Press, 2023.

———. *Three Addresses on the Relations Subsisting Between the White and Colored People of the United States*. Washington, DC: Gibson Bros., 1886.

Draper, Nicholas. *The Price of Emancipation: Slave-Ownership, Compensation, and British Society at the End of Slavery*. Cambridge University Press, 2010.

Du Bois, W. E. B. (William Edward Burghardt). *Black Reconstruction in America, 1860–1880*. With an introduction by David Levering Lewis. Free Press, 1992.

———. "The Freedmen's Bureau." *Atlantic Monthly* 87 (1901): 354–65.

———. "Niagara Movement Speech." 1905, Teaching American History, accessed November 13, 2024. https://teachingamericanhistory.org/document/niagara-movement-speech/.

Edwards, Justene Hill. *Unfree Markets: The Slaves' Economy and the Rise of Capitalism in South Carolina*. Columbia University Press, 2021.

Egerton, Douglas R. "Slaves to the Marketplace: Economic Liberty and Black Rebelliousness in the Atlantic World." *Journal of the Early Republic* 26, no. 4 (2006): 617–39.

Emberton, Carole. *Beyond Redemption: Race, Violence, and the American South After the Civil War*. University of Chicago Press, 2013.

———. "Unwriting the Freedom Narrative: A Review Essay." *Journal of Southern History* 82, no. 2 (2016): 377–94. https://doi.org/10.1353/soh.2016.0139.

Ernest, John. *A Nation Within a Nation: Organizing African American Communities Before the Civil War*. John R. Dee, 2011.

Feimster, Crystal N. *Southern Horrors: Women and the Politics of Rape and Lynching in the South*. Harvard University Press, 2009.

Fitzgerald, Michael W. *Splendid Failure: Postwar Reconstruction in the American South*. Ivan R. Dee, 2007).

Foner, Eric. *Free Soil, Free Labor, Free Men: The Ideology of the Republican Party Before the Civil War, with a New Introductory Essay*. Oxford University Press, 1995.

——. "The Meaning of Freedom in the Age of Emancipation." *Journal of American History* (Bloomington, Ind.) 81, no. 2 (1994): 435–60. https://doi.org/10.2307/2081167.

——. *Nothing but Freedom: Emancipation and Its Legacy*. Louisiana State University Press, 1983.

——. *Reconstruction: America's Unfinished Revolution*. Updated ed. Harper Perennial, 2014.

Foner, Philp Sheldon. *The Life and Writings of Frederick Douglass*. 5 vols. International Publishers, 1950–1975.

——, ed. *The Voice of Black America: Major Speeches by Negroes in the United States, 1797–1971*. Simon and Schuster, 1972.

Foner, Philip S., and Ronald L. Lewis, eds. *The Black Worker*. Vol. 1: *The Black Worker to 1896*. Temple University Press, 1978. https://doi.org/10.2307/j.ctvn1tbr6.

Foner, Philip S., and Yuval Taylor, eds. *Frederick Douglass: Selected Speeches and Writings*. Chicago Review Press, 2000.

Fortune, Thomas T. *After War Times: An African American Childhood in Reconstruction-Era Florida*. Ed. Daniel R. Weinfeld. University of Alabama Press, 2014.

——. *Thomas T. Fortune, the Afro-American Agitator: A Collection of Writings, 1880–1928*. Ed. Shawn Leigh Alexander. University Press of Florida, 2008.

Fortune, Timothy Thomas. *Black and White: Land, Labor, and Politics in the South*. Introduction by Seth Moglen. Washington Square Press, 2007.

Gabriel, Dexter J. *Jubilee's Experiment: The British West Indies and American Abolitionism*. Cambridge University Press, 2023.Gates, Henry Louis, Jr., ed. *Frederick Douglass's Autobiographies*. Library of America, 1994.

Gerteis, Joseph. *Class and the Color Line: Interracial Class Coalition in the Knights of Labor and the Populist Movement*. Duke University Press, 2007.

Getachew, Adom, and Jennifer Pitts, eds. *W. E. B. Du Bois: International Thought*. Cambridge University Press, 2022.

Giddings, Paula J. *Ida: A Sword Among Lions: Ida B. Wells and the Campaign Against Lynching*. Amistad, 2008.

Glotzer, Paige. *How the Suburbs Were Segregated: Developers and the Business of Exclusionary Housing, 1890–1960*. Columbia University Press, 2020.

Gourevich, Alex. *From Slavery to Cooperative Commonwealth: Labor and Republican Liberty in the Nineteenth Century*. Cambridge University Press, 2015.

Griffin, Sean. "A Reformer's Union: Land Reform, Labor, and the Evolution of Antislavery Politics, 1790–1860." PhD diss., City University of New York, 2017.

———. *The Root and the Branch: Working-Class Reform and Antislavery, 1790–1860*. University of Pennsylvania Press, 2024.

Gronningsater, Sarah L. H. *The Rising Generation: Gradual Abolition, Black Legal Culture, and the Making of National Freedom*. University of Pennsylvania Press, 2024. https://doi.org/10.9783/9781512826326.

Guglielmo, Jennifer, and Salvatore Salerno. *Are Italians White? How Race Is Made in America*. Routledge, 2003.

Gura, Philip F. *The Life of William Apess, Pequot*. University of North Carolina Press, 2015.

Guyatt, Nicholas. "America's Conservatory: Race, Reconstruction, and the Santo Domingo Debate." *Journal of American History* 97, no. 4 (2011): 974–1000.

———. *Bind Us Apart: How Enlightened Americans Invented Racial Segregation*. Basic Books, 2016.

———. "'The Outskirts of Our Happiness': Race and the Lure of Colonization in the Early Republic." *Journal of American History* 95, no. 4 (2009): 986–1011.

Hahn, Steven. *A Nation Under Our Feet: Black Political Struggles in the Rural South from Slavery to the Great Migration*. Belknap Press, 2003.

Haley, Sarah. *No Mercy Here: Gender, Punishment, and the Making of Jim Crow Modernity*. University of North Carolina Press, 2016.

Hardesty, Jared. *Unfreedom: Slavery and Dependence in Eighteenth-Century Boston*. New York University Press, 2016.

Hardt, Michael. "Jefferson and Democracy." *American Quarterly* 59, no. 1 (2007): 41–78. https://doi.org/10.1353/aq.2007.0026.

Harris, Cheryl I. "Whiteness as Property," *Harvard Law Review* 106, no. 8 (1993): 1707–91. https://doi.org/10.2307/1341787.

Hartman, Andrew. "W. E. B. Du Bois's 'Black Reconstruction' and the New (Marxist) Historiography." Society for U.S. Intellectual History, November 1, 2017. https://s-usih.org/2017/11/w-e-b-du-boiss-black-reconstruction-and-the-new-marxist-historiography/.

Hartman, Saidiya V. *Lose Your Mother: A Journey Along the Atlantic Slave Route.* Farrar, Straus and Giroux, 2007.

———. *Scenes of Subjection: Terror, Slavery, and Self-Making in Nineteenth Century America.* Oxford University Press, 1997.

Hébert, Keith S. *Cornerstone of the Confederacy: Alexander Stephens and the Speech That Defined the Lost Cause.* University of Tennessee Press, 2021.

Hild, Matthew. *Greenbackers, Knights of Labor, and Populists: Farmer-Labor Insurgency in the Late-Nineteenth-Century South.* University of Georgia Press, 2007.

Hill, Herbert. "The Problem of Race in American Labor History." *Reviews in American History* 24, no. 2 (1996): 189–208.

Hinks, Peter P. *To Awaken My Afflicted Brethren: David Walker and the Problem of Antebellum Slave Resistance.* Pennsylvania State University Press, 1997.

History of Wages in the United States from Colonial Times to 1928. Bulletin of the Bureau of Labor Statistics No. 499. Government Printing Office, 1934.

Hodes, Martha. "The Sexualization of Reconstruction Politics." *Journal of the History of Sexuality* 3, no. 3 (1993): 402–17.

Holt, Thomas C. *The Problem of Freedom: Race, Labor, and Politics in Jamaica and Britain, 1832–1938.* Johns Hopkins University Press, 1992.

Horton, James Oliver, and Lois E. Horton. *In Hope of Liberty: Culture, Community and Protest Among Northern Free Blacks, 1700–1860.* Oxford University Press, 1997.

Huang, Mingwei. *Reconfiguring Racial Capitalism: South Africa in the Chinese Century.* Duke University Press, 2024. https://doi.org/10.1515/9781478059998.

Hudson, Peter James. *Bankers and Empire: How Wall Street Colonized the Caribbean.* University of Chicago Press, 2017.

Huston, James L. "Abolitionists, Political Economists, and Capitalism." *Journal of the Early Republic* 20, no. 3 (2000): 487–521. https://doi.org/10.2307/3125066.

Huston, Reeve. *Land and Freedom: Rural Society, Popular Protest, and Party Politics in* Antebellum. Oxford University Press, 2000.

Huzzey, Richard. *Freedom Burning: Anti-Slavery and Empire in Victorian Britain.* Cornell University Press, 2012.

Jacobs, Donald M. "William Lloyd Garrison's *Liberator* and Boston's Blacks, 1830–1865." *New England Quarterly* 44, no. 2 (1971): 259–77.

Jackson, Kellie Carter. *Force and Freedom: Black Abolitionists and the Politics of Violence*. University of Pennsylvania Press, 2020.

———. *We Refuse: A Forceful History of Black Resistance*. Seal Press, 2024.

Jenkins, Destin. *The Bonds of Inequality: Debt and the Making of the American City*. University of Chicago Press, 2021.

Jenkins, Destin, and Justin Leroy, eds. *Histories of Racial Capitalism*. Columbia University Press, 2021.

Johnson, Walter. *River of Dark Dreams: Slavery and Empire in the Cotton Kingdom*. Harvard University Press, 2013.

———. "To Remake the World: Slavery, Racial Capitalism, and Justice: How the History of Slavery Prompts Us to Rethink Our Notion of Justice." *Boston Review*, February 1, 2017.

Jones, Douglas A., ed. *Maria W. Stewart: Essential Writings of a Nineteenth-Century Black Abolitionist*. Oxford University Press, 2024.

Jones, Jacqueline. *No Right to an Honest Living: The Struggles of Boston's Black Workers in the Civil War Era*. Basic Books, 2023.

Jung, Moon-Ho. *Coolies and Cane: Race, Labor, and Sugar in the Age of Emancipation*. Johns Hopkins University Press, 2006.

———. "What Is the Coolie Question?" *Labour History* 113 (2017): 1–8.

Kantrowitz, Stephen. *More Than Freedom: Fighting for Black Citizenship in a White Republic*. Penguin, 2012.

Karuka, Manu. *Empire's Tracks: Indigenous Nations, Chinese Workers, and the Transcontinental Railroad*. University of California Press, 2019. https://doi.org/10.1525/9780520969056.

Katz, Philip M. *From Appomattox to Montmartre: Americans and the Paris Commune*. Harvard University Press, 1998.

Kazanjian, David. *The Colonizing Trick: National Culture and Imperial Citizenship in Early America*. University of Minnesota Press, 2003.

Kelley, Blair L. M. *Right to Ride: Streetcar Boycotts and African American Citizenship in the Era of Plessy v. Ferguson*. University of North Carolina Press, 2010.

Kenny, Gale L. *Contentious Liberties: American Abolitionists in Post-Emancipation Jamaica, 1834–1866*. University of Georgia Press, 2010.

Kerr-Ritchie, J. R. *Rites of August First: Emancipation Day in the Black Atlantic World*. Louisiana State University Press, 2007.

Koshy, Susan, Lisa Marie Cacho, Jodi A. Byrd, and Brian Jordan Jefferson, eds. *Colonial Racial Capitalism*. Duke University Press, 2022. https://doi.org/10.1515/9781478023371.

Krupa, Christopher. *A Feast of Flowers: Race, Labor, and Postcolonial Capitalism in Ecuador.* University of Pennsylvania Press, 2022.

Kundnani, Arun. *What Is Antiracism? And Why It Means Anticapitalism.* Verso, 2023.

Lai, Walton Look. *Indentured Labor, Caribbean Sugar: Chinese and Indian Migrants to the British West Indies, 1838–1918.* Johns Hopkins University Press, 1993.

Leong, Nancy. "Racial Capitalism." *Harvard Law Review* 126, no. 8 (2013): 2151–26.

Levesque, George A. "Black Crime and Crime Statistics in Antebellum Boston." *Australian Journal of Politics and History* 25, no. 2 (1979): 216–227.

Lewis, Davis Levering. *W. E. B. Du Bois, 1868–1919: Biography of a Race.* Henry Holt, 1993.

Linebaugh, Peter. *The Many-Headed Hydra: Sailors, Slaves, Commoners, and the Hidden History of the Revolutionary Atlantic.* Beacon, 2000.

Litwack, Leon F. *North of Slavery: The Negro in the Free States, 1790–1860.* University of Chicago Press, 1961.

Logan, Rayford W. *Howard University: The First Hundred Years 1867–1967.* New York University Press, 1969.

Lopenzina, Drew. *Through an Indian's Looking-Glass: A Cultural Biography of William Apess, Pequot.* University of Massachusetts Press, 2017.

Lowe, Lisa. *The Intimacies of Four Continents.* Duke University Press, 2015.

Lye, Colleen, and Christopher Nealon. *After Marx: Literature, Theory, and Value in the Twenty-First Century.* Cambridge University Press, 2022.

Lynerd, Benjamin T. "Emancipation, the *Ager Publicus*, and Black Political Thought." *American Political Thought: A Journal of Ideas, Institutions, and Culture* 12, no. 1 (2023): 28–53.

———. "Republican Ideology and the Black Labor Movement, 1869–1872." *Phylon* 56, no. 2 (2019): 19–36.

Lynn, Denise. "Charisse Burden-Stelly. Black Scare/Red Scare: Theorizing Capitalist Racism in the United States." *American Historical Review* 130, no. 1 (2025): 493–94. https://doi.org/10.1093/ahr/rhae626.

Mahoney, Michael. "'The Great Experiment': Explaining the Advent of Indenture to the West Indies." The National Archives blog, January 26, 2021. https://blog.nationalarchives.gov.uk/the-great-experiment-explaining-the-advent-of-indenture-to-the-west-indies/.

Mancini, Matthew J. *One Dies, Get Another: Convict Leasing in the American South, 1866–1928.* University of South Carolina Press, 1996.

Mandell, Daniel R. "Shifting Boundaries of Race and Ethnicity: Indian-Black Intermarriage in Southern New England, 1760–1880." *Journal of American History* 85, no. 2 (1998): 466–501.

———. *Tribe, Race, History: Native Americans in Southern New England, 1780–1880.* Johns Hopkins University Press, 2008.

McKivigan, John R., Julie Husband, and Heather L. Kaufman, eds. *The Speeches of Frederick Douglass: A Critical Edition.* Yale University Press, 2018.

Manjapra, Kris. *Black Ghost of Empire: The Long Death of Slavery and the Failure of Emancipation.* First Scribner hardcover edition. Scribner, 2022.

Martin, Scott, ed. *Cultural Change and the Market Revolution in America, 1789–1860.* Rowman and Littlefield, 2005.

McPherson, James M. "Grant or Greeley? The Abolitionist Dilemma in the Election of 1872." *American Historical Review* 71.1 (1965).

McQuiad, Kim, "William Apes, Pequot: An Indian Reformer in the Jackson Era." *Journal of New England History* 50, no. 4 (1977): 605–25.

Melamed, Jodi. "Racial Capitalism." *Critical Ethnic Studies* 1, no. 1 (2015): 76–85. https://doi.org/10.5749/jcritethnstud.1.1.0076.

Melish, Joanne Pope. *Disowning Slavery: Gradual Emancipation and "Race" in New England, 1780–1860.* Cornell University Press, 1998.

Minar, Claudia Miner. "The 1886 Convention of the Knights of Labor." *Phylon* 44, no. 2 (1983): 147–59.

Money and Prices in Foreign Countries, Being a Series of Reports upon the Currency Systems of Various Nations in Their Relation to Prices of Commodities and Wages of Labor: Volume XIII—Part I. Government Printing Office, 1896.

Morgan, Jennifer. *Reckoning with Slavery: Gender, Kinship, and Capitalism in the Early Black Atlantic.* Duke University Press, 2021.

Moriah, Kristin, ed. *Insensible Boundaries: Studies in Mary Ann Shadd Cary.* University of Pennsylvania Press, 2025.

Muhammad, Khalil Gibran. *The Condemnation of Blackness: Race, Crime, and the Making of Modern Urban America, with a New Preface.* 2nd ed. Harvard University Press, 2019. https://doi.org/10.4159/9780674240919.

Murphy, Sharon Ann. *Banking on Slavery: Financing Southern Expansion in the Antebellum United States* University of Chicago Press, 2023.

Myers, Ella. *The Gratifications of Whiteness: W. E. B. Du Bois and the Enduring Rewards of Anti-Blackness.* Oxford University Press, 2022.

Laws of the African Society, Instituted at Boston, Anno Domini 1796. Boston: Printed for the Society, 1796.

Newell, Margaret Ellen. *Brethren by Nature: New England Indians, Colonists, and the Origins of American Slavery*. Cornell University Press, 2015.

Nicholas, Mark A. "Mashpee Wampanoags of Cape Cod, the Whalefishery, and Seafaring's Impact on Community Development." *American Indian Quarterly* 26 no. 2 (2002): 165–97.

Nielsen, Donald M. "The Mashpee Indian Revolt of 1833." *New England Quarterly* 58, no. 3 (1985): 400–20. https://doi.org/10.2307/365039.

Nimtz, August H., and Kyle A. Edwards. *The Communist and the Revolutionary Liberal in the Second American Revolution: Comparing Karl Marx and Frederick Douglass in Real-Time*. Brill, 2024.

O'Brien, Jean M. *Dispossession by Degrees: Indian Land and Identity in Natick, Massachusetts, 1650–1790*. Cambridge University Press, 1997.

———. *Firsting and Lasting: Writing Indians Out of Existence in New England*. University of Minnesota Press, 2010.

O'Connell, Barry ed. *On Our Own Ground: The Complete Writings of William Apess, a Pequot*. University of Massachusetts Press, 1992.

Olsavsky, Jesse. "The Abolitionist Tradition in the Making of W. E. B. Du Bois's Marxism and Anti-Imperialism." *Socialism and Democracy* 32, no. 3 (2018): 14–35. https://doi.org/10.1080/08854300.2018.1563447.

———. *The Most Absolute Abolition: Runaways, Vigilance Committees, and the Rise of Revolutionary Abolitionism, 1835–1861*. Louisiana State University Press, 2022.

Paton, Diana. *No Bond but the Law: Punishment, Race, and Gender in Jamaican State Formation, 1780–1870*. Duke University Press, 2004.

Peck, Gunther. "Labor Abolition and the Politics of White Victimhood: Rethinking the History of Working-Class Racism." *Journal of the Early Republic* 39, no. 1 (2019): 89–98. https://doi.org/10.1353/jer.2019.0007.

———. *Reinventing Free Labor: Padrones and Immigrant Workers in the North American West, 1880–1930*. Cambridge University Press, 2000.

Penn, Garland I., and Frederick Douglass. *The Afro-American Press and Its Editors*. Springfield, MA: Willey, 1891.

Pfeifer, Michael J. *Rough Justice: Lynching and American Society, 1874–1947*. University of Illinois Press, 2006.

Power-Greene, Ousmane K. *Against Wind and Tide: The African American Struggle Against the Colonization Movement*. New York University Press, 2014.

Rana, Aziz. *The Two Faces of American Freedom*. Harvard University Press, 2010.

Reddy, Chandan. *Freedom with Violence: Race, Sexuality, and the US State*. Duke University Press, 2011.

Reed, Adolph L, and Kenneth W. Warren. *Renewing Black Intellectual History: The Ideological and Material Foundations of African American Thought*. Paradigm Publishers, 2010.

Reidy, Joseph P. *From Slavery to Agrarian Capitalism in the Cotton Plantation South: Central Georgia, 1800–1880*. University of North Carolina Press, 1995.

Rexhepi, Piro. *White Enclosures: Racial Capitalism and Coloniality Along the Balkan Route*. Duke University Press, 2022.

Rice, Alan J., and Martin Crawford. *Liberating Sojourn: Fredrick Douglass and Transatlantic Reform*. University of Georgia Press 1999.

Richardson, Marilyn ed. *Maria W. Stewart, America's First Black Woman Political Writer: Essays and Speeches*. Indiana University Press, 1987.

Ripley, C. Peter, ed. *The Black Abolitionist Papers*. 5 vols. University of North Carolina Press, 1985–1992.

Roberts, Neil. *Freedom as Marronage*. University of Chicago Press, 2015.

Robinson, Cedric. *Black Marxism: The Making of the Black Radical Tradition*. University of North Carolina Press, 2020. First published in 1983.

Rockman, Seth. *Plantation Goods: A Material History of American Slavery*. University of Chicago Press, 2024.

———. *Scraping By: Wage Labor, Slavery, and Survival in Early Baltimore*. Johns Hopkins University Press, 2009.

Roediger, David. "'Not Only the Ruling Classes to Overcome, but Also the So-Called Mob': Class, Skill and Community in the St. Louis General Strike of 1877." *Journal of Social History* 19, no. 2 (1985): 213–39.

Rose, Willie Lee. *Rehearsals for Reconstruction: The Port Royal Experiment*. University of Georgia Press, 1962.

Rosen, Deborah. *American Indians and State Law: Sovereignty, Race, and Citizenship, 1790–1880*. University of Nebraska Press, 2007.

Rosen, Hannah. *Terror in the Heart of Freedom: Citizenship, Sexual Violence, and the Meaning of Race in the Postemancipation South*. University of North Carolina Press, 2009.

Rosenthal, Caitlin. "Abolition as Market Regulation." *Boston Review*, February 1, 2017.

———. *Accounting for Slavery: Masters and Management*. Harvard University Press, 2018.

Rothman, Adam. *Slave Country: American Expansion and the Origins of the Deep South*. Harvard University Press, 2007.

Rothman, Joshua D. *Flush Times and Fever Dreams: A Story of Capitalism and Slavery in the Age of Jackson.* University of Georgia Press, 2012.

———. *The Ledger and the Chain: How Domestic Slave Traders Shaped America.* Basic Books, 2021.

Royce, Edward. *The Origins of Southern Sharecropping.* Temple University Press, 1993.

Rugemer, Edward Bartlett. *The Problem of Emancipation: The Caribbean Roots of the American Civil War.* Louisiana State University Press, 2008.

Rusert, Britt. "Disappointment in the Archives of Black Freedom." *Social Text* 125 (2015): 19–33.

Saba, Roberto. *American Mirror: The United States and Brazil in the Age of Emancipation.* Princeton University Press, 2021.

Saunt, Claudio. "The Invasion of America." Video, 1 minute, 27 seconds, Facing History & Ourselves, updated November 17, 2022. www.facinghistory.org/resource-library/invasion-america.

———. *Unworthy Republic: The Dispossession of Native Americans and the Road to Indian Territory.* Norton, 2021.

Saxton, Alexander. *The Indispensable Enemy: Labor and the Anti-Chinese Movement in California* .University of California Press, 1971.

Saville, Julie. *The Work of Reconstruction: From Slave to Wage Laborer in South Carolina, 1860–1870.* Cambridge University Press, 1996.

Scanlan, Padraic X. *Slave Empire: How Slavery Built Modern Britain.* Robinson, 2022.

Schermerhorn, C. "The Thibodaux Massacre Left 60 African Americans Dead and Spelled the End of Unionized Farm Labor in the South for Decades." *The Smithsonian*, November 21, 2017.

Schermerhorn, Jack Lawrence. *The Business of Slavery and the Rise of American Capitalism, 1815–1860.* Yale University Press, 2015.

Schoeppner, Michael A. "Black Migrants and Border Regulation in the Early United States, *Journal of the Civil War Era* 11, no. 3 (2021): 317–39.

Schuessler, Jennifer. "Emory University Acquires W. E. B. Du Bois's Copy of Rare Early Abolitionist Appeal." *New York Times*, March 7, 2016.

Scott, Julius S. *The Common Wind: Afro-American Currents in the Age of the Haitian Revolution.* Verso, 2018.

Seeley, Samantha. "Beyond the American Colonization Society." *History Compass* 14, no. 3 (2016): 93–104.

———. *Race, Removal, and the Right to Remain: Migration and the Making of the United States*. Omohundro Institute of Early American History and Culture and the University of North Carolina Press, 2021.

Seguin, Charles, and Sabrina Nardin. "The Lynching of Italians and the Rise of Antilynching Politics in the United States." *Social Science History* 46, no. 1 (2022): 65–91. https://doi.org/10.1017/ssh.2021.43.

Sell, Zach. *Trouble of the World: Slavery and Empire in the Age of Capital*. University of North Carolina Press, 2021.

Sharpe, Christina Elizabeth. *In the Wake: On Blackness and Being*. Duke University Press, 2016.

Singh, Nikhil Pal. "Black Marxism and the Antinomies of Racial Capitalism." In *After Marx: Literature, Theory, and Value in the Twenty-First Century*, ed. Colleen Lye and Christopher Nealon. Cambridge University Press, 2022.

———. *Race and America's Long War*. University of California Press, 2017.

Sinha, Manisha. *The Slave's Cause: A History of Abolition*. Yale University Press, 2016.

Smith, Shannon M. "'They Met Force with Force': African American Protests and Social Status in Louisville's 1877 Strike." *Register of the Kentucky Historical Society* 115, no .1 (2017): 1–37.

Smith, Stacey L. *Freedom's Frontier: California and the Struggle over Unfree Labor, Emancipation, and Reconstruction*. University of North Carolina Press, 2013.

Snyder, Terri L. *The Power to Die: Slavery and Suicide in British North America*. University of Chicago Press, 2015.

Speed, Shannon. *Incarcerated Stories: Indigenous Women Migrants and Violence in the Settler-Capitalist State*. University of North Carolina Press, 2019.

Stanley, Amy Dru. *From Bondage to Contract: Wage Labor, Marriage, and the Market in the Age of Slave Emancipation*. Cambridge University Press, 2010.

Staudenraus, P. J. *The African Colonization Movement, 1816–1865*. Columbia University Press, 1961.

Stauffer, John. *The Black Hearts of Men*. Harvard University Press, 2009.

———, ed. *The Works of James McCune Smith*. Oxford University Press, 2006.

Sterling, Dorothy, ed. *Speak Out in Thunder Tones: Letters and Other Writings by Black Northerners, 1787–1865*. 1973; repr., Da Capo, 1998.

Stewart, Maria. *Meditations from the Pen of Mrs. Maria W. Stewart, (Widow of the Late James W. Stewart), Now Matron of the Freedmen's Hospital, and Presented in 1832 to the First African Baptist Church and Society of Boston, Mass.* (Washington: n.p., 1879).

Stovall, Tyler. *White Freedom: The Racial History of an Idea*. Princeton University Press, 2021. https://doi.org/10.1515/9780691205366.

Tadiar, Neferti X. M. *Remaindered Life*. Duke University Press, 2022. https://doi.org/10.2307/j.ctv2j86bp5.

Tejada, Vivien. "Unfree Soil: Empire, Labor, and Coercion in the Upper Mississippi River Valley, 1812–1861." PhD diss. Duke University, 2024.

Temin, Peter, ed. *Engines of Enterprise: An Economic History of New England*. Harvard University Press, 2000.

Thirteenth Report of the Railroad Commissioners of Kentucky, for the Year 1892. Frankfort, KY: Capital Office: E. Polk Johnson, Public Printer and Binder, 1892.

Thomas, Bettye C. "A Nineteenth Century Black Operated Shipyard, 1866–1884: Reflections Upon Its Inception and Ownership." *Journal of Negro History* 59, no. 1 (1974): 1–12.

Thornbrough, Emma Lou. *T. Thomas Fortune: Militant Journalist*. University of Chicago Press, 1972.

Towers, Frank. "Job Busting at Baltimore Shipyards: Racial Violence in the Civil War-Era South." *Journal of Southern History* 66, no. 2 (2000): 221–56.

Trotter, Joe William. *Workers on Arrival: Black Labor in the Making of America*. University of California Press, 2019. https://doi.org/10.1525/9780520971172.

Turner, James ed. *David Walker's Appeal, in Four Articles: Together with a Preamble, to the Coloured Citizens of the World, but in Particular, and Very Expressly, to Those of the United States of America*. Third and Last Edition, Revised and Published by David Walker, 1830. Black Classic Press, 1993.

Usner, Daniel H., Jr. "American Indians on the Cotton Frontier: Changing Economic Relations with Citizens and Slaves in the Mississippi Territory." *Journal of American History* 72, no. 2 (1985): 297–317.

Walcott, Rinaldo. *The Long Emancipation: Moving Toward Black Freedom*. Duke University Press, 2021. https://doi.org/10.1515/9781478021360.

Walia, Harsha. *Border and Rule: Global Migration, Capitalism, and the Rise of Racist Nationalism*. Haymarket Books, 2021.

Walker, David. *Walker's Appeal, in Four Articles: Together with a Preamble to the Colored Citizens of the World, but in Particular, and Very Expressly to Those of the United States of America*. Sept 28th, Boston, 1829.

Walker, David, and Henry Highland Garnet. *Walker's Appeal, with a Brief Sketch of His Life, by Henry Highland Garnet, and Also Garnet's Address to the Slaves of the United States of America*. New York: J.H. Tobitt, 1848.

Warren, Wendy. *New England Bound: Slavery and Colonization in Early New England*. Liveright, 2017.
Washington, S. A. M. *George Thomas Downing: Sketch of His Life and Times*. Milne Printery, 1910.
Waters, Kristin Waters. *Maria W. Stewart and the Roots of Black Political Thought*. University Press of Mississippi, 2021.
Weir, Robert E. *Beyond Labor's Veil: The Culture of the Knights of Labor*. Penn State University Press, 1993.
Wells, Ida B. *Crusade for Justice: The Autobiography of Ida B. Wells*. Ed. Alfreda M. Duster. University of Chicago Press, 1970.
———. *The Light of Truth*. Ed. Mia Bay. Penguin, 2014.
Wells, Ida B., Frederick Douglass, Irvine Garland Penn, and Ferdinand L. Barnett. *The Reason Why the Colored American Is Not in the World's Columbian Exposition: The Afro-American's Contribution to Columbian Literature*. Ed. Robert W. Rydell. University of Illinois Press, 1999.
White, Lisa A. "The Curve Lynchings: Violence, Politics, Economics, and Race Rhetoric in 1890s Memphis." *Tennessee Historical Quarterly* 64, no. 1 (2005): 43–61.
White, Richard. *Railroaded: The Transcontinentals and the Making of Modern America*. Norton, 2011.
Wilentz, Sean. *Chants Democratic: New York City and the Rise of the American Working Class, 1788–1850*. 20th anniversary ed. Oxford University Press, 2004.
———, ed. *David Walker's Appeal, In Four Articles; Together With A Preamble, to the Coloured Citizens of the World, but In Particular, and Very Expressly, to Those in the United States of America*. Hill and Wang, 1995.
Williams, Kidada E. *I Saw Death Coming: A History of Terror and Survival in the War Against Reconstruction*. Bloomsbury, 2023.
Wirzbicki, Peter. *Fighting for the Higher Law: Black and White Transcendentalists Against Slavery*. University of Pennsylvania Press, 2021.
Witgen, Michael J. *Seeing Red: Indigenous Land, American Expansion, and the Political Economy of Plunder in North America*. Omohundro Institute of Early American History and Culture and University of North Carolina Press, 2022.
Wolff, Gerald. "The Slaveocracy and the Homestead Problem of 1854." *Agricultural History* 40, no. 2 (1966): 101–12.
Wood, Gordon S. *The Radicalism of the American Revolution*. First Vintage Books edition. Vintage Books, 1993.

Wright, Theodore S., Gerrit Smith, Charles B. Ray, and James McCune Smith. *An Address to the Three Thousand Colored Citizens of New-York: Who Are the Owners of One Hundred and Twenty Thousand Acres of Land, in the State of New-York, September 1, 1846.* New-York, n.p., 1846.

Wynes, Charles E. "T. McCants Stewart: Peripatetic Black South Carolinian." *South Carolina Historical Magazine* 80, no. 4 (1979): 311–17.

Yacovone, Donald. "The Transformation of the Black Temperance Movement, 1827–1854: An Interpretation." *Journal of the Early Republic* 8, no .3 (1988): 281–97.

Yates, Joshua and James Davison Hunter, eds. *Thrift and Thriving in America: Capitalism and Moral Order from the Puritans to the Present.* Oxford University Press, 2011.

NEWSPAPERS

"Address, Delivered Before the General Colored Association at Boston, by David Walker." *Freedom's Journal*, December 19, 1828.

"An Address to the Colored People of the United States." *North Star.* September 29, 1848.

"Adulterated Republicanism." *New National Era.* April 6, 1871.

"The Annual Meeting of the American Anti-Slavery Society." *Frederick Douglass' Paper.* Part of African American Newspapers Collection, Rochester, NY, May 20, 1852.

"Aristocracy of Wealth." *Colored American.* April 1, 1837.

"Benefits of Protection to Home Industry." *New National Era.* April 3, 1873.

"Can the Proud Anglo-Saxon Be Enslaved?" *New National Era.* April 3, 1873.

"Capital and Labor." *Frederick Douglass' Paper.* Part of African American Newspapers Collection, Rochester, NY, March 4, 1853.

"A Case in Point." *New York Freeman.* May 22, 1886.

"Cheap Labor." *New National Era.* August 17, 1871.

"Chinamen and Anarchists." *New York Freeman.* May 15, 1886.

"Colorphobia in Labor Organizations." *New York Globe.* January 26, 1884.

"Colored Communism." *The New National Era.* September 25, 1873.

"Colored Convention Nonsense." *New York Freeman.* January 1, 1887.

"Colored Knights of Labor in Arkansas." *New York Freeman.* July 17, 1886.

"Colored Men, Reflect." *New York Freeman.* December 4, 1886.

"The Colored Press Association." *New York Freeman.* March 6, 1886.
"The Coming Man." *New National Era.* June 22, 1871.
"The Coolie Trade." *New National Era.* August 10, 1871.
"Communications." *Frederick Douglass' Paper.* Part of African American Newspapers Collection, Rochester, NY, January 1, 1852.
"Communism in the United States." *New York Globe.* May 5, 1883.
"Constitution of the Afric-American Female Intelligence Society of Boston." *The Liberator* (Boston). January 7, 1832. Library of Congress (website). www.loc.gov/resource/sn84031524/1832-01-07/ed-1/?sp=2&st=image&r=0.425,1.098,0.465,0.231,0.
"Convention of Colored Mechanics." *Christian Recorder.* Part of African American Newspapers Collection, Philadelphia, August 14, 1869.
"Co-Operation Among the Colored People." *New National Era.* December 4, 1873.
"The Danger of the Republican Movement." *Radical Abolitionist,* July 1856.
"Dangerous Power of Railroad Monopolies." *New National Era.* April 3, 1873.
Delany, Martin. [Untitled.] *North Star.* July 7, 1848.
"A Difficulty Explained." *Colored American.* July 27, 1839.
"Doctrines of the Southern Democracy." *National Era.* Part of African American Newspapers Collection, Washington D.C., April 23, 1857.
"Does the Colored Laborer in the South Receive Less Wages." *New York Freeman.* October 2, 1886.
"Don't Come to England." *The Liberator.* July 25, 1851.
"Effect of Emancipation—Remarkable Error." *National Era.* November 11, 1847.
"Emigration of Colored People to Jamaica." *The Liberator.* October 24, 1851.
"An Example Worth Imitating." *New National Era.* October 16, 1873.
"Exiled." *New York Age.* June 25, 1892.
"Failure of Labor." *New York Freeman.* April 10, 1886.
"A Florida Strike." *New York Freeman.* February 12, 1887.
"The Folly, Tyranny, and Wickedness of Labor Unions." *New National Era.* May 7, 1874.
"Frederick Douglass at the Cooper Institute." *Douglass' Monthly.* Part of African American Newspapers Collection, Rochester, NY, March 1863.
"Frederick Douglass on the Crisis." *Douglass' Monthly.* Part of African American Newspapers Collection, Rochester, NY, June 1861.
"The Freedmen Rejoice Over Their Release from the Bonds of Slavery." *National Republican.* April 17, 1888.

"From Alabama." *New National Era.* May 28, 1874.
"From Our Brooklyn Correspondent." *Frederick Douglass' Paper.* Part of African American Newspapers Collection, Rochester, NY, January 22, 1852.
"From Rhode Island." *National Era.* February 20, 1851.
Garrison, William Lloyd. "Working Men." *The Liberator,* January 1, 1831.
"Grievances in Kentucky." *New York Freeman.* March 20, 1886.
"A High Tariff a Necessity." *New National Era.* January 5, 1871.
"A Home Market." *New National Era.* November 16, 1871.
"The Homestead Bill." *New York Times.* May 4, 1852.
"Important to Workers." *Colored American.* August 3, 1839.
"An Inconsistent Demagogue." *New National Era.* October 16, 1873.
"An Industrial Servitude." *New York Age.* March 17, 1888.
"The Industrial College." *Frederick Douglass' Paper.* Part of African American Newspapers Collection, Rochester, NY, January 2, 1854.
"Industrial Slavery in the South." *New York Freeman.* December 25, 1886.
"Injustice at the South." *New York Age.* June 1, 1889.
"Iola's Southern Field." *New York Age.* November 19, 1892.
"The Knights of Labor." *New York Freeman.* October 16, 1886.
"The Knights of Labor Show the White Feather." *New York Freeman.* October 23, 1886.
"Italian Slaves in the South." *New York Age.* April 4, 1891.
"Labor and Capital." *National Era.* November 9, 1848.
"Labor Demonstration." *New York Freeman.* March 20, 1886.
"Labor in Iron-Manufactories and Workingmen." *New National Era.* December 28, 1871.
"Labor Union." *New National Era.* May 28, 1874.
"Labor Upheavals." *New York Freeman.* March 20, 1886.
"The Laboring Men." *North Star.* November 3, 1848.
"The Labor Question." *New National Era.* October 12, 1871.
"Land and Liberty." *National Era.* March 2, 1848.
"Land Reform." *Frederick Douglass' Paper.* Part of African American Newspapers Collection, Rochester, April 1, 1852.
"Land Reform." *Frederick Douglass' Paper.* Part of African American Newspapers Collection, Rochester, May 27, 1852.
"Land Reform." *National Era.* May 30, 1850.
"Land Reform." *North Star.* February 25, 1848

"Land Reform—Wages Slavery." *National Era*. March 18, 1847.
"Land Reform and Its Prospects." *Frederick Douglass' Paper*. part of African American Newspapers Collection, Rochester, NY, June 3, 1852.
"Land Reform in the Senate." *National Era*. February 7, 1850.
"A Lesson to Be Taught." *New National Era*. September 10, 1874.
"Letter from Communipaw." *Frederick Douglass' Paper*. Part of African American Newspapers Collection, Rochester, February 12, 1852.
"Letter from Communipaw." *Frederick Douglass' Paper*. Part of African American Newspapers Collection, Rochester, February 26, 1852.
"Letter from H.H. Garnet." *Frederick Douglass' Paper*. Part of African American Newspapers Collection, Rochester, September 2, 1853.
"Letter from Philadelphia." *New National Era*. October 19, 1871.
"Letter of Charles Stuart." *The Emancipator*. December 26, 1839.
Massachusetts General Court, House of Representatives No. 11. *Memorial of the Marshpee Indians: A Voice from the Marshpee Indians, Jan. 1834* (1834).
"The Mission of Democracy No. 2." *National Era*. April 20, 1848.
"More Enmity to Workingmen." *New National Era*. December 28, 1871.
"Mr. Douglass as a Partisan." *New York Freeman*. May 9, 1885.
"Mr. Fortune Declines." *New York Freeman*. December 25, 1886.
"Mr. Fortune on the West: Glances at Indianapolis and Chicago." *New York Age*. August 11, 1888.
"National Labor Union." *New National Era*. January 19, 1871.
"Natural History of Slavery—No. 1." *National Era*. Part of African American Newspapers Collection, Washington, DC. March 31, 1853.
"Natural History of Slavery—No. 2." *National Era*. Part of African American Newspapers Collection, Washington DC. April 7, 1853.
"The New Exodus." *New York Freeman*. January 16, 1886.
"A New Future." *New York Freeman*. March 14, 1885.
"The North Star." *Homestead Journal and Village Register*. December 22, 1847.
"Novel Argument in Support of Slavery—Immigration and Wages." *National Era*. November 9, 1848.
"Odds and Ends." *New York Freeman*. January 15, 1887.
"A One-Sided View." *New National Era*. December 14, 1871.
"Our Republicanism." *New York Globe*. May 17, 1884.
"Outrages in Louisiana." *New York Age*. December 3, 1887.
"The Pathway of Success." *The New National Era*. October 30, 1873.

"Peril to the Free." *Colored American*. September 1, 1838.
"Pernicious Labor Teachings." *New York Freeman*. May 1, 1886.
"The Poor Whites of the South." *North Star*. March 1, 1850.
"The Public Lands." *National Era*. February 13, 1851.
"Public Lands." *North Star*. February 25, 1848.
"The Question of the Hour." *New York Freeman*. May 1, 1886.
"The Real Enemies of the Workingman." *New National Era*. November 23, 1871.
"Results of Protection at the South." *New National Era*. November 30, 1871.
"Santo Domingo—No. 8." *New National Era*. June 15, 1871.
"Senator Clemens." The *National Era*. March 28, 1850.
""Secession." *Weekly Anglo-African*. December 22, 1860.
Should a Conference Be Held to Protest Against Injustice?" *New York Freeman*. April 10, 1886.
"Slavery Missionaries at the North." *National Era*. November 12, 1857.
"Socialistic Literature." *New York Freeman*. February 14, 1885.
"Socialistic Riot in England." *New York Freeman*. February 13, 1886.
"Southern Brutality." *New York Freeman*. May 23, 1885.
"The Southern Chaingang." *New York Freeman*. March 13, 1886.
"The Southern Labor Question." *New York Freeman*. January 23, 1886.
"Southern Manufactures." *New National Era*. June 22, 1871.
"The Southern Problem." *New York Globe*. February 3, 1883.
"A System of Slavery." *New York Freeman*. August 7, 1886.
"'Thrifty Americans' and Hayti." *New York Age*. August 2, 1890.
"To 'Ethiop' and 'Observer.'" *Frederick Douglass' Paper*. Part of African American Newspapers Collection, Rochester, NY, April 8, 1852.
"Tyranny Among Laborers." *New National Era*. April 20, 1871.
"The Unholy Alliance of Negro Hate and Anti-Slavery." *Frederick Douglass' Paper*. Part of African American Newspapers Collection, Rochester, NY, April 5, 1856.
[Untitled]. *Colored American, Black Abolitionist Papers, 1830–1865*. October 2, 1841.
[Untitled]. *Colored American, Black Abolitionist Papers, 1830–1865*. December 25, 1841.
[Untitled]. *North Star*. January 7, 1848.
[Untitled]. *London Times*. BAP British Volume, July 3, 1851.
[Untitled]. *The Liberator*. National Era. Jan. 25, 1834.
[Untitled]. *New York Freeman*. April 3, 1886.

"Virginia Democracy." *National Era*. Part of African American Newspapers Collection, Washington, DC. September 14, 1854.

"Virginia Going Backward." *Christian Recorder*. Part of African American Newspapers Collection, Philadelphia, December 21, 1861.

"Vital Truths for Workingmen." *New National Era*. March 14, 1872.

"Wages and Chattel Slavery—The Elevation of the Working Class." *National Era*. Part of African American Newspapers Collection, Washington, DC, March 25, 1846.

"A Warning to Business Men!" *New National Era*. August 15, 1872.

"West India Emancipation." *National Era*. Part of African American Newspapers Collection, Washington, DC, November 25, 1858.

"White and Colored Laborers Detrimental." *New York Freeman*. December 4, 1886.

"Who Is the Parasite?" *New York Globe*. February 16, 1884.

"Why We Advocate Protection." *New National Era*. November 30, 1871.

"Wisdom in the Counsels of Washington." *New National Era*. June 15, 1871.

"The Word 'White.'" *Frederick Douglass' Paper*. Part of African American Newspapers Collection, Rochester, NY, March 17, 1854,

"The Work of the Future." *Douglass Monthly*. Part of African American Newspapers Collection, Rochester, NY, November 1862.

"Workingmen Betrayed in the House of Their Friends." *New National Era*. March 7, 1872.

"The Workingman's Party." *New National Era*. September 5, 1870.

"Young America—Land Reform—Wages Slavery." *National Era*. March 11, 1847.

"Young America—Reform—'Wages Slavery.' &c." *National Era*. February 11, 1847.

INDEX

abolition democracy, xv–xvi, xxiv–xxvi, 123, 170–73, 181n37. *See* Du Bois, W. E. B.
abolitionists, xvi, xxvi, 3–6, 45, 47–48, 76, 169, 181n39; and annexation, 199n46; on capitalism, 43, 190n10; on the Civil War, 75–76; on labor reform, 42–46; on land reform, 50, 53–54, 56–62, 71–72, 74–75, 79–80; on wage slavery, 51–53; on West Indian emancipation, 63–71
Alabama Labor Union, 111–12
American Colonization Society, 26, 28
Apess, William, 3, 12–13, 30, 32–36, 185n44; on dispossession, 12–13, 19–20; and engagement with Black and Native communities, 6; on guardianship, 33–35; *A Son of the Forest* (Apess), 6; time with the Mashpee, 30–35. See also *Indian Nullification of the Unconstitutional Laws of Massachusetts*; Indigenous communities

Asian Americans: anti-Chinese racism, 89, 149–51, 206n53; and coolie labor, 100–101, 199–200n48. *See* West Indian emancipation

Bailey, Gamaliel: and land reform, 53–55, 57–59; and *National Era*, 53, 57–58. *See also* Evans, Henry
Birney, James, 45–46
Black and White (Fortune), 127–30, 132–33, 137–38, 140, 152
Black intellectual history, xviii, xix, 170, 173, 175n9
Black Marxism (Robinson), xxii–xxiii. *See also* Robinson, Cedric
Black press, 45–48, 55–56, 124–25, 182n5; on abolition and capitalism, 45–48, 55–57; on Knights of Labor, 138–40; on West Indian emancipation, 63, 66, 68
Black radical tradition, xxii, xxiv; and abolition, xxiv, xxvi–xxvii, 170, 172–73, 181n39

Black Reconstruction in America, 1860–1880 (Du Bois), xv, xvi, 121, 123, 137, 202n77
Brown, William Wells, 65–66. *See* West Indian emancipation

capitalism: histories of, xix; liberal, xx, 93; and relationship to abolition, 42, 80, 84, 97–98, 102; state's role in, 132–34, 170–71; theories of, 132–35, 141. *See* racial capitalism
Caulkers' Association, 86–88
Colored Caulkers Trade Union Society, 88
Civil War, and persistence of slavery, 39, 63, 75–79. *See also* abolition
Clay, Henry, 27–28. *See* colonization
Collins, John, 53. *See* land reform
colonization, 8, 23–24; critiques of 27–30; economic motivations, 28; Liberia, 26–27, 30. *See also* American Colonization Society
Colored American, 45–48
Colored National Labor Convention, 90–96; *New National Era*, 97. *See* Colored National Labor Union
Colored National Labor Union, 90–96, 110
communism, 76; Frederick Douglass on, 107–12, T. Thomas Fortune on, 122–23, 126; and Paris Commune, 107–10
Convention of Colored Mechanics, 88–89, 91. *See* Myers, Isaac
convict leasing, xxi, 170
Cornish, Samuel, 63. *See also* Black press; *Colored American*

Delany, Martin, 49–50
Democratic Party: critiques of, 96, 99, 125, 129, 154; and slavery, 96, 98–99
Douglass, Frederick: and Colored National Labor Union, 96–97; on communism, 107–11, on freedom, 72–75, 81–85, 129–30; on Irish poverty, 52; on labor, 40–41, 43, 96–104, 113–19, 196n9, 200–201n59; on land reform, 52–53, 55–56, 62, 77–78; "The Lessons of the Hour," 81–83; and *North Star*, 49, 55–57, 85–86, 157; slaves of society, xxi, 73, 77–78, 100, 115; on West Indian emancipation, 69–70. *See also* abolitionists; Black press; *Frederick Douglass' Paper*
Downing, George, 90, 93–94, 195n80. *See* Colored National Labor Convention
Du Bois, W. E. B., xvii, 123; on abolition democracy, xv–xvi, xxiv–xxv, 123, 170–72; "The African Roots of War," 171; on economic slavery, xxi. *See also Black Reconstruction in America, 1860–1880*

Evans, George Henry, 50, 51, 53–54; and debate with Wendell Phillips, 51; and National Reform Association, 51; *Working Man's Advocate*, 50; Workingmen's Party, 50; *Young America*, 51, 53. *See* land reform

INDEX ❧ 235

Ferrell, Frank, 146–47. *See also* Knights of Labor
Fortune, T. Thomas, 121, 123–26, 162, 166–68, 203–4n7, 204n21; on abolition and communism, 121–23; on capitalism, 126–27, 131–36; on class solidarity, 140–48, 152–53; on freedom, 130, 132, 137; on Knights of Labor, 138–43, 145–48; National Afro-American League, 166; *New York Age*, xvii, 138, 152, 157, 160, 163; *New York Globe*, 121, 124. See also *Black and White* (Fortune); freedom: Black freedom
Frederick Douglass' Paper, 59, 62, 66, 68, 72–73
freedom, 77, 95; Black freedom, 28, 45, 48, 62, 71, 73, 75, 77–80, 83–85, 97, 119, 127, 130, 132, 137, 141, 163, 168, 172–73; and continuity with slavery, xx, 71–73. *See* racial capitalism; slavery
free labor ideology, 40–42, 57, 63–65, 69–70, 78, 83–84, 93, 103, 116, 119, 123
free trade, 96, 98, 106, 112–13

Garnet, Henry Highland, 66–67. *See* West Indian emancipation
Garrison, William Lloyd, 42; *The Liberator*, 5–6, 51. *See* abolitionists
George, Henry, 131, 136, 144. See also *Black and White* (Fortune)
Gibbs, Mifflin Wistar, 71. *See* West Indian emancipation

Hartman, Saidiya, xx; on afterlife of slavery, 178n20

immigration: debates about, 72, 94, 100–2, 150–52. *See* Asian Americans
Indian Nullification of the Unconstitutional Laws of Massachusetts (Apess), 18
Indigenous communities, 6–7; and dispossession, 1, 7, 10–11, 19, 20; and guardianship, 8, 10–11, 23–24, 27, 31–36, 184n19; Mashpee, 30–36; racist ideologies about, 14, 26–27, 31–32; and reservations, 22

Jackson, Kellie Carter, 170, 181n39. *See* Black intellectual history; Black radical tradition
Jim Crow, 155, 159–60. *See also* lynching
Johnson, Walter, xxi, 37. *See* racial capitalism: theories of

Knights of Labor, 138–40, 143, 145–49, 166

land reform, 43, 50, 136; abolitionists, 43–44, 51, 130, 136; Black homesteaders, 49–50; in Black press, 59–62; Homestead Bill of 1852, 59–60, 193n46; *Homestead Journal*, 55; relationship to labor reform, 50–51; wage slavery, 44, 50–56, 58, 60, 62, 80, 128–30
Langston, John Mercer, 94. *See also* Colored National Labor Convention; Colored National Labor Union; unions

Liberator, The, 5–6, 51
lynching, 153–57, 170; Curve lynchings, 154–55, 159, 161; justifications given for, 158, 166, 206–7n66. *See also* Wells, Ida B.

Marx, Karl, xv; theories of class formation by, xxii–xxiii. *See also* Robinson, Cedric
McCune Smith, James, 39, 78–80, 189n4, 195n80; on Black freedom, 71, 73, 78–80; on slavery and wage labor, 39–41, 43; on West Indian emancipation, 68–69
mutual aid, 4, 14, 20–21
Myers, Isaac, 87–89, 144. *See also* Colored Caulkers Trade Union Society; Convention of Colored Mechanics; unions

National Afro-American Council, 167. *See also* Fortune, T. Thomas
National Era, 53, 57–58
National Labor Union, 89, 91
North Star, 49–50, 55–57, 85–86

Panic of 1873, 105–6, 200n54, 200–201n59
Philanthropist, The, 45–46
Pickens, Francis Wilkinson, 47, 57, 192n40
Powderly, Terence, 139, 146–47. *See* unions: Knights of Labor

racial capitalism, xv–xvi, xxi, xxiv, 1, 2, 9, 37, 170–73; and attacks on Black success, 25, 153, 161; and criminalization, 2, 13–14, 115, 117, 156; and economic oppression, 2, 9–10, 15, 16–17, 83, 114–17, 120, 126; and lack of legal power, 11–12; racist ideologies, xxiii, 2, 14, 20, 22–26, 121, 135, 142, 147–48, 153–58, 160, 162–63, 168; and segregation, 24; theories of, xxii–xxiv, 97–98, 102–3, 114–20, 160, 162–63, 166, 178n22; and violence against Black people, 82, 114, 127, 135, 140, 148, 153–56; 200–201n76. *See also* Indian communities: and dispossession; Robinson, Cedric
Rainey, Joseph Hayne, 95–96. *See also* Colored National Labor Convention; Colored National Labor Union; unions
Reconstruction, xv–xvi, 82, 115, 118–19; and Black labor, 97–104, 116–19; failure of, 119, 126, 128–29, 132, 168, 171; racial violence, 114–15
Red Record, A (Wells), 163–65. *See also* lynching
Republicanism: in Black political thought, 92–93, 95, 97, 107, 109, 112, 150, 197n26; and Foner, 42. *See also* free labor ideology
Republican Party, 89, 125, 131; critiques of, 111, 124–26, 129, 131, 140, 154; Douglass and

the, 97–98, 106, 109, 113, 118
Robinson, Cedric: *Black Marxism*, xxii–xxiii; on Marxism, xxii–xxiii. *See also* Black radical tradition

Shadd Cary, Mary Ann: on Black women, 94–95; on land, 198n33. *See also* Colored National Labor Convention; Colored National Labor Union; unions
sharecropping, xxi, 118, 170
slavery, 5, 26, 28; chattel, xvi, xxi, xxiii–xxiv, 1, 44, 58; histories of, xv, xix, xxiii, xxvi, 17, 169; as labor competition, 86, 113, 131; racial capitalism, 208n1; relationship to capitalism, xviii, xxi, xxiii–xxiv, xxvi, 1, 17, 18, 39–47, 51–52, 59, 76–78, 115–16, 137; theories of, 44, 58, 114–15, 131, 190n12, 192n32. *See also* abolitionists; freedom; land reform
Smith, Gerrit: on land reform, 48–50, 56; and the Liberal Party, 59; on slavery and capitalism, 47–48; work with James McCune Smith, 48–49
socialism, xvi, xxiii, xxvii, 93, 111, 112, 120, 122, 126–27, 134, 171–72
Southern Horrors (Wells), 157–59. *See also* lynching
Stewart, James, 5, 12
Stewart, Maria, 3, 12, 13, 15, 36; analogizing of race and gender, 16; on colonization, 29; on Black women's economic empowerment, 16, 22; *Productions of Mrs. Maria W. Stewart*, 5–6; *Religion and the Pure Principles of Morality*, 5
Stuart, Charles, 64–65. *See also* West Indian emancipation
Swinton, John, 144–45. *See also Black and White* (Fortune); Fortune, T. Thomas

Thibodaux Massacre of 1887, 148–49. *See also* Knights of Labor; unions
Thomas, John, 59–62. *See also* Douglass, Frederick; *Frederick Douglass' Paper*; land reform

unions, 85–87, 107–8, 111–12, 116; racism of, 85–89, 96, 98–99, 146–51. *See also* Alabama Labor Union; Caulkers' Association; Colored Caulkers Trade Union Society; Colored National Labor Union; Knights of Labor; National Labor Union

Vashon, George Boyer, 95–96. *See* Colored National Labor Convention; Colored National Labor Union; unions

Walcott, Rinaldo, and long emancipation, xx
Walker, David, 3–8, 13, 20, 35–36; on colonization, 27–29; on the lowest freedom, vii, xvii, xix–xxi, 173

Walker's Appeal, in Four Articles . . . (Walker), 4, 5, 11, 14–15, 35–36, 183n14, 188n111. *See also* abolitionists

Washington, Booker T., 167

Wells, Ida B., 121, 123–24, 126, 167–68; on Black labor, 159–63; on boycotts, 159–62, 166; lynching investigations, 153–57, 161, 163–66; *Memphis Free Speech*, 125, 156–57, 159, 163; *New York Age*, 125, 157, 160, 163; on racial violence and economics, 154, 158–59, 161, 166. *See also* Black press; lynching; *Red Record, A* (Wells); *Southern Horrors* (Wells)

West Indian emancipation, 63, 68–70, 193n53, 194n68; and coolie labor, 100–102; Slavery Abolition Act of 1833, 63

GPSR Authorized Representative: Easy Access System Europe, Mustamäe tee 50, 10621 Tallinn, Estonia, gpsr.requests@easproject.com

www.ingramcontent.com/pod-product-compliance
Lightning Source LLC
Chambersburg PA
CBHW031239290426
44109CB00012B/354